BAULS OF BENGAL

In the Quest of Man of the Heart

BAULS OF BENGAL

IN THE QUEST OF MAN OF THE HEART

R. M. SARKAR

GIAN PUBLISHING HOUSE
New Delhi-110002

GIAN PUBLISHING HOUSE
4-C, Ansari Road, Darya Ganj
New Delhi-110002

ISBN 81-212-0320-1

PRINTED IN INDIA

Published by Mrs. Gayatri Garg for Gian Publishing House, New Delhi 110002.
Laser type set by Shiva Shakti Laser Typesetters, New Delhi 110002.
Printed at : Goyal Offset Printers, Delhi.

DEDICATED TO

THE BAULS OF BENGAL
WHO CONSECRATE THEMSELVES
TO THE CAUSE OF
UNIVERSAL BROTHERHOOD
OF MANKIND

Preface

India is well-known in the world perspective as a land of traditions. The tradition-bound societies of this country have got certain specialities of their own. The land of diversities has specifically become unity-oriented only through the possession of rich cultural heritage. It cuts across all sorts of differentiation and inequalities. In spite of the presence of conspicuous differences in the life-ways and thought-ways of the diversified communities having variegated philosophy of life, here exists an internal current of integration which marks the speciality of India. The social heritage in respect of a particular community vis-a-vis a country is conditioned by slow cultural transmission through space and time. The norms, traditions, folkways and mores as well as behaviour-patterns of the people synthetically constitute what is called cultural heritage. On categorical analysis through multifarious view-points it will be seen that the heritage is totally influenced by the overall life-philosophy of the country in which the particular group or community has developed. Therefore, through the various patterns of movement and different features of actions of these groups or communities the total picture of the cultural heritage of the country is seen to be reflected. There are variegated folk communities in India which possess distinctive cultural heritage of their own that have developed through their time-long march for adjustment with the surroundings. The intensive study of these tradition-bound communities does a great deal in understanding the cultural heritage of the country where they live and work. It is true that these small groups "with which conformity identification are sought is relatively small, both areally and numerically but its time dimension aims to be long, its consciousness of conformity with the past is strong" (Kroeber, 1948 : 611).

The Bauls of Bengal, the subject-matter of the present study, constitute such a small group in numerical strength but they exceed all sorts of limits and bindings in their age-long effort to propagate their philosophical understandings and deep-rooted modes of behaviour through melodious songs and artful dances. Being belonged to the tradition-bound community of Bengal, the Bauls bear a rich cultural heritage of the country which has developed through a long process of interactions and harmonization of different life-ways and thought-ways pertaining to various socio-religious traditions. The persons belonging to their tradition-bound community represent the indigenous ethnic groups of rural Bengal. In course of their various performances they maintain a close and direct link with the peasant communities. People belonging to these communities are the genuine patrons of the Bauls.

The specific appeal for this study, therefore, lies in the attempt of exploration of the life and thought of the Baul community in the realistic view-points and to evaluate the various elements in the close-set background of the rural society. Unlike the former works in this line, though very limited, the Bauls have not been isolated here to highlight only their deep-rooted philosophical thinking and the nature and extent of their spiritualism. The present work claims a speciality of its own because of the fact that it is exclusively based on direct field work-oriented data which have been collected by a long-term, painstaking field work organised through the application of categorical scientific methodologies. The Bauls have been studied here as parts of the integrated rural society characterized by various inequalities and interactions. Thus, it, very naturally, has needed exclusive close observations on the behaviour-patterns of the Bauls during various general and special situations. The life and activities of the Bauls are highly characterized by many peculiarities which sometimes create so much complications that it becomes difficult to understand them on mere superficial observations. The Baul life is specifically oriented with overt and covert behaviour-patterns, and until and unless these two perspectives are explored properly the very attempt of focussing light on the Baul life would be futile. The covert behaviours of the Bauls are not very easy to explore, rather it becomes impossible for the outsiders to have a look into the situation. It needs deep-based and time-long rapport as well as very close living with the people under study. In order to serve the specific purpose of study both intensive and extensive types of field investigations were conducted for a long period. There was an urgent need to become well-acquainted with some code terminologies very often used by the Bauls.

To work among the Bauls becomes very difficult until and unless the investigators understand the basic nature of application of the code terms in the conversations amongst themselves. The Bauls are always on the move--they wander from one place to another; sometimes they cover a very wide region. It, therefore, requires travelling over a vast area in search of the Bauls for collecting information. This study pledges from the very beginning to satisfy all these needs to focus the unexplored horizon of Baul life.

The study has been planned to focus the basic nature of the traditional perspective of Baul life characteristically governed by spiritualism. Thus their modes of bahaviour in relation to the rural-based society have been focussed through empirical data. Their love for humanity and the continuous search for *Maner manus* have been explained here through the application of their actual behaviour-patterns in the midst of rural society. It also depicts that the Bauls are the traditional carriers of the message of profound love for man and universal brotherhood which they have been communicating through their melodious songs.

Changes are inevitable in human society, and there are multiple forces of change through the time. The life of the Bauls is not an exception to this. It has been shown here that Baul life has been fast changing and sometimes these changes have been so effective that their very existence is at stake. Despite multifactorial changes, the Baul way of life is in a continuous process. It is still exerting its specific influence on the people and society. The spontaneous Baul gatherings during various age-old socio-religious occasions are still highly effective. The Bauls still carry the message of love, integration and in artificial sense of fraternity to the people. They are still very much vocal against social inequality based on caste and class, religious feuds, untouchability and disintegration, and they continuously advocate for the futility of religious commotion and thereby want a peaceful assimilation of all religions conditioned by the love for humanity. All these traditional and modern features of activities are seen to be reflected in the different chapters of the present study.

Of late, Baul songs, by virtue of their specific wordings, rhythm, tuning and mode of presentation, have found a conspicuous place throughout the world. The popularity of Baul songs is on the rise with every passing day. But the want of any broad-based book on this particular community, in English language, has conspicuously been noted by the interested persons. I do believe that this book would cater to the need of these persons. Moreover, it would arouse special interest amongst those who seriously think about full-fledged national integration through the obliteration of all types of inequalities found within the society. The traditional flame of integration amongst the people in the background of love and respect for humanity is being incessantly carried by this community, and thus they are serving specifically for the cause of the nation. Let us join our hands with these eternal lovers of mankind and celebrated searchers of *Maner manus* in their going ahead with their conspicuous philanthropic appeal.

R.M. Sarkar

Acknowledgements

This book is the outcome of a long-term field investigation done mostly in the inaccessible rural setting in West Bengal, and naturally, my indebtedness rests on a large number of persons belonging to the different spheres of the society. The shortage of space here would not provide me the opportunity to record such a long range of names. The field investigation was conducted, under my direct control, by a competent team of investigators composed by Sri Swadesh Laha, Sri Mani Sarkar, Sri Rasamoy Sutradhar, Sri Jiten Dhibar, Sri Aditya Mukhopadhyay and Sri Nıladri Sarkar. The investigators took all possible care to collect empirical data through painstaking field work. I am thankful to all of them. Sri Ashanandan Chattaraj, a reputed folk song composer and a close friend of mine, was all along highly helpful to me in making contacts with the Bauls and in understanding the different facets of their life and thought. I owe a deep debt of gratitude to him. During the period of my study and analysis I have been fortunate enough in getting the blessings from Swami Sachchidananda Giri, Mohanta Maharaj Sri Harikant Smaran Dev Brajabasi, Sri Harekrishna Goswami-Brahmacharibaba, belonging to the different *Ashrams* at Jaydev-Kenduli-the centre of Baul culture. I consider it is a rare opportunity to get direct support from such stalwarts in the spiritual world as Kavi Kumud Kinkar, an ascetic as well as a noted local journalist, was conspicuously helpful to me for his lively discussions with me during the various phases of work. Sri Ajit Kumar Mitra, a reputed folklorist and rural litterateur, encouraged me profusely at the time of my tour through the rural settings. Sri Santu Sengupta and Sri Samarpan Sengupta of Kotasur Ashram extended all possible help in studying the Bauls from close quarters during Baul assemblage at Kotasur *Madhukari* festival. Without their positive help my study on the covert behaviour of the ascetic Bauls could not be conducted. I take this opportunity to record my gratefulness to all of them individually. Sri Srikumar Ghose, a pupil of mine, was by my side constantly during my painstaking field tour through the rural districts of West Bengal. Sri Aditya Mukhopadhyay, a young litterateur of Birbhum, provided me with some concrete information on Baul way of life and took part in occasional discussions. My special thanks are due to them.

Many of my Baul friends and well-wishers have helped me in many ways during field work amongst them and in understanding the inner recesses of their life and behaviour-patterns through depth-oriented discussions. Special mention may be made of Sudhir Das Baul (Sainthia), Biswanath Das Baul, Nirnoy Das Baul, Kumaresh Das Baul, Sudhir Das Baul (Tamaltala), Tinkari Das Baul and Gour Das Baul. I sincerely express my gratitude to all of them. I shall be failing in my duty if I do not acknowledge with thanks the help and cooperation extended to me in the form of providing of accommodation for my short stay and substantial care during my tour through the remote villages.

I have deliberately used the findings of previous authors in respect of Bauls and other allied matters during discussions of my own data. I am specifically indebted to the different authors of these books and articles. A number of songs composed by Nagababa, Ashnanandan Chattaraj, Thakurdas, Jhingey Kshepa have been rendered into English for presentation here. For this I am grateful to them.

My two daughters, Km. Soma Sarkar and Km. Nivedita Sarkar, helped me a lot in drawing the sketches used in this book. Thanks are due to them.

I like to put on record with requisite acknowledgement the help and cooperation rendered by my wife who has unflinchingly and clamly put up with my lack of attention to many of the familial basic needs owing to my frequent absence from home during field investigation and constant library work. I am indebted to M/S Gian Publishing House, one of the leading publishing organisations in India, for the specific attention and effective care provided by them to bring out this book in such a nice manner.

I am grateful to the Indian Council of Social Science Research, New Delhi, for providing me necessary funds for conducting the research project on the Bauls. The full-fledged co-operation of this research organisation in various phases of the work is thankfully acknowledged.

List of Tables

List of Illustrations

Contents

1

Introduction

I

The Bauls represent the folk tradition of Bengal as a particular cult, encircling Baul way of life, and has its origin from diverse folk beliefs and ideas. The Bauls have been recognised by eminent scholars as the conspicuous representatives of Indian folk-religion. It redounds to the credit of the celebrated poet Rabindranath Tagore for throwing considerable amount of light on this particular community. Ultimately it attracted many scholars to explore the different phases of life of the Bauls. Rabindranath Tagore's address on the "Philosophy of our People", given before the learned participants of the Indian Philosophical Congress held at the Senate House of Calcutta University, in 1925, depicted the general nature and behaviour-patterns of the Bauls. The efforts for depicting the Baul life and their evaluation in the background of Indian folk-religion became important when Tagore delivered a course of lectures on "The Religions of Man". He was invited to deliver the Hibbert Lectures of 1930, at Manchester College, Oxford, when Tagore categorically mentioned the nature and extent of the Bauls who have no organised religion, images, temples, scriptures or ceremonials, who declare in their songs the divinity of man, and express for him an intense feeling of love (Tagore; 1958: 18). Through these lectures the great thinkers of the then world, who had been to Oxford, became readily acquainted with this peculiar community of rural Bengal. Before this

Rabindranath had made a successful attempt to meet a few Bauls at their natural habitat *i.e.*, in rural surroundings of Bengal villages and had some concrete discussions with them. In course of his observation he has marked that "they live outside social recognition, and their very obscurity helps them in their seeking, from a direct source, the enlightenment which the soul longs for, the eternal light of love" (1959 : 76). In this perspective he did not hesitate to express that he had neither the training nor the opportunity to study that mendicant religious sect in Bengal from an ethnological view-point (1959 : 88). All that he could make a fruitful attempt "to find out how the living currents of religious movements work in the hearts of the people" (1959 : 88). Rabindranath felt an essential need for an anthropological interpretation of the tradition-bound Baul community. He always stressed the need for an anthropological study of the primitive and small communities to find out their peculiarities in their life, and also their overall nature of adjustment with the Indian society. Being impressed by the clarion-call of Rabindranath to know the people, few eminent scholars responded to the call to study the Baul community. But all these works are based on the spiritual meditational patterns of the Bauls. A few are centred around the nature and extent of songs of the Bauls and in the latter endeavour, all possible efforts are made to highlight their songs having deep metaphysical meaning as well as to focus them as the age-old bearers of this traditional art. The studies so far made on the Bauls are undoubtedly very insignificant in comparison with the vastness of the multiple nature of thoughts, ideas and behaviour-patterns of the community concerned. The theological interpretations of the Baul life have been the central theme of all such studies and in almost all the works that have already been made parallel lines of thinking are met with. No attempt has been made to focus the realistic life of the Bauls. The thinking pattern of the Bauls have not been evaluated in the background of their day-to-day life-situations. The Bauls have complicated ideas in the different worldly and divine phenomena, and these ideas have been centred around a set of philosophical principles based on deep-rooted critical observations. They bear double meaning in each item of the phenomena concerned. But this particular line of Baul life has never been assessed in the background of reality. The Baul life has all the time been discussed, both superficially and critically , on the basis of theoretical understanding and in rare cases these Bauls have been met with and a few Baul gatherings have been attended by the scholars concerned. To have a concrete idea on the life of the Bauls whose life is influenced by diverse thoughts and ideas an organised field work is essential with a view to interrogating a considerable number of Bauls in their places of work as well as in their routes of wandering through the country. A close observation on their movements and reactions is to be made very minutely to enter into the realm of their life and thinking without which a proper evaluation of Baul life can never be made. The present study is a departure from all the studies made on the life of the Bauls and it is completely based on direct field investigation. The attempt of understanding the Bauls in this study is to be regarded as the pioneer because of the fact that the evaluations of the Baul life and activities have been made here on the basis of data collected through various methodological principles of research. The previous works on the Bauls are characterised principally by the library-based collection of data with biased as well as sentimental outlook. The Bauls have been presented in these works as the carriers of the high-level tradition and the thinkers of a deep-rooted philosophy. The readers are made in these studies, to look at the Bauls as a group of mendicants with the highest influence of metaphysical nature of thinking and sometimes it becomes so rigid and pin-pointed that the Bauls are automatically bestowed with a spiritual position which is completely aloof from worldly affairs. But what about the day-to-day realistic life of the Bauls? How do they maintain themselves? What are the patterns of interactions with the society in the midst of which they stay and meditate? Do they actually follow or can be able to follow the deep-rooted philosophical principles, as have been depicted in different studies, in their daily mode of life and *sadhana*? What are their actual understandings on the principles of the esteemed Bauls philosophy? These pertinent questions are to be answered properly before presenting a broad picture on the life and activities of the Bauls. Mention may be made that satisfactory answers to these questions can be given only through direct and personal interviews with the Bauls and with the help of systematic field study. This is the main objective of the present study. It promises to throw discernible light on the neglected sphere of the Baul life though it is the inevitable part of the whole structure on which the Baul way of life has obtained its proper shape.

II

In this study emphasis is being laid on examining the traditional background of the Baul life as well as its changing pattern, on the basis of data collected from various angles. The Bauls have been given a supreme position in the realm of truth and philosophy and they have been focused as the mendicants who go against all sort of social and religious institutions. While moving about in search of their only personality, the Man of the Heart, the Bauls devote their own self completely at the feet of the Ultimate Reality. They are against the idol worship and they think that the temples, where the idols are installed, are the barriers to reach the realm of God. Therefore, the holy visits to these temples, mosques or churches, and the performances of ritualistic rites do not show any devotee the right path to get the eternal bliss after coming in association with the Man of the Heart. The present study seeks to cover the different ideas and realistic attitude on this particular background.

The Bauls are regarded as the representatives of a particular community, which has been formed through the direct and indirect interactions of ritualistic and cultural traditions through the ages. It has been observed in the different scholarly studies made at different times that the Bauls are nothing but the products of diverse religious interactions which reached its culmination during the Buddhist influence through the length and breadth of the then Bengal. The Buddhist beliefs and ideas that have permeated the life-ways and thought-ways of the emerging community known as the Bauls faced certain new modes of behaviour when the Vaishnavite rulers became the dominating figures in the country. The phenomenon in question resulted in deep-rooted interactions between the two sets of values and remarkable clashes and conflicts had been the ultimate results that, in due course, led to the trends of cohesion and compromise. The impact of Muslim rulers and their religion brought terrific influence on the life and living of the people and it also infiltrated into the life of Bauls. Some scholars advocate the view that owing to the broad impact of the Islamic beliefs and ideas, the Baul community has evolved specific characteristic features of compromise between the Buddhist and Islamic traditions. It is, no doubt, very difficult to explore the exact nature of interactions with conspicuous time factors that have found place in the mode of life of the Bauls and its development through the ages. The Islamic mysticism which has ultimately given a new perspective *i.e. Sufism* has caused a great deal in the moulding of the Baul sect marked by the concrete analogy between the two. The present study tries to evaluate all these factors from the available data and then it takes a turn to focus the dark horizon prior to the Buddhist dominated period to some extent through the analysis of the behaviour-patterns of the Bauls in association with various socio-historical and theosophical trends found reflected in the minds of the Bauls as well as the people who are the patrons of the Bauls. The Baul culture is essentially a folk culture of Indian origin which is highly characterized by love for the people. There is every probability that the Baul way of life originated before the advent of Buddhism in Bengal when it was not widespread to have a full view of the situation. The fact that this particular community has got no written scripture or any other view of life in writing proves its antiquity. Discernible light has been focussed here to explore this glorious past of the Baul way of life on the basis of information available both from direct and indirect sources. The social status of the people embracing the Baul life have been studied and it is seen that a great percentage of them belong to the lower rungs of the Hindu as well as Muslim communities. The higher caste groups more or less, keep themselves aloof from the Baul mode of life. The members belonging to the lower caste groups even the untouchables greatly come under the fold of the Baul sphere of life. This particular phenomenon indicates the folk basis of the Baul trend of life. Thus it is a pertinent point to evaluate this way of life in the perspective of the traditional folk behaviour-patterns of India. The cultural patterns of India are especially noted for the spirits of accommodation and compromise. These never resisted or tried to strive against any alien belief or practice, rather these created a neutral field for its own development in its line of thinking. Most of the time remarkable interchange of thoughts and ideas have taken place to a large extent which ultimately has given the institution or beliefs concerned a complicated look with the imposition of diverse characteristic features. The Bauls of Bengal represent a neat picture of such interactions of diverse thoughts arising out of Indian as well as alien sources. While passing through a considerable long period of time the basic folk traditions of India had been and is being strikingly influenced by different socio-religious thoughts and ideas like Buddhism, Jainism, Vaishnavism and other sects of Hinduism, Sufism, as well as other aboriginal beliefs in Indian perspective. The present study tries to explore this point from socio-historical background of various institutions and their development in India.

III

The Baul community should not and must not be depicted as an offshoot of Buddhism as believed by most of the scholars or as an integral part of Vaishnavism as some researchers feel. The Baul community has its own identity, developed in the soil of pre-Buddhist India, which, in later periods, has been heavily influenced by multiple thought-patterns. The Bauls have been depicted in all the previous works as the followers of high philosophical principles and they are inextricably interwoven with these deep-rooted understandings. The present work looks into this particular aspect and through various ways it tries to pinpoint the original understandings of the Bauls in the perspective of high philosophical orders.

Apart from the spiritual aspects of the Bauls, the present work explores the less-known phase of Baul existence. The Bauls carry the message of love and friendship to all. This is done through their general mode of behaviour, as well as through the presentation of songs. How far the Bauls are acquainted with these principles, and how do they feel about these ? In a categorical study on the attitude of the Bauls towards these basic principles and on the explanation of terminologies of different beliefs and practices, discernible light has been thrown to understand the practicability of the situation packed up with philosophical view points.

The former studies conspicuously lack one aspect of Baul life which is the pattern of interactions with the non-Bauls. There is a section of Bauls, the members of which lead domestic life and their other family members may or may not lead Baul way of life. These domestic Bauls live in villages characterized by heirarchical patterns and for most part they acquiesce in observing the local rites and rituals as members of the village, though mentally they try to remain free from all such social customs. How are these Bauls interact with their co-villagers ? How are their feelings when they are compelled to the local customary regulations? These questions have been answered as far as possible through the data collected.

The ascetic Bauls are those who are devoted to the life of true asceticism. They are rigid in maintaining their own philosophical principles. But they lead conjugal life with their respective consorts. At the same time they do not like to enter into any normal family life. The whole situation, it is stated, is controlled by the deep-rooted *sadhana* based on the control of the body and mind through the application of some *sexo-yogic* practices. In this perspective the behaviour of the ascetic Bauls has been brought to light and their interactions with their counterparts in the domestic sphere has been evaluated through the mental attitude, social behaviour and cultural patterns. The Bauls belonging to their two sections strongly believe in the principle of *sadhana*, but they differ from each other in their daily mode of life. The domestic Bauls are to proceed with a large number of limitations. How do they compensate ? Are they looked down upon by the ascetic Bauls because of the leading of family life? These questions have been treated with sincerity and seriousness.

In recent years owing to a variety of reasons the educated urban people have been very much attracted towards the Baul way of life. The Bauls are invited to present their songs in the public performances in the urban settings, in the Akashvani and Doordarshan programmes. The Bauls have visited different western countries with their rich heritage of songs and through this they have been able to win over the hearts of the alien audience who are far away from their homes and totally different from their own mode of life and value patterns. The rural Bauls have migrated and are still migrating, in the urban sittings they are being attracted by various allurements. This phenomenon has certainly brought many abrupt changes in the Baul community on the whole and the impact of which have resulted in various conspicuous alterations which go both in favour and against the Baul tradition. Specific explanations of these aspects of Baul life have been attempted.

Through the invaluable songs having a rich cultural heritage, the Bauls spread the message of love for humanity. Though the Bauls are the travellers on the path of spiritualism, they are impatient in the search of intangible, and their songs are not only directed towards God but also towards life. The Bauls accept the varieties of life, and their path is not influenced by rigid stoicism and apathy to life. The Bauls criticise through their songs the utter irrelevancies in life--they criticise through powerful languages the futile rigidity of customary rites in the name of religion, the artificial barriers of caste and religion in man. From time immemorial the Bauls have been singing and thereby preaching the message of love and sympathy to the people. They boldly resist the feuds amongst various castes and religious groups. Above all, the Bauls are the successful mediators who try to establish universal brotherhood. But those untiring efforts of the Bauls towards the establishment of communal harmony has not found any place in the history of communal feuds and caste struggles that have been written through the ages. It is, a remarkable lapse in the attempt of evaluation of Baul life. Their traditional contribution in the perspective of the amelioration of human integrity and total abolishment of communal inequality must be acknowledged and assessed with due honour, otherwise the Baul philosophy cannot be properly understood. The Bauls are promised to earn their living through *madhukari, i.e.*, begging, and they do not earn more than their daily necessities. The central theme of their *sadhana* is based on the universal brother hood and profound love for mankind. These features of the Bauls find parallel in Indian philosophy. The Bauls act as sincere teachers of the common people and their method of teaching is direct which is characterized by numerous concrete examples gathered from the society of the people. The Bauls look at the world differently in comparison to the common people. The study of the world-views of the Bauls has given much importance in the present work to highlight the internal features of actions in the minds of the Bauls. Analysis of a few representative songs collected through extensive field tours focus the line of action of the Bauls in the establishment of fellow-feeling and universal fraternity.

It has been discovered that the rapid changes in the social values and the impact of urban thoughts and ideas on the Bauls, have made the community at the cross-roads of remarkable alterations. The Bauls of the present period have been facing the challenges arising out of the changed pattern of the society in the midst of which they wander about. In the perspective of the changing situation the continuity of the Baul cult has been shown through various presentations of their traditional mode of life that runs through the time without any interruption. Despite the present day popularization of Baul songs vis-a-vis Baul way of life in the minds of the general people has induced the urge to know their activities. In consequence of their continuous inartificial endeavour to provide the people of the world with the overall information on life-philosophy based on mutual love, reciprocal sympathy and universal friendship through the amelioration of mental attitude, the Bauls deserve supreme position in the human society of the world.

IV

The present study is based on such a community which is characterized by wandering habit and complicated modes of behaviour resulted from diverse thoughts and ideas drawn from various socio-religious understandings. In order to conduct a close study amongst this community certain special steps were taken at the very outset in preparing the background for approaching the people concerned in assessing their modes of behaviour. The area over which the Bauls stay and wander about is vast. It is situated in the western part of West Bengal. Five districts in this region, namely Birbhum, Murshidabad, Bankura, Burdwan and Nadia have been taken up to conduct detailed field study on the Bauls. Out of these districts the first one, *i.e.*, Birbhum can be called the homeland of the Bauls. The Bauls are seen to spread throughout the length and breadth of this district. It is the birth place of many eminent Bauls. With these five districts, another neighbouring district known as Purulia has also been taken into consideration. Efforts have been made to find out and to meet a number of Bauls who stay at the family *ashrams* in the Bengali-speaking areas of the neighbouring district of the Santal Pargana in Bihar as well. As the Bauls of the Santal Pargana and Purulia districts have close links with those of the area under study, they are also included in this study. A few Bauls from Hooghly district especially those who attended the famous Rathajatra at Mahesh were also brought under investigation. A number of Bauls from 24 Parganas in West Bengal and some from Dhanbad and Singhbhum districts, both in Bihar, who were also met at different Baul fairs in the western part of West Bengal was included in this investigation. They seem to regularly attend different Baul gatherings in this area under study.

The universe of study was spread over a large geographical area--it was extensively scattered. The selection of the universe was conducted on the basis of a short term pilot survey on different districts in the region of study to understand the actual nature of the population to be studied. It was seen that the concentration of the people to be studied was very much conspicuous in the district of Birbhum. From the very beginning special stress was laid to cover the district of Birbhum as far as possible and for this reason it was taken up first of all; possible measures were adopted to bring many Bauls under the investigation. During pilot survey, the points of concentration of the Bauls in the different districts, the location of various *akhras* or *ashrams* and also the date and time of performance of annual or other customary gatherings of the Bauls in these centres were carefully enquired.

The Bauls represent peculiarities and they are different from the common people in respect of their way of life. They stay amongst the people but do not share their day-to-day life and activities. They refuse to be guided by any convention--social or religious. They proceed in a direction which is completely at variance with the path followed by the common people. Owing to this, the Bauls depict their path as *ulta* or reverse, and they place themselves as the followers of a trend which proceeds against the current. The Bauls are not internally free to converse with the outsiders and non-Bauls though they in appearance show all sorts of co-operation. The Bauls always follow dualism in their talk with the people as well as in their nature of songs presented before the people. In short, all their activities carry double meaning.

In order to cope with the situation, a few special techniques were adopted in gathering information from amongst the Bauls who follow the *ulta* path in their life. At the very outset efforts were made to pick up a few local energetic and educated young men having special inclination towards Baul life and to train them up as ground workers. The author with his thorough understanding of the region and basic knowledge on the universe of the study, made contacts with some persons, who were very close to the Bauls and were engaged in the observations and discussions on Baul life and activities. Most of them were prolific composers of Baul songs as well as the writers of Baul philosophy. With the help of these persons having direct contact with the Baul life the author was able to make tours through the districts, and having a considerable first-hand knowledge on the geography and society of the region of study, was able to pick up a few devoted and enthusiastic persons for the spade work. These persons had acquaintance, familiarity and knowledge on the peculiar terminologies and local dialects particularly used by the Bauls. It is to be noted, in this connection, that the Bauls, most of the time converse amongst themselves and also with the outsiders in some sorts of code dilects which can only be deciphered instantaneously by the people having thorough command over the local dilect as well as the local mentality. Until and unless proper efforts are made to grasp these code dialect-influenced conversations the proper entry into the inner recess of Baul life cannot be made. At first these persons who have closeness with the Baul life were trained up in the line of basic investigation and they were extensively used as first hand informers on the basis of which an integrated frame of reference had been chalked out.

The author's constant visit to the different people interested in the Baul life in the whole region of study and his former acquaintance with a number of influential and devoted Bauls who have been organising *akhras* or Baul centres made it possible to establish a congenial atmosphere for this in-depth study. Picking up of the Bauls roaming over a vast stretch was indeed a very difficult task and a few categorical techniques were adopted to do the particular job. It was done by the use of what is called snowball sampling technique. The Bauls, in a region, are very much known to each other. After interviewing an individual Baul, he was asked to give some concrete instruction to know the whereabouts of the others. In this way the linking members of this population were gradually found out and brought under investigation. In this study the district of Birbhum being the birth place of Baul culture in the western part of West Bengal was given special importance and all of them were met and interrogated. In the case of other adjoining districts the respondents were selected by the stratified sampling method. It helped categorically in presenting the entire qualities of the universe proportionately. It was also associated with quota sampling. But sometimes due to the scattered and wandering nature of the universe there was no alternative but to use convenience-sampling to serve the purpose. In the district of Nadia the cluster sampling technique was very much effective and it was done during the agglomeration of the Bauls at the important fairs. While working on the Fakirs, the cluster sampling was the only way out, for searching them scattered over the vast geographical region, entailed enormous wastage of money as well as non-productive time spending during travelling. The sampling of cluster from the population was done through the adoption of random sampling method.

The study was based on the different types of interviews, observations and case-studies from the selected respondents. During field investigations altogether 229 Bauls and 42 Fakirs have been interrogated individually. According to nature and extent of the way of meditation and specialized behaviour-patterns the Bauls were divided into three distinct categories---the *Ascetic, Domestic* and *Others*. The Bauls who follow the rigid rules of Baul life and maintain asceticism all through the time have been termed as 'Ascetic Bauls'. The Bauls, who lead family life, and perform all sorts of family duties in addition to their *sadhana* as per their initiation in the Baul life, are called 'Domestic Bauls'. Those Bauls who identify themselves as the Bauls but do not follow the strict regulations of Baul life, rather they depict a loose pattern of life, are brought under the sphere of 'Others'.

Both structured and unstructured types of interviews were made with the three categories of the Bauls, and for this a large number of villages and *akhras* covered. It was a troublesome affair and which aroused many problems during work. On getting information about a particular Baul, it became indispensable to walk for a long distance to reach his village or *akhra* and on going over there it had been seen that the particular Baul was out for *madhukari*. It was really very difficult to make successful contact with the Bauls at the very first attempt. Sometimes it so happened that on reaching a particular *ashram* the investigator came to know that the Baul concerned was engaged in *sadhana* and it would take time to be free. It repeatedly happened in case of the ascetic Bauls. Whatever might be the fact the investigator could create an impression that he is interested in understanding the greatness of the Baul life and as an essential part of knowledge it should be circulated to the people having deep regard for the same. The uniqueness of the life of the Bauls as well as the greatness of their songs were highlighted profusely through the constant appeal of the investigator which made the Bauls sympathetic towards him. There were large number of instances in which the respondents became active in coming forward to the investigator to answer their questions and sometimes they did not hesitate to stop their routine activities. At times they escorted him to other places for meeting with more respondents.

A detailed questionnaire depicting all aspects of life and thoughts of the Bauls through the insertion of 103 different questions was used all through the time to collect information from all types of Bauls. In addition to this two short questionnaires were prepared, one for the Bauls and the other for the *Fakirs*, to collect rapid information during survey. Over and above these, various familial and village-level information were collected from the Domestic Bauls through a schedule. Unstructured interview was the only useful source to collect information on the personal as well as intimate nature and much time and energy was devoted for the application of this method. At the time of investigating into the inner recess of life of the respondents, the focussed interview method was sharply adopted. At the mature stage of investigation, measures were adopted to take in-depth interview of some eminent Bauls, to go deep into their minds for having some information on psycho-social situations. Post-interview conversations were conducted wherever possible to maintain the tempo of interview. A mailed questionnaire was prepared with 20 different questions to collect information about the Bauls from the lovers and scholars in the line of Baul research. It was felt in course of investigation that the reflections in the minds of many Baul lovers and efficient thinkers about the Bauls should be given due importance for getting possible avenues to go deep into the various phases of life of the Bauls. With this end in view a list was prepared during the course of investigation with the names and addresses of some conspicuous persons in the line just discussed, and arrangements were made to mail the questionnaires with the requisite appeal and stamped addressed envelopes for getting replies. The nature of response was satisfactory and in some cases the answers to the different questions given by the rural intelligentsia provoked many new angles for study and analysis in respect of the investigation concerned. As most of the replies are based on personal observations from close quarters through a long span of time, these depicted the total pictures of every perspective.

The success of this type of work was largely dependent on the different types of observations, and efforts have been made all through the time to prepare fertile fields for taking observations of participant and non-participant nature. Special alertness was always maintained to keep close observations on the behaviour-patterns of the respondents. In order to adopt this method proper arrangements had been made to attend the different Baul fairs and assemblages throughout the year. In the region of study a large number of traditional Baul gatherings are held at different centres especially on some fixed dates in which the Bauls gather spontaneously. There are also occasions when the Bauls are invited formally to attend the fair or *mahotsab, i.e.,* great festival. These *mahotsabs* are not to be regarded as mere assemblages of the Bauls but these are the occasions when various activities relating to social, philosophical and religious spheres are performed many socio-religious problems in connection with the conjugal life of the Bauls, taking of initiation or reciprocal misunderstanding, *etc.* are readily solved. From the very beginning a programme had been chalked out as regards the places and dates of such Baul *mahotsabs* or gatherings and were attended in time. It was really very difficult thing. Maintenance of the time schedules in attending the fairs and *mahotsabs* of the Bauls became a considerable problem. Most of the *mahotsabs* were held in inaccessible places and there were no particular arrangements for boarding and lodging. At places the minimum facilities for staying even in an uncomfortable way were absent. Despite all sorts of disadvantages and obstacles the author along with the field assistants made it a point to attend all the important *mahotsabs* for a few days, starting from inauguration to the closing function of the ceremonies concerned. During the performance of such observational studies special emphasis was laid to live with the Bauls, to talk freely with them and to eat side by side with them in the general feasts of the *mahotsabs*. From close quarters it has been possible to observe their different modes of behaviour, manner of conversation, smoking of *ganja*, nature of meditation, presentation of songs and various other activities of related nature. Specific observation-oriented eyes were constantly put on the spontaneous and unexposed pictures of life led by the respondents. In these gatherings the Bauls became free from all sorts of obligations, if any, and they used to dedicate themselves fully in the presentation of songs to the accompaniment of rhythmic dances. It was the opportune moment in having a full view of the performance. Some representative songs had been collected and the dance peculiarities were carefully noted. The observations that were made on dance patterns were thoroughly recorded through the method of photography. The photographic 'eyes' were always applied to record the dance and other related behaviour patterns of the Bauls with authenticity and impartiality. Most of the actions, organised or spontaneous, were given a full-fledged view through the camera lens to keep off the records from the preconceived notions and selective interests. Attempts have been made in this study to take some serial photographs relating to the different activities of Bauls for getting a more or less perfect visual understandings of the fact. Some representative songs were also recorded through tape-recorders. These observations were made years after years and the data collected on the events during different years were compared and systematically analysed.

The case-study method had been adopted largely to explore the internal facets of the *ashram* units composed of the Bauls, both males and females. In order to delve deep into the emotional side of the socio-cultural phenomena the application of case-study method became very much fruitful. The Bauls have got varied personal experience in their life and all these experiences given proper shape of the community as a whole. In order to have a full view of the actions and reactions on the community the whole life of the respondents was portrayed through the taking of cases and analysing the elements of the actual life-situations. Various events of the respondent's life were collected carefully through long-term discussions and those were categorically analysed to find out their social significance.

The biographies that have been gathered from a number of Bauls were utilized to focus the different strands of discussion of Baul thought.

By thorough analysing of the compact biographies of the Bauls some concrete information could be gathered on the personality type of the community.

The Bauls have two sets of life--overt and covert. The overt view of life is accessible to a considerable extent by the outsiders and the genuine field workers having the knowledge of all methodological principles can be able to enter into this area of life for getting information. But the covert view of life of the Bauls is very difficult to look into. The Bauls, both ascetic and domestic, are very much sensible to this aspect of life and in no circumstance, they allow any outsider to have a knowledge about it. It is their own affair and they think that no non-Baul has any right to peep into it. It is really a very difficult situation. The covert view of life is characterized by the actual nature of *sadhana* organised by the Baul, the manner of conjugal life based on *sexo-yogic* principles, their basic philosophy of obtaining Realistic Love through the full enjoyment of worldly love, based on the bodily union of the *Purusha* and *Prakriti.* When anybody goes to have some idea about it, the Baul readily declines to throw any light on it by saying that they have got nothing of that kind. But in reality there are definite evidences of having such type of life within the Baul community. The Guru of the Bauls imparts practical training to the male and female disciples for going through the bodily union by the total control of the sexual passion. It was done through the critical psycho-physiological procedures. It is not possible for the outsiders to enter deeply into this realm of activities of the Bauls. But some efforts were made to have some idea about this covert life through a particular way devised for this purpose. The Bauls show aversion to discuss these covert activities with the non-Bauls, and whatever may be the strength of rapport or closeness of personal understanding they always stick to this point. In course of investigation into the Baul way of life it was seen that there were some persons who took initiation from the Baul *Guru,* but they did not take to the mendicant life. Rather they led family life like others, and by having formal education they established themselves as teachers, writers, journalists and other professional persons. The author had close friendship with a few of those initiated Bauls which was established by the long connection through his literary activities and various types of social works. In order to cope with the situation those initiated Bauls were approached to make contact with the mendicant Bauls for making the atmosphere for discussions in this line. It was a sort of close door interview and none except the author and his initiated Baul friend was allowed to sit with the Baul. It was conveniently seen that after a short-term intensive discussions on the spirit of the survey work the interviewee became highly articulate about the situation. During the time of taking interview there was ample advantage to check, control or instruct the mediator as per convenience and necessity. All possible efforts were made to have some basic and practical knowledge about the covert behaviour of the Bauls through this specially devised way. It is not only a painstaking affair but it needs long and close set acquaintence with the Bauls conditioned by friendship, love and mutual understanding.

The data relating to the documentary sources were collected from the beginning of the survey work. Like the acutely scattered universe the documentary data are spread over a wide perspective and to collect these needs a tremendous labour and sufficient time at hand. There are a few authentic books on the Baul life but most of the other works are scattered in the shape of stray articles. A large part of these works belong to the literary perspectives and many of these are based on superficial observations. There are a few literary works, done in Bengali language, which obviously depict the well-knit picture of the behaviour-patterns of the Bauls. All these works have been searched out as far as possible and were primarily consulted to examine their range of discussions. These works, it is natural, could not extend any help to conduct serious sociological works but certainly these threw some light on the formulation of some concrete categories for baseline study. The serious types of works on the Bauls, though put forward in a different way, were consulted deeply to understand the basic nature of the Baul life and philosophy. The author was all along alert in collecting the nature and extent of large number of articles on Baul life that appeared in the little magazines published from the different districts of West Bengal. Sometimes these may communicate many new ideas as these works are mainly based on personal observations made by the writers born and brought up amongst the Bauls. The historical accounts of different fairs and festivals held in the rural areas were collected from the historical records as well as other officially published data supervised by the State and the Central Government. Various works on Buddhist, Islam, Hindu and Sufistic religious literatures had been consulted to evaluate various data on the Baul philosophy and working principles gathered during field work.

To get quantitative indices of the dimensions and for obtaining the frequency counts in respect of the replies to the various questions the coding was carefully made. After getting a sufficient mass of data of qualitative nature the different categories of replies were identified through the use of code number. In this way the qualitative replies of the respondents were changed to specific numbers. With the help of these simple statistics, calculations were attended and the relevant tables were made.

V

Rabindranath Tagore is unquestionably regarded as the pioneer in the celebrated effort of bringing the tradition-bound Baul life to the scholastic world. As mentioned earlier, he presented the behaviour-patterns of the Bauls, first of all, before the international scholars through his Presidential Address given at the Philosophical Congress held on the 18th December, 1925 under the auspices of the Calcutta University. While putting forward the deep-rooted philosophical principles in the life-style of the people of India he made a relevant reference to the Baul community following a characteristic philosophy of their own. It was followed by a broad-based article entitled "The Bauls and Their Cult", and which was published in the *Visvabharati Quarterly* in 1928. The article in question was written by Professor Kshitimohan Sen, a close associate of Rabindranath Tagore. It was based on the observations in respect of Baul Life in the perspective of their philosophical settings. It attracted the attention of the scholars in that particular field of study. Rabindranath from the very beginning of his poetic works became very much interested in the Bauls. While he was in Silaidaha, a picturesque spot under his zamindary in Eastern Bengal (now in Bangladesh), he had the chance to come in close contact with a few eminent Bauls in that locality. In course of time Rabindranath became very much influenced by the life and activities of the Bauls and this influence was visible in his literary works also. In 1905, when Rabindranath came forward to put a resistance on the partition of Bengal planned by the then British rulers, he composed a few patriotic songs in the Baul tuning. In that year he published a booklet named *Baul* in which a few songs were composed on Baul line of thinking.

In 1915 (corresponding to 1322 B.S. (the leading Bengali monthly *Pravashi* (first published in 1308 B.S. or 1901 A.D.) opened a sectional discussion department named "Haramani". It was started with an editorial request put forward to the readers of the journal to send their personal collection of folk songs and related matters for their serial publications. In the first issue the famous Baul song of Gagan Harkara was published which was collected by Rabindranath Tagore. It was associated with required musical notations. His poetic works were very much influenced by the direct and indirect impact of Baul life and thinking. He was aware of that impact. He was always against the distortion of Baul songs as he believed that there was an inartificial speciality in Baul songs which was to be collected with great caution. There were so many songs composed by him which were cast in the Baul line but he did not try to imitate these. Those were conspicuously composed by Rabindra-Baul (Mansooruddin, 1972 : 195). In Birbhum, Rabindranath came very close to the Bauls and here he started finding out the inner recess of the Baul line of thinking for understanding their philosophy based on simple deeds and talks. Rabindranath met *Sarva-Khepi* in a remote village and he was overwhelmed by her simple talk to him which contained profound meaning. He "felt that the woman, in her direct vision of the infinite personality in the heart of all things, truly represented the spirit of India" (1922 : 77). In his '*Creative Unity*' (1922) a chapter was devoted to Indian region in which a brief discussion of his own findings of the Baul way of life and philosophy was made. Rabindranath's contribution to the sphere of Baul study took world wide recognition when he presented the life and thinking patterns of the Bauls before the scholarly gathering of the world through his famous Hibbert Lecture delivered at Oxford University in the year 1930. In his celebrated lecture on the broad topic like "The Religion of Man" he emphasised that "coming from men who (the Bauls) are unsophisticated, living a simple life in obscurity it gives us a clue to the inner meaning of all religions" (Tagore, 1930 : 19). Sashi Bhusan Dasgupta (1940), came forward with an analytical standpoint to evaluate the various aspects of Baul life. He made a very fascinating study on the nature of Baul philosophy and did a scholastic evaluation of the different historical processes through which the Baul community had emerged. The different religious complexes in the background of Buddhism, Hinduism and Islamic beliefs had been categorically analysed to fit the various situation of Baul thoughts and ideas. While studying the Baul he observes that the "freedom of spirit is their watch-word and they take to an unsophisticated way of life in which the more natural inclinations of the mind are not restrained by social institution" (1946 : 185). This particular study takes a departure from the earlier works because of the fact that it tries to put analytical methodology in the emergence and development of the Baul cult in the background of the

Buddhist Sahajiya and Vaishnava Sahajiya ideas along with Sufistic perspective. On this ground it is to be considered as the pioneer work in the sphere of the analytical phase of study on the Baul community. Chittaranjan Dev, a reputed worker in the sphere of folk songs has made some passing remarks on the Baul and Vaishnava songs and their interpretations in his book entitled *Palligeeti O Purbabanga* or 'Village Songs and East Bengal', published in the year 1957. In his observatio s through tour along with village paths the author noted many features of integrity and fusion of Bauls mode of living.

Professor Kshiti Mohan Sen's work in Bengali, entitled *Banglar Baul,* or 'The Bauls of Bengal', appeared in 1954. It was the outcome of the "Lila Lecture Series" delivered before the Calcutta University a year prior to its publication. In this book Professor Sen has presented the Baul philosophy in a sophisticated background. He has accounted for the origin of the Baul community as a non-Shastric, scripture-free spiritual entity nurtured by the non-Aryan people beyond the boundary of the Aryan territory. He has depicted the Baul religion as one which is based on eternal truth of humanity. Therefore, it had its origin with the emergence of man. *The Vedas are too junior in comparison to it and this is why these are artificial* (1954 : 3). Professor Sen, in this work, has tried to put a comparative statement between the Baul philosophy and Vedic line of thinking. In a number of places he has put forward different Sanskritic extracts from various *Shastras* and has tried to make a comparison between these two lines of approaches. At one place he has made some discussions on the non-availability of the real Bauls and the preponderance of the fake Bauls. All through this work Professor Sen has become vocal in putting forward the theology and the procedure of *sadhana* of the Bauls. It can be said with certainty that Professor Sen's study is completely based on library work though he has pointed out the incidents of a few visits with some eminent Bauls.

Professor Upendranath Bhattacharya entered the field of investigation on the Bauls with majestic gait. He surpassed all other works on the subject by his study in Bengali entitiled - *"Banglar Baul O Baul Gian"* or 'The Baul and the Baul songs of Bengal' published in 1957. It supersedes all the former works by virtue of its deep approach as well as its voluminous size. Professor Bhattacharya did not accept the nature and extent of study made by his predecessors, especially that made by Professor Kshiti Mohan Sen. He criticised Prof. Sen's approach to the study on the Baul by saying that most of the time he based his views on imagination and not on facts. He went to the extent of saying that Prof. Sen's observations on the Baul philosophy and the nature of *sadhana* did not tally with those behaviours as followed by the Bauls of Bengal. The way in which the Bauls of the present day sing their songs, the manner through which they perform religious activities have got no similarities with the nature of songs and the procedures of *sadhana* as depicted by Prof. Sen (1957 : 73). Leaving everything aside, Professor Bhattacharya began to tour throughout the rural areas in search of the Bauls and thereby having their close association. In course of his time-long painstaking tour through the districts, he was able to collect a large number of songs and during which he mixed freely not only with the Bauls but also with the *Fakir* and *Vaishnava* mendicants. All his findings were systematically incorporated in his epoch-making voluminous book as mentioned. The book in question is broadly divided into two parts,--first part is devoted to the analytical study on the Bauls and their philosophical principles with critical statements on their every stage of development, whereas the second part is packed up with as many as 679 songs collected by him. In this voluminous work Prof. Bhattacharya politely admitted that the actual time of origin of Baul line of thinking could not be traced. It was rather impossible to search out the source because of the lack of materials of the social and religious history of the 17 the Century Bengal (1957: ix). In 1957, a book entitled *Study of Changes in Traditional Culture* was edited by Prof. K.P.Chattopadhyay and it was the outcome of a Seminar organised by the Department of Anthropology, Calcutta University. In an article published in that book Prof. Somendranath Bandhopadhyay made a valuable discussion on the nature of Baul songs of Bengal and the impact of changes on these due to modernism. It categorically pointed out the changing patterns of the songs in the perspective of the changed economic life of India.

Das and Mahapatra edited an anthology of Lalan songs. Lalan was a devoted Baul of East Bengal and he came in close contact with Rabindranath Tagore. The book entitled, *Lalan Gitika* (1958) provided as many as 462 songs said to have been composed by Lalan with hints and running notes at the end. Another anthology of Baul songs collected mostly from Eastern Bengal had been presented by Muhammad Mansoor Uddin and it was entitled *'Haramoni'* (1961). The collection was characterized by orginality. In the same year another book of Baul songs compiled by Tarachand Das appeared. It contained various types of songs with short analysis of the different phases underlying these. Kalidas Roy in his study on Padavali Literature (1961), made some passing remarks on the Baul life in the perspective ofVaishnava literature. In this connection, Sitanath Roy's work, entitled *Brihat Baul Sangit*, or "The Great Baul Songs" deserves mention. It contained different types of songs sung by the Bauls. In her work on *Banglar Sadhak Baul* (1962), Indira Devi threw discerning light on the ascetic Bauls of Bengal . The study in question focussed considerable light on the nature and extent of asceticism in the Baul way of living. In 1964, P. Chattopadhyay edited a book entitled *Baul Sangit*, or "The Baul Songs" following the former principles of preparing anthology. Another book on Baul songs edited by Nandalal Seal deserves mention in this connection.

The year 1965 was marked by the publication of an analytical book on the Bauls written by a veteran author, Dr. Somendra Nath Bandyopadhyay. The book entitled "*Banglar Baul: Kavya O Darsan*", or "The Bauls of Bengal - Poetry and Philosophy", was devoted to the the - analytical study on the history and specialities of the Bauls. He wanted to understand the nature of the Bauls through songs based on rich heritage of philosophical principles. The author efficiently discussed the various corners of Baul philosophy and he rightly pointed out the life-oriented *sadhana* of the Baul community; it was not totally directed towards God. Throughout his discussions the writer tried to pick up the underlying truth on which the Baul *sadhana* rested and flourished.

Dr. Bhattacharya a noted litterateur and a scholar in the field of folk culture, gave a fascinating discussion on the origin and development of the Baul in his voluminous study entitled-*Bangiya Lok--Sangeet Ratnakar*, or the "Quarry of Gems of Bengali Folk Songs", published in 1967. He claimed the Baul cult as the very ancient folk cult of Bengal having the traditional Indian life-ways and thought-ways, which, in course of its travel through the ages, assimilated many features, beliefs and ideas of alien and sophisticated religions. He carefully pin-pointed the course of development of two branches namely the Muslim Baul and the Vaishnava Baul - the latter in turn branched off into two sections, *e.g.*, Nabadwipi branch and Rarhiya branch. As many as 214 Baul songs collected by him had been presented at the end of main discussion on the community.

Sanat Kumar Bose has depicted a very fascinating picture on the Baul songs in his thought-provoking article entitled, "Baul Songs of

Bengal'' appeared in an anthology *Folk Music and Folklore,* edited by the noted musicologist Hemango Biswas, in 1967. In his article, Bose has shown that the different types of folk-songs in Bengal are characterized by fusions and integrations and these have emerged from a very right and highly complex type of cultural life. He has emphasized that the Baul songs symbolize exclusively the spiritual quests of the people belonging to a particular community. But the people, are not being able to evaluate these in their proper perspective. They generally mix these up with other folk songs. He has tried all through his article to pin-point the spiritual nature of all types of songs which form the quintessence of each of these. In spite of the rich tradition, the author laments, the Baul Songs are disappearing for ever. The Baul singers have now been attracted to the professional musical programmes of the urban sittings. They are now mainly interested in earning money and fame amongst the middle class intelligentsia in urban setting. In an earlier article entitled, ''The Bauls of Birbhum'' (1966), appeared in the Annexure of the *Birbhum District Handbook* under 1961 Census, the same author has pointed out the life and thought of the Bauls in a limited perspective. He has emphasized that as a typical figure in rural Bengal the Baul is the bearer of the richest cultural heritage which is reflected in his folk-songs. He has felt that for some inevitable reasons the Baul community is gradually dying out.

The renowned litterateur Samaresh Bose, under pseudonym 'Kalkut', has given a picturesque description of the Baul centres throughout Bengal and the different modes of behaviour of the Bauls and the Fakirs in his famous novel entitled, '*Kothai Pabo Tarey*', or ''Where shall I meet him ?", published in 1968. Unlike other novels this particular work is the manifestation of the lively reflection of the author's thorough tour in the Baul concentrated region and personal contact with the people of the said community. The very title of the work has been taken from the first line of the famous Baul song of Gagan Harkara collected by Rabindranath Tagore. This book is not only a unique contribution to the field of literature, but it also presents tremendous interest in the sphere of social science.

Mani Bardhan, the reputed folk dancer, has presented the systematic description of his tour and study in the different Baul concentrated regions of West Bengal in a book entitled, *Banglar Loknritya O Giti Bichitra,* or ''Folk Dances of Bangal and Diversities of Songs'' published by the Government of West Bengal in 1969. In course of his discussions on the selected songs sung by the Bauls at the different centres he has brought to light many intrinsic features of Bauls philosophy. While analysing the nature of dances performed by the Bauls he has highlighed many distinctive features of folk dances practised by the Bauls of the different regions of the country. D.Bhattacharya rendered English translation, in a very lucid and rhythmic way, of a large number of Baul songs which were published in a book form entitled, *The Mirror of the Sky* (1969). The songs were in original Bengali and collected from the different published works as well as direct from the field. The songs are beautifully translated keeping the original tempo of Baul songs intact. These are systematically arranged to explore the different recesses of Baul life.

Dilip Mukhopadhyay, in his book, entitled, *Uttar Rarher Lok Sangit*, or "The Folk Songs of Northern Rarrh" (1979), has devoted a few pages on the discussion on the Baul community. In a brief perspective he has tried to depict the different theological principles followed by this community. He has categorically discussed the constituent elements of Baul religion as well as the nature and extent of the working patterns of the prophets. At the end of the discussion 24 songs of different nature in the sphere of the Baul have been presented.

Rabindranath Gangopadhyay contributed some basic nature Baul line of thinking in the background of metaphysical understanding of things. In course of his study entitled, "A Glimpse into the Baul Culture of Bengal", published in *The Contemporary* (1972), he highlighted the way of intermingling of the Baul culture with the Vaishnavite faith as well as with Sufistic mentality. A few conspicuous Vaishnava dominated fairs and festivals attended by the Bauls throughout the years have been brought under discussion.

Another book on the anthology of the Baul songs after translating these into English from original Bengali deserves mention here. Aloke Ranjan Das Gupta and Mary Ann Das Gupta presented 57 songs collected from both the published and field sources in the book entitled, *Root in the Void - Baul Songs of Bengal*, published in 1977. The book in question is divided into five sections each of which has been provided with a number of representative songs befitting the central theme of the sections concerned. The English rendering of the songs are elegantly done. The five sections are - *Roots in the Void, The Winged Flute, Troubadours of Love, The Sea of Beauty* and *Wedding Palanquin.*

Dr. Sanat Mitra, in his book *Lalan Fakir - Kavi O Kavya*, or 'Lalan Fakir - Poet and Poetry', published in 1979, has given a new line of thinking on the life and works of Lalan, the famous Baul in East Bengal. He has claimed his observations on Lalan and his connection with Rabindranath as original. While discussing the eventful life of the great Baul, he has categorically discussed the nature and extent of Baul philosophy. At the end of second part of the book as many as 225 songs strongly believed to have been composed by the poet himself, have been appended. The songs have been classified into sixteen categories according to their central themes. In his another earlier edited work on Kartabhaja sect, Dr. Mitra tried his level best to pinpoint the different lines of thinking of the sect pertaining to the Baul way of life as well as the history of development of the sect including its impact on the people. The book *Kartabhaja : Dharmamat O Itihas*, or "*Kartabhaja:* Religious Ideas and History" (1975) deserves attention in this line of thinking.

Surath Chandra Chakravorty has presented the Bauls in a very high esteem of philosophical perspective in his book. *The Bauls - the Spiritual Vikings*, published in 1980. The author has established his ability in focussing the Baul line of thinking from various angles of theological priciples. Various mysteries of Baul life and activities have been analysed here in the background of diverse religious faiths flourishing in the soil of India. From his analytical study on the Baul thoughts and ideas he has observed that the "Bauls are the spiritual Vikings in the turbulent ocean of spiritual life" (1980 : 2). The work is fully based on library findings and the songs utilised here have been taken from the published works of Prof. Upendranath Bhattacharya. Tripti Brahma in her works on folk religious songs of Bengal has highlighted the Baul life from diverse angles. She has analysed the patterns of impact of various religious practices on the development of Baul cult and has categorically shown, by arranging for concrete examples, the direct and indirect influences of different religious beliefs on the way of *sadhana* of the Bauls. Her works contained in the book *Lokajibane Banglar Loukik Dharma-Sangit* or "Folk Relgious Songs of Bengal in Folk Life", published in 1982, have focussed discernible light on the nature of songs and their origin. The recoginition of the composers of Baul songs and various categories of songs divided on the basis of their central theme. While analysing the songs and putting these in the systematic orders the author has shown considerable efficiency in focussing the actual purpose of these in the light of deep-rooted philosophy.

Prof. Carol Solomon of Pennsylvania University has made an enchanting study on the interpretation of the Bilvamangal Chintamani legend through the songs as characteristically sung by the devoted Baul Sanatan Das. It is a love episode of Vaishnava tradition which has been given an artistic touch by the sincere interpretation of Sanatan Das through his melodious tune and heartfelt presentation. In an article entitled" A Contemporary Sahajiya Interpretation of the Bilvamangal Cintamani Legend, as sung by Sanatan Das Baul and published in the *Folklore* (Bangladesh) in 1982 under the editorship of Dr. Anwarul Karim. By way of depiction of the love episode the article discusses many points on the Baul *sadhana* especially those are based on Sahajiya sexual *sadhana*. In his study Prof. Solomon feels that the mythical episodes of India "continues to be reworked, changed and revitalized in accordance with the needs of every century" (1982 : 21).

In a booklet entitled *Banglar Lokajibane Baul*, or "Baul in the folk-life of Bengal" published in 1983, Amit Gupta has given his observations made through occasional haphazard tour in the Baul fairs and festivals. The subject - matters are displayed in different solitary and brief chapters but these are placed in a descriptive nature. At the end of the booklet there is a brief directory of Baul fairs and festivals held in the different districts. Besides this, 31 Baul songs in original Bengali have been appended here. In a long article on the *Aul*, written in Bengali, published in the *Saptaha* (1983), a Bengali Weekly, Saktinath Jha has attempted at evaluating the opinions given by the different scholars of India and Bangladesh on the *Aul* community. Various close similarities and broad differences between *Aul* and Baul have been highlighted here in the background of empirical evidence adduced from the religious texts of diferent sects. In spite of its dependency on published work the study is thought-provoking.

Dr. Sarkar in his article entitled "Conflict Compromise and Diversity-Unity Oriented Life-Philosophy of a wandering community" published in 1984, has categorically focussed how the wandering community of singers like the Bauls are centralised on a theme of unity in diversity - a particular trend in the thinking pattern of these people - and how their behaviour- patterns are moulded according to this particular principle. They are always eager to establish compromising atmosphere in these sorts of conflicting situations. They are against any type of discrimination based on caste, class, religion or any other factor, because they find man as an ultimate reality. In Baul cult love for humanity is given supreme position. It is the way of love through which one can make an entry into the realm of man. He has shown how the Bauls attempt to consider human body as the microcosm of the Universe - it is the sacred abode of the Absolute. This Absolute is the Baul's Soul's Companion popularly known to them as *Maner Manush* or Man of the Heart. This study basically explores the underlying principles maintained by the Bauls to find out the way to reach that Man of the Heart. The traditional long-term journey of the Bauls through the ages is devoted to the search of the *Maner Manush.*

In another article entitled "The Bauls of Bengal: Their diverse nature and pattern of Thinking", published 1988, Dr. Sarkar has put forward variegated dimensions of Baul life and philosophy. Starting from the origin of this community in the soil of Bengal through the presentation of different factual evidences he has tried, in this paper, to highlight the development of the community concerned through the ages and its impact on the regional life-pattern. It has been shown with the help of concrete field data how the tradition-bound and rigidity - oriented Bauls are being moulded in a different way according to the changing society. The traditional classification pattern of the Bauls has to be re-oriented on the basis of their changing mode of life. The inter-actions of these newly developed categories of the Bauls have been put forward in a compact way to understand the values in intragroup and intergroup perspectives of the newly formed and traditional categories of the Bauls. The continuity and change of the rich cultural heritage nurtured by the Bauls have been focused through different angles.

Above are the various types of systematic studies made on the Baul community which deserve mention in connection with this work. Besides these, there are a good many articles published in the popular journals in Bengali which depict the different spheres on the life and thinking of the Bauls. But as all these are either based on superficial studies or are centred around much discussed subject matter with same conference as depicted by the eminent authors in this line so these are not included in this review. But a record has been kept at the bibliography as far as possible through a time-long drive in the different libraries at the National and State levels and also in the allied sources throughout the districts of study.

2

Bauls in Traditional Perspective

The Baul community is unique. This particular community represents the concrete portrait of the rich cultural heritage of the traditional land and people of Bengal. There is no denying the fact that Bengal has always been the fertile field for the development of various cultural traits conditioned by the direct and indirect patterns of interactions amongst diverse life-ways and thought-ways of the people. The rural life of Bengal is highly characterized by indigenous beliefs and practices centered round the network of rivers and creeks as well as vast tracts or fields covered by green vegetations and golden crops. The villages of Bengal have the tradition of rich cultural perspective which developed over a long span of time. The people of Bengal were mainly dominated by the native rites, rituals, and communal ceremonies which developed out of their own philosophy of life. The Aryan and other immigrants in later years could exert influence on the indigenous belief-pattern, but it was not possible for the outsiders to wipe out all the traditional elements constituting the principal theme of life and activities of the people. As a dominant group with new outlook and understanding the Aryans could ultimately penetrate into the inner recess of life of the people and thereby to bring into effect striking changes in the way of life of the people, though, restricted to the higher sections with conspicuous economic background. The Aryans began to teach the people their way of life and the natives were, most of the time, compelled to imbibe all those ideas and beliefs of the conquerers. Sometimes they deliberately accepted some elements of the Aryan life due to immediate benefit of socio-economic nature. The process of Aryanization took a long way to inflict the foreign ideas upon the very way of life of the indigenous people or Bengal. But, mention may be made that, the lower sections of the people with meagre economic means and tribal perspective could maintain their traditional patterns of life to a considerable extent. Amongst the lower sections of the people these characteristics, *i.e.*, non-Aryan elements are still noticeable in their life. In the rural areas especially which are highly dominated by the lower sections of people, the trend of Aryanization seem to be less effective and at times the non-Aryan features supersede the Brahminical procedures. There are numerous folk deities and attached folklore and traditions which have been maintaining the indigenous philosophy to a considerable extent. There are tremendous interactions between the Aryan and non-Aryan traditions and these have been playing an essential role in shaping the form and function of life through the ages. Rural Bengal, therefore, exhibits a clear picture of retaining the traditional culture, despite large scale impact of alien influence.

After the large scale Aryanization of the land and people two distinct traditions became apparent. Sometimes they indulged in direct clashes and at other times they found a way of mutual understandings. In the later phases the whole of Bengal became heavily disturbed through the conflicts and clashes amongst different religious sects. The Jainism, the Buddhism, the Islam, the Hinduism and its various factions started exerting influence on the people of Bengal at different times. There are evidences that the various religious groups, in course of their spread throughout the country, have aroused many unfortunate situations. Thus the history of ancient Bengal is characterized by conflict and cohesion had existed. The social history of Bengal pinpoints an idea of conflict and compromise, clash and tolerance. There are a few human communities in this part of the country, the members of which contribute to this particular perspective in their day to day life. .Sometimes these are so manifest that it seems they are the living embodiments of traditional Bengal. The Baul community is regarded as the best example of such kind of living embodiment, the life and activities of which are highly characterized by contradictory ideas and conflicting attitudes but conditioned by deep-rooted compromise and tolerance.

The Bauls are the subject-matter of profound surprise. From time immemorial they have been attracting the people belonging to various grades. Many scholars have tried to analyse the way of life of this particular community but have failed to highlight all the aspects of life of these variegated people. The Bauls are undoubtedly the products of the villages of Bengal, nurtured by the air and water of the same. All of them have been derived from the peasants and as a natural consequence they share the very philosophy of peasant community that has been moulded in the background of the stresses and strains of the society as a whole. The Bauls characteristically keep themselves aloof from the society within which they move about and perform various activities, especially relating to their spiritual aspects. But they are not detached completely from the society - they love the land and show profound respect to the people as Baul philosophy is rooted from the selfless love for the humanity.

The word 'Baul' has a great antiquity. This particular word has been used many a time in the ancient literatures. It was first used in the *Krishnavijay* by Sri Maladhar Basu. The word 'Baul' was used there to understand the care-free and dishevelled nature of a particular person depicted in the book in question. In the *Chaitannya Charitamrita,* written by Sri Krishnadas Kaviraj, the word 'Baul' has been used profusely. In this book Lord Gauranga has been depicted as the Great Baul. Some references to the word 'Baul' also occur in the writings of the great poet Chandidas. On close analysis it is observed that the word 'Baul' has been applied here and there in these books to mean the craziness or madness of the persons concerned.

The etymological meaning of the term 'Baul' is mad. It has been derived from the Sanskrit word 'Vatula' or from 'Vyakula'. The meaning of the former is mad, whereas the latter one indicates impatiently eager. There is a Hindi variant of this particular word and it is known as 'Baura'. It signifies the person with incoherent behaviour. The Sufi word 'Diwana' indicates the particular mode of behaviour centralized on the word 'Baul'. Some are of the opinion that the word 'Aul' is used to point out a class of Muslim prophets. The very word 'Aul' or 'Aulia' is said to have derived from 'Akul' meaning extremely worried. There is a word 'Baura' which is greatly used in rural Bengal. The very meaning of this particular word is indifference to worldly interest. This attitude of indifference may be outcome of profound grief as well as extreme joy. The man becomes indifferent of this nature due to his total submission at the feet of the God or the Supreme Controller of the world. Therefore, the term 'Baul' might have been originated from the word 'Baura'. The people who have become *baura* or have developed indifference to the wordly affairs, ultimately have come to be known as the *Bauls*.

It should be pointed out, in this connection, that this particular nature of human community is to be found amongst both the Hindu and the Muslim religious groups. Generally, these people in Muslim religious fold are given the appellation 'Fakir'. In order to make a distinction with the ordinary Fakir they are called *Nerar Fakir* or Fakirs who have got their heads shaved. It has a historical background and in the history of Bengal we find a particular trend of religious interactions and assimilations through the ages. It was the customary rite of the Buddhists to have their heads shaved. It is still in vogue amongst the present-day followers of Buddhism. During the Pala Dynasty in Bengal the spread of Buddhism reached its peak. The Tantrik faction of the Buddhists became highly dominant. With them the *Vajra-Yana* and *Sahaja-yana* also spread widely. A large number of people belonging to the lower section of the Hindu society embraced Buddhism and they were the followers of the Sahajiya tradition. Then after the Muslim invasion they had to convert themselves into Islam due to multiple reasons. But in spite of their introduction into the new fold of religion they did not leave the former mode of life and thinking. They have been transformed into the Islamic fold but they continued to shave their heads as Buddhists and also stuck to other previous thoughts and ideas. It is because of this reason they have been termed as the shaven *Fakirs*. It has been observed from close scrutiny that there is practically no difference in the line of thinking of the Tantrik Buddhist Sahajiyas and the Muslim *Fakirs*. Then the influence of *Sufism* as well as the Chaitannya-oriented Vaishnavism has fallen on them. But the groups concerned did not lose its identity because of the maintenance of the main line of thinking. The other section of the lower class of people who did not embrace the Islam, but were neglected by the Brahmin-oriented society, took shelter in the Vaishnavism after keeping their inclination towards Tantra-based Buddhist meditation. It is because of their coming into the sphere of Vaishnavism from Buddhism they are called by the terms *Nerah-Nerhi* or the shaven-headed men and women. It is said that Birabhadra, the son of the great Vaishnavite Nityananda, has caused a great deal in bringing these Buddhist Sahajiyas under the spell of Vaishnavism.

Thus according to the opinion of the scholars, the Bauls might have originated from the Buddhist Sahajiyas, and in course of time they have been largely influenced by the Vaishnava Sahajiya cult. During the Pala Dynasty in Bengal the whole society and culture were highly influenced by the various thoughts and ideas of Buddhist philosophy. A large section of people became converted to Buddhism to get various advantages from the rulers of the country. As a natural consequence, the cultural horizon of the then Bengal bore deep imprint of the Buddhist thinking. The reflection of this particular feature was largely found amongst the Baul way of life.

The Bauls have become the main point of attraction because of their unparallel mode of thinking. The Baul cult has got certain distinctiveness and is provided by its own peculiar characteristic features. It is to be noted that the social and religious life of the Bauls is not guided by any conventional social customs or religious rituals. The attempt for realization of the Absolute is the basis of their way of life. The human body is the shelter of the Absolute and this body is regarded as the microcosm of the Universe. The Absolute cannot be understood through knowledge and intellect or through the idol worship. The Absolute is the Baul's soul's companion or *Maner Manus, i.e.* 'Man of the Heart'. It can be perceived only through subjective understanding. It is very hard to come in line with this mode of understanding. In order to reach this state of perfection one is to pass through a number of ordeals both in the spiritual as well as material levels. Throughout his life and activities the Baul is always busy in the eternal quest for the Ultimate Reality. The Ultimate Reality is known as the Supreme Beloved. He is all the time in the search of 'Man'. He believes that the Man of the Heart dwells in the human being but it cannot be understood owing to inadequate knowledge and improper realization. The attempt for realization of the Ultimate Being is in other words the self-realization. From time immemorial the Baul has been in the deep search of himself. The very understanding of human self gives vent to the realization of the Divine Self. When these two spheres meet, a unique perspective is brought to light in which is seen a broad reflection of the total picture of man. It is this Man for whose search the Bauls have started their long-term journey through the ages.

In the cult of the Bauls, love is given the supreme position--it attains the highest order of the society and culture. This feeling of love has its origin from the core of the heart and which tries to embrace all the human beings of he world. Love for mankind is the basis of Baul way of thinking. Love is eternal; love is divine. Without love between each other, mankind will cut a sorry figure. The Bauls move about here and there in the search of this divine love and when they find it necessary to implant this love in the inner recess of man they do it with full devotion. The religion of the Bauls does not aim at the collective observance of rituals, worship of images and the like or individual performance of religious procedures where god is conceived to be outside the body of man. The Baul philosophy is based on the idea that god resides in each human being. On this ground the total emphasis is given on the individual human being. It is expected that the individual human being should dedicate himself at the feet of the Ultimate Reality through constant effort for making himself worthy to prepare his body and mind for self-realization.

The Bauls engage themselves in the deep meditation or *sadhana* which is the yogic practice to realise the self. This self does not mean the human self. Human self is regarded as the finite manifestations of infinite divine Self. The spiritual realization of the Bauls is attained only when this human self annihilates and the body remains above the physical sensation. This leads to the melting away of the human self into the divine Self. The *sadhana* of the Bauls is highly influenced by the process of sexo-yogic practices. The Baul accepts the female consort as *sadhika*. Both of them must be purified by ritualistic procedures and the body should be the ideal one to endure the austere practices. The mind must be under the complete control of any base passions and *sadhana* is centred round the successful attempt of making complete control over the body and sense organs and total command over the breathing system. It is to be practiced for a long period to be successful in the full sense of the term. Through a continuous and painstaking procedure the Baul *sadhaka* acquires full command over the sexual performances and by this he can withdraw the semen at the extreme moment of sexual intercourse and thereby throws it back in the upward direction. This is the very secret act practised by the Bauls and they consider it a compulsory as well as honourable activity for a Baul wandering in the domain of the particular belief and attitude system. There is a worth-mentioning way of *sadhana* practised by the Bauls and it is, however, peculiar to some extent, and naturally befitting to this community with notable diversities. The special cult which the Bauls must perform is known as the ritual of the 'four moons'. At a particular period of the *sadhana* it is the compulsion to perform the application of the four moons. It helps the body to become mature or *pukka* and proficient or *Siddha.* It is nothing but a very secret practice to purify the body and mind in the way of proper performance of the *sadhana.* The four moons are composed of four essential elements of the body--semen, the menstrual flow, stool and urine. On an appointed day the 'piercing of the four moons' or *charichandrabhed* ceremony is performed when the *sadhaka* and the *sadhika* exchange these four elements between each other in such a way that one cuts across the other, of course psychically, so that each of them would acquire a perfect mind to win over all the bodily and worldly affairs. The Baul philosophy advocates the view that until and unless this particular situation is firmly established in the minds of the persons concerned no successful attempt can be made for the desired *sadhana.* There is no short-cut to this and naturally all concerned must take it as a challenge. The ultimate is that the *sadhaka* and the *sadhika* gradually overcome the worldly feelings and emotions for sexual desires and they develope a sort of purified love of divine nature. At the last stage of the ceremony of *Charichandrabhed* the *sadhaka* and the *sadhika* realise the basic nature of purified love and ultimately reach the metaphysical state of tranquillity. This psycho-physiological condition of the body and mind brings the *sadhaka* and the *sadhika* concerned to the realm of man--the eternal field of realization.

In course of their rigid performance of rites and rituals to reach the sphere of Man the Bauls are to depend on the preceptors or the *Guru.* In the Baul philosophy the *Guru* is held in the supreme position. Without the instructions of the *Guru* the the Bauls cannot move forward. The *Guru* works as the mediator between the man and the Absolute. In a troublesome journey to the Absolute conducted by the Bauls, the *Guru* unhesitatingly takes the role of path-indicator and it is he who has the ability to show the correct way to reach the realm of Man. As an anchor sheet for the devotees the *Guru* of the Bauls takes all possible care to bring the disciple to the eternal sphere of knowledge where the latter could establish himself with requisite honour and prestige. It is seen that in all religious spheres in India the importance of *Guru* is highly acknowledged. He is inevitable--he is inseparable from religious performance conducted by the people. In all the societies the place of *Guru* attains the most exalted position. He is next to God--he should be venerated from the deepest corner of the heart. But the Bauls look to the *Guru* in a somewhat different way. The *Guru* is not God or a part of God, according to the Bauls; he is really the spiritual guide who does a great deal in clearing the darkness of ignorance and imperfect feelings in the mind of man. The *Guru* inserts the perfect knowledge of realization of the different earthly phenomena in the mind of the Baul disciples and by virtue of which the latter find ample opportunities to realize the Truth. The essence of Baul philosophy conveys the idea that the cloud of ignorance, such as ritualistic formalities, imperfect knowledge about various religious scriptures, heavy attraction for fulfilling carnal desires and above all constantly irksome resistance of the sense organs covers up the bright moon of intelligence and truth. These can be overcome at a considerable distance by uprooting these through the direct assistance of the *Guru*, who is the right person to resist the tentacles of ignorance and then to clarify the horizon of knowledge around him for the proper realization of the disciples. The *Guru* is called as the *Murshid* who is to be followed minutely and seriously to enter into the threshold of the Religion of Man. The *Adhar Manus* or uncatchable man of Baul philosophy can be recognised through the direct assistance of the Guru. Thus *Guruvada* or cult of *Guruhood* is the central theme of Baul philosophy. The individual Baul relies on his own potentialities for the performance of his *sadhana* but he is always aware of the fact that his real success lies with the support of the *Guru* and his blessings. In all spheres the disciple is not in favour of seeking the grace of God, rather he seeks it through the medium his Guru.

In Baul philosophy the human body is given the highest value. As mentioned before the human body is conceived by them as the microcosm of the universe. In Baul *sadhana* the human body deserves the ultimate importance due to the fact that it is considered the seat for all yogic--*sadhanas*--it is the centre of spiritual performances. Bauls try to draw an analogy between the human body and the universe. Bauls think that the human body is the abode of all senses and truth. It is the sacred seat for the Ultimate Reality, who stays there in the form of human being known as the *Manus* or man. The body is inevitable for *sadhana* and it is a rare privilege and fortune to be born in this earth. The gods in heaven express their desire to come down to the earth to get a human body as it is the greatest manifestation of the creation of the Almighty. As the body is the abode of gods, there is no need for visiting the places of pilgrimage. The Bauls feel no necessity to go to Mecca, Gaya or Kashi. The basic elements constituting the body are thought to be the sky, earth, water, fire and air. The Bauls think that the human body is composed of multitude of apartments which are provided with numerous windows and somewhere with latticed openings in the rooms and nine doors. The Bauls have a characteristic yogic physiology. They attach great importance on the location of the different *chakras* or wheels and the *padmas* or lotus in the body. In between the rectum and the male organ in the abdominal region the lowest *chakra* is believed to exist - it is known as the *Muladhara Chakra*. In this, exists a coiled serpent power known by the term *'Kula-Kundalini Sakti'* which is a passive female force. The *Kundalini* is sometimes called *Jogamaya*, a passive female force characterized by the potential power of creation. A lotus is said to exists in the *Muladhara Chakra* having four red coloured petals. Sometimes it is imagined as having six or eight such petals. The three essential nerves of the bodily system, viz : the *Ida*, the left nerve, *Pingala*, the right nerve and the *Susumna* and the middle nerve, meet at the *Muldhara*. The particular meeting point is known as *Triveni* or the confluence of three streams of life force. At the centre of the eye-brows there is the highest *Chakra* known as *Ajna Chakra*. In this *chakra* there is a lotus with two white coloured petals. It is also regarded as the upper meeting point of the three important nerves. Thus *Muladhara* is jointed with *Ajna Chakra* by these three nerves. There are two other important *chakras* - the *Manipura Chakra* and the *Visuddha chakra*. The former is found to exist at the nerval point with a lotus of ten petals, and the latter is represented by the lotus of sixteen petals and is situated nearest to the throat. At the cerebrum region the highest plexus is to be located. It is known as *Sahasrara*. A lotus of thousand petals is believed to exist here. In between *Muladhara* and *Sahasrara* there are seven floors. Eighteen cells of *mokams* are to be found in *Sahasrara*, and in the central cell lives the Man of the Heart. In *Muladhara* the female force of creation and in *Sahasrara* the male force of creation is found. It is believed that from *Sahasrara* continuous flow of eternal light is maintained. The Man of the Heart stays and performs his plays at the *Ajna Chakra*, the lotus with two petals. At times he comes down to *Manipur Chakra*, the lotus of ten petals, and *Visuddha Chakra*, the lotus of sixteen petals. He may also come down to *Muladhar Chakra*, the lotus of four petals at some particular moment. In these network of nerves or the living channels of life, the Man of the Heart moves about according to the situation of the body. But there is always a tendency in his movement to come in the downward direction. Through his painstaking *sadhana* the Baul tries his best to push the Man of the Heart in the upward direction. First of all, it is his prime duty to establish Man of the Heart at the *Ajna Chakra* by bringing him up through the vital nerves. Then he takes all possible attempts to place him in *Sahasrara,* the lotus of thousand petals. It is really a very strenuous task and it requires deep devotion, profound sincerity, sustained efforts and firm conviction. When it is done, *i.e.*, he is successful in placing the Man of the Heart in the *Sahasrara,* the Baul concerned reaches the level of deep-rooted *sadhana* and thereby he loses his material existence. Thus the Baul *sadhaka* reaches the particular state which is called *Jayente mara, i.e.*, death while living. It indicates the celebrated mixing of the self with the Ultimate Being which further lead to the Ultimate realization--the essence of Baul philosophy. Thus in Baul understanding the body is viewed from two different angles namely material and physiological. The body is composed of materials of diverse nature, and most of the time this materialistic body is compared with cage, boat, building and other similar-phenomena. This material body is subject to destruction at any moment and, therefore, it is advised to try to achieve the ultimate realization without delay. The physiological concept of the body is centred round the complicated idea on the arrangement and functions of the plexuses with the special reference to the main three vital nerves. The latter form of understanding is based on deep-rooted thinking governed by the complexities of diverse ideas.

In Baul philosophy much stress is laid on the mind. It is said that all spiritual life is rooted in the mind. Owing to this principle the Bauls put high premium on the nature and extent of the mind of the *sadhaka* concerned. The mind is taken by him as an instrument of action in the full sense of the term. The Bauls are keen in the following conception, the polarity of force which is known as the *Surya-Soma Tattwa, i.e.*, the Sun-Moon theory. This theory is the base of all the religious philosophies. The Bauls categorically accept this theory and they have moulded it according to their line of thinking. The Sun represents *Prana* which may be individual or cosmic. It represents the vital force of the cosmic energy. The *Pingale* of the human body represents the *Prana. Soma* stand for moon. It indicates mind or *Ida* of the human body. Sun is the essential factor for energy, activity and vitality, whereas moon is meant for sustenance. The Bauls consider *Prana* and mind as the cosmic principle of evolution. These two separate factors, according to them, work together as a rigid entity in the process of evolution. The full control of the mind is an essential part of *sadhana* for which the Bauls move forward. To reach the climax of metaphysical attainment it is inevitable that the mind must be well trained to throw away the worldly pleasures. Man possesses five *indriyas* or sense organs and six inherent vices or *ripus* : these stand in the way of man's progress towards the Ultimate Reality. Without proper control *sadhana* is impossible. The *indriyas* and the *ripus* exert tremendous influence on the mind and if it is not properly trained, one is dragged behind. Naturally, the *Sadhaka* concerned will fall down from the higher seat of *Sadhana*. The *Guru* of the Bauls throw discernible light on this problem and it is he who can lead the Bauls to adopt requisite firmness in having a full command over the activities of these sense organs and inherent vices. The Bauls are made conscious by their *Gurus* for being alert throughout so that the mind does not travel in the wrong direction. The mind should move forward, after throwing away all the untoward happenings aside, aiming at the desired and characterized by the heavenly deeds. The mind is recognized in two forms--good mind and bad mind. The former moves in the correct way and it has affiliation to good activities whereas the latter one runs after wrong performances leading the persons concerned in unwanted path. The mind is considered the root of all sorts of success as well as failure.

The Baul philosophy is characteristically influenced by the understanding of *Rupa* and *Svarupa*. The *Rupa* means the form whereas the *Svarupa* indicates the real nature. The latter is sheltered on the former and its innate character is exposed through the illumination of the inner phases of the *Rupa*. The *Rupa-Svarupa* concept is based on a significant principle in the Baul way of life. The manifested existence is the *Rupa* and the metaphysical existence is the *svarupa*. One is outer view and the other is related to the internal perspective. The physical form and beauty of men and women is known as *Rupa* and the spiritual form and sublime activities are called as *Svarupa*. The spiritual nature is dwelt in the physical form and the former is always existent in an unrealized state. The attempt of understanding of this spiritual nature through physical existence forms the core of Baul *sadhana*. The divine Self is manifested in the human self, and in order to understand the true nature of Divine Self the *Sadhaka* must proceed through the human self. Likewise *Svarupa* is manifested in *Rupa* and *Svarupa* can properly be understood only through the keen analysis of *Rupa*. *Svarupa* can only be realised in the midst of *Rupa* through purified love and sincere devotion. *Rupa* stands for the gross existence and *Svarupa* signifies the divine existence. *Rupa* relates to the finite manifestation of the infinite *Svarupa*. The Bauls believe that the innate nature of a particular phenomenon can be realised through gross material existence. The Bauls, in course of their time-long *sadhana* put special emphasis on the attribution of divinity to man. It is a process through which the gross love is transformed into the Divine Love. Thus the physical existence is raised to the level of metaphysical existence and ultimately it is seen that the physical existence is put to an end. In this way it is seen that *Rupa* ultimately fuses with the *Svarupa* and there remains no basic difference between the two.

It is seen that in the Baul *sadhana,* the worldly love between men and women as well as the six passions have been given due importance. It is accepted that the purified and divine love is raised from the gross love. The gross love is nothing but a passion in which the human beings desire for complete union with the lover and in this hunger for sex union all sensuousness concentrates. In this particular perspective of love, the frantic passion leads to the sexual activities based on the bodily union of the male and female, and there worldly pleasure is drawn. In Baul *sadhana* the primary importance of this sexual union is accepted and the eternal truth behind this is categorically acknowledged. In this affair the Bauls agree with Freudian psychology that sex activities are the basic phenomena in human life. These cannot be kept aside, rather these should be properly evaluated and given proper importance for full flourishing of human life. Freud is of the opinion that all the activities of mankind are fundamentally based on the sexual impulse and, therefore, he tries to analyse everything of man and his society through the line of sex. The Bauls are in parallel line with Freud when they say that the sex is the basic factor of human movement. But they deviate from him when the Bauls attempt to move beyond the worldly activities relating to sexual desires. The Baul philosophy does not stick to the Freudian explanation that the sex is everything of human nature. The Bauls go beyond this point - they surpass the activities of bodily enjoyment through sexual activities and ultimately reach the domain of divine love. In order to achieve this end the Bauls are to pass through a time-long and painstaking training of secret nature they are educated in the controlling of the bodily passions by letting these away in reversed directions.

These are the basic characteristic features of the Baul community. These have no doubt, developed through a long process conditioned by conspicuous interactions of diverse thoughts and ideas. As a separate entity this homogeneous group has accepted and assimilated many distinguishing features of society encircling it from time immemorial and has developed a distinctive feature of its own. The process of acceptance and assimilation is still continuing. Thus the Baul way of life has been facing various changes through the ages.

The Baul community is the result of fusion of many religious groups. The Bauls are neither Hindus nor Muslims. But it is to be noted that people belonging to all castes, classes and communal groups have come under the shade of Baul cult. Thus people of various castes have come together through the clarion call of a particular philosophy of love and mutual understanding. The trend of activities of the Bauls indicate a close resemblance of this community with the Buddhist Tantra, Hindu Tantra and the Vaishnavas. Sometimes their mode of thinking dates back to the Pre-Vedic period. The Bauls have some resemblances with the Sufis. The Sufis are against all religious formalities. The ritual performances act as the barrier between man and God. The God is regarded as the Absolute and he can be realised only through love. The Sufis believe that the true love brings man nearer to God. The Ultimate realization of the Absolute goes by the name of *Fana* state of life in which total annihilation of individual existence takes place. It has similarity with the *Jyante-mara* or death while living as believed by the Bauls. According to Sufism, the God is the Real Truth in the Universe. He is not only the Truth but is provided with endless love. It is the ultimate aim of man to have this divine love. The purpose of propitiation is to become one with Him and to feel the impulse of extreme delight that comes out of the celebrated union. This is the main principle of Sufistic idea and in these the Bauls have got basic similarities. The Bauls are famous for their unique songs and dances. The Sufis also give expression of their ecstatic mood through dance. At a particular point of maturity of joyous mood, the Sufis as well as the Bauls become completely still. This particular mood is resulted through deep-rooted devotion and profound sincerity to the mode of activities concerned. This *samadhi* - like mood is known by the term *Mahabhava.* This is the topmost level of devotion conducted in the background of spiritual practices.

The Baul tradition finds its fullest reflection in the songs known as Baul songs. These songs are the part and parcel of Baul philosophy as the outer and inner facets of Baul way of life are conspicuously expressed through various songs composed and sung by themselves. These songs are said to be the mirrors through which the overall reflection of Baul life are seen clearly. The Baul philosophy, as has been stated, is based on heavily complicated ideas and findings. It is highly characterized by the expression of various thoughts and ideas on which the life and activities of the Bauls are based. But most of the time these expressions are made through indirect perspective. The songs bear double meaning in general --one is external and the other is internal. The songs not only give shelter to the diverse philosophical understandings but also act as the store-house of various evidences of social interactions that have been taking place through the ages. The speciality of the Baul songs is that these not only present vast amount of materials relating to the complicated way of thinking of the Bauls, but also melodious tuning and ideal presentation of these songs bring the listeners to the highest level of performance. The songs of Bauls play the essential role in bridging the gap between the Baul community and the public. The popularity of this particular community lies principally on their melodious songs.

Table No. 2.1 reveals that many respondents (24.45%) feel that it is the special tuning of the songs which makes the audiences spell-bound at the time of listening. Similarly, a good number of them point out the realistic and catchy wordings of these which attract the people very much. The high philosophy of these songs is also the special characteristic feature for their popularity according to many of the respondents (19.21 %). The Table highlights the various other features of Baul songs that act in favour of their popularity which are put forward by the different categories of the respondents separately. It helps in assessing the various types of responses given by the Ascetic, Domestic and Other types of Bauls. The impact of these songs on the minds of the public is deep and obvious. These songs emphatically nourish and bear the rich cultural heritage of this part of the country. Therefore, the life of the Bauls cannot be properly evaluated without giving due importance to these songs.

The song is sung to the accompaniment of a number of musical instruments which are indigenous in nature and the mechanisms of these are based on simplified principles. The Ektara, Dotara, Dugi, Ananda Lahari or Gabgubi and Sarinda are the popular instruments which the Bauls use at the time of presenting songs. These instruments become full of life by the live touch of the Bauls and these collectively do a great deal in changing the total atmosphere by their joint appeal. These instruments are made and repaired by themselves. Most of the components of these instruments are the local products and there are a few indigenous experts

TABLE 2.1

Reasons for Special Attraction of the Baul Songs

Sl. No.	*Particulars*	*Ascetic*	*Percentage*	*Domestic*	*Percentage*	*Others*	*Percentage*	*Total*	*Percentage*
1.	Special Tunings of the songs ..	24	25.26	25	24.75	7	21.21	56	24.45
2.	High Philosophy of the songs ..	19	20.00	20	19.80	5	15.16	44	19.21
3.	Special Types of Musical Instruments ..	4	4.21	6	5.94	3	9.09	13	5.67
4.	Unique Appeal of the singers ..	9	9.47	16	15.84	6	18.18	31	13.53
5.	Realistic and Catchy wordings of songs ..	27	28.42	20	19.80	6	18.18	53	23.17
6.	Not Clear ..	12	12.64	14	13.87	6	18.18	32	13.97
	Grand Total ..	95	100.00	101	100.00	33	100.00	229	100.00

who look into the matter. Many of the Bauls are skillful in the preparation of these instruments. The instruments are considered by them as the life force of their *sadhana*, the principal part of which is centralized on the presentation of songs in honour of the Man of the Heart. The offering of songs, they consider, must be made from the very core of the heart by sincere appeal, and the instruments through which the songs get animation should be provided with due sacredness and genuineness. It is for this reason the Bauls take all possible care to maintain the sanctity of the instruments used during the song recital.

The dance is regarded as the integral part of Baul song. The body of the Baul is subject to various movements during the presentation of songs. The movement is conditioned by rythmic circulation of different bodily parts and the whole process is characterized by a particular idealistic procedure which is entirely personal to the Bauls. Through these rhythmic movements the Baul singer finds it easy to place his appeal at the feet of the Man of the Heart. An individual Baul is expert in the joint presentation of song and dance with the playing of musical instruments by taking no help from anybody. The dance is conducted through rigid procedures and everything is based on technical perspective. In these perspectives the Bauls no doubt represent the typical features of rural Bengal. They are notable not only in the manner of living but also they bear speciality in their dress and other related adornment of the body. The Bauls are very particular about their dress. Generally, the Bauls are seen to wear *dhotis* which are wrapped round the waist ; and sometimes they are seen to wear saffron coloured *lungis*. The upper part of the body is covered by long saffron gown which hangs below the knees. It is the characteristic upper garment of the Baul community. Sometimes they also use white coloured dress of similar nature. A few of them prefer multi-coloured garments which are prepared by joining the small pieces of diverse coloured cloths. The head is covered by turban which may be of different colour. In a few rare cases red and yellow coloured dresses are seen. Various types of bead necklaces are worn by them. Bangles made of copper, iron and some other metals are worn by them in the right arm. All the Bauls keep long hair and they regularly spend some time for the care of these hair. After bath the hairs are dried up and through continuous combing these are processed and tied up high above the head. They are in the regular habit of decorating the forehead and the body with various sectarian marks with the help of the holy clay of the Ganges. The Bauls are conscious about the colour of the dress and they think that the colour of their dresses has got significant relation with their nature of thinking. Table No. 2.2 reveals that most of the respondents(45.41 %) believe that this relationship is weak but it exists. The colour of the dresses has got, according to them, spiritual worth and the Bauls must follow the required principle in the wearing of dresses. In Table No. 2.3, 54.58 % of respondents go in favour of saffron colour dresses and next to it comes (18.77 %) in favour of white colour dresses. 10.04 % of the respondents put their opinion in favour of multi-colour dresses. This Table (No. 2.3) categorically highlights the different opinions given by various categories of respondents on the colour of dresses.

Thus the mental attitudes and outward expression of the Bauls while being with common people always exhibit specialities which are based on high philosophical understanding. But they do not go far away from the people amongst whom they live and from the land on which they have taken birth. The main cause of this is the overall simplicity of their approach towards people as well as to the Man of the Heart. The Bauls are the real mystics. This mysticism is expressed inwardly and outwardly in different courses of activities of the devoted personalities of this community. It is this mysticism which has given this community a special position in the society.

The Bauls give due consideration for the society in the midst of which they move about and perform their mendicant activities. Most of them are conscious of their roles that are to be played for the society. Table No. 2.4 presents the various responses of the respondents as regards their consciousness about their devoted duties towards the society of man. Most of the respondents believe that they must do something which establishes sweet relationship amongst mankind and they must alert the people in following the honest and open-hearted life. It is true that a small percentage of them is not very particular about this consciousness but they indirectly, rather emotionally do the same through their way of life.

With these sorts of consciousness of duties the Bauls, as a natural consequence, have developed a particular mental attitude for performing noble activities which, in course of time, have found place in their value-oriented system. On an enquiry into the particular likeness of the Bauls for the performance of different types of work, a large percentage of them

TABLE 2.2

Relationship Between Colour of Dress and Baul Thinking Pattern

Particulars	*Conspicuous relation exists*	*No relation exists*	*Very faint relation exists*	*Indifferent*	*No idea*	*Total*
Ascetic ..	42	11	32	6	4	95
Percentage ..	44.21	11.57	33.68	6.33	4.21	100
Domestic ..	45	12	33	7	4	101
Percentage ..	44.55	11.88	32.67	6.94	3.96	100
Others ..	17	1	8	3	4	33
Percentage ..	51.51	3.04	24.24	9.09	12.12	100
Grand Total ..	104	24	73	16	12	229
Percentage ..	45.41	10.48	31.89	6.98	5.24	100

TABLE 2.3

Preference for Colour of Dress Amongst the Bauls

Particulars		*White colour*	*Saffron colour*	*Blue colour*	*Black colour*	*Different combined colours*	*Other type*	*No definite colour*	*Total*
Ascetic	..	32	47	1	2	9	1	3	95
Percentage	..	33.68	49.47	1.05	2.10	9.47	1.08	3.15	100
Domestic	..	9	61	3	2	9	3	14	101
Percentage	..	8.91	60.39	2.97	1.98	3.9	2.99	13.36	100
Others	..	2	17	1	-	5	3	5	33
Percentage	..	6.06	51.51	3.04	-	15.15	9.09	15.15	100
Grand Total	..	43	125	5	4	23	7	22	229
Percentage	..	18.77	54.58	2.18	1.74	10.04	3.09	9.60	100

prefer to serve man through singing and dancing according to them, it is the supreme way of rendering service to God as well as to humanity. Table No. 2.5, illustrates the different modes of likeness of the Bauls in respect of their performance of work closely allied to their own line of thinking.

In Table No. 2.5 it is seen that some respondents (21.57 %) put forward their likeness in favour of searching out *Maner Manus* in emotional mood. The *Maner Manus* or the Man of the Heart is regarded as the essential and earnestly desired factor for propitiation, as has been discussed elsewhere in this chapter. It is an abstract entity and, according to the Baul philosophy, all the efforts of man are pointed towards this particular entity. The Bauls sacrifice themselves in the painstaking process of searching the existence of the Man of the Heart. Whatever may be the high philosophical perspective in providing an idea about the Man of the Heart the Bauls have developed some basic understandings as regards the nature of this particular entity and they maintain this idea as per their basic realization. A broad-based enquiry was conducted on the line of perceiving the ideas on *Maner Manus* by the Bauls belonging to the three distinct categories. Table No. 2.6 will illustrate the different trends of responses given by the various respondents. It is seen that a good number of them (27.94 %) like to connect *Maner Manus* with Radha-Krishna, some (17.90 %) desire to describe him as an impersonal force, whereas a few (12.66 %) realise him as *Guru* and others (12.22 %) signify him as God. This Table shows that except a few (4.80 %) all the respondents possess some sorts of ideas on the *Maner Manus* in whatever direction it might have led.

It has been pointed out in the earlier part of this Chapter that the Bauls do not worship any idol as they cannot assume the existence of God outside the body of man. None of them is found to worship any god or support the practice of worshipping during investigation. But they keep portraits of different gods, goddesses and various incarnations of God in their possession with which they always like to keep mental connection. Table No. 2.7 will reveal that a large number of them (39.30 %) keep the portrait of Radha-Krishna, some (14.84 %) keep the portrait of Durga and Kali and some respondents put forward their responses in favour of keeping the portraits of miscellaneous deities. They do not worship the deities - it has become the established truth about the Bauls. But what is the way of adoration ? Table No. 2.8 pin-points the different procedures

TABLE 2.4
Special Duty of the Bauls Towards Society

Sl.No.	Particulars		Ascetic	Percentage	Domestic	Percentage	Others	Percentage	Total	Percentage
1.	To instruct people for following honest life	..	18	18.94	15	14.85	8	24.24	41	17.90
2.	To draw people towards the ideals of the Bauls	..	39	41.05	32	31.68	7	21.22	78	34.06
3.	To teach people the love for humanity	..	13	13.68	10	9.90	3	9.09	26	11.35
4.	To influence people for warding off caste and community differences	..	7	7.36	10	9.90	3	9.09	20	8.73
5.	To impart sweet relationship in society through songs	..	10	10.52	12	11.88	4	12.12	26	11.38
6.	No particular duty	..	5	5.30	10	9.90	4	12.12	19	8.29
7.	Not Clear	..	3	3.15	12	11.89	4	12.12	19	8.29
	Grand Total	..	95	100.00	101	100.00	33	100.00	229	100.00

TABLE 2.5

Particular Types of Work Bauls like most

Sl. No.	Types of works	Ascetic	Percentage	Domestic	Percentage	Others.	Percentage	Total	Percentage
1.	Singing and dancing in meditative mood ..	23	24.24	45	44.55	19	57.57	87	38.06
2.	Serving the people through love and sympathy ..	15	15.78	18	17.82	3	9.09	36	15.79
3.	Adoration of Radha-Krishna, Gour-Nitai, etc. ..	24	25.26	9	8.91	3	9.09	26	15.79
4.	To search out *Maner Manus* in emotional mood ..	21	22.10	25	24.75	4	12.12	50	21.57
5.	To follow the path of *Guru* ..	12	12.63	3	2.98	1	3.04	16	6.98
6.	Crafts and other self works ..	-	-	-	-	3	9.09	3	1.38
7.	Cultivation ..	-	-	1	0.99	-	-	1	0.43
	Grand Total ..	95	100.00	101	100.00	33	100.00	219	100.00

TABLE 2.6

Categorical Ideas about *Maner Manus*

Particulars		*Imperso-nal force*	*Sri Chai-tannya*	*Radha-Krishna*	*Guru*	*God*	*Kali*	*Soul*	*No Idea*	*Others*	*Total*
Ascetic	..	16	2	35	20	5	2	6	4	5	95
Percentage	..	16.84	2.10	36.84	21.05	5.26	2.10	6.34	4.21	5.26	100
Domestic	..	17	5	25	7	14	4	13	6	10	101
Percentage	..	16.83	4.95	24.75	6.93	13.86	3.96	12.87	5.95	9.90	100
Others	..	8	1	4	2	9	0	6	1	2	33
Percentage	..	24.24	3.03	12.12	6.06	27.27	-	18.18	3.04	6.06	100
Grand Total	..	41	8	64	29	28	6	25	11	17	229
Percentage	..	17.90	3.49	27.94	12.66	12.22	2.62	10.91	4.80	7.46	100

TABLE 2.7

Keeping of different portraits by the Bauls

Particulars		*Radha & Krishna*	*Nitai & Gour*	*Durga & Kali*	*All Gods*	*Siva*	*Others.*	*No idol or Portrait*	*Total*
Ascetic	..	46	8	9	4	2	15	11	95
Percentage	..	48.45	8.45	9.50	4.23	15.73	11.53	2.13	100
Domestic	..	37	9	17	4	5	14	15	101
Percentage	..	36.65	8.95	16.85	3.95	4.95	13.85	14.85	100
Others	..	7	2	8	2	2	8	4	33
Percentage	..	21.21	6.06	24.2	6.06	6.06	24.2	12.12	100
Grand Total	..	90	19	34	10	9	37	30	229
Percentage	..	39.30	8.29	14.84	4.36	3.93	16.15	13.13	100

adopted by the Bauls in the propitiation of *Parameswar, i.e.* God. It reveals and His activities does everything. A few of them (12.12 %) like to pay respect to Him through the infliction of love. Though the others differ amongst themselves in the procedure of propitiation, there is an internal link amongst the diverse responses and all such responses acknowledge the essentiality of paying respect to the deities, as well as to the *Guru*, and infliction of love towards humanity.

The Bauls possess idealism in their life and all categories of the Bauls honour the different idealistic attitudes that have allured them towards the life-philosophy of the Bauls. Table No. 2.9, indicates that 32.31 % of respondents think the honest and mendicant life is the ideal of the Baul life, whereas 31.44 % believe that the idealism of the Baul way of life centres round the feeling of love and respect for man. According to some respondents (18.34 %) the cultivation of Vaishnavism is the ideal of Baul life. The Table concerned illustrates the different other ideals that have been taken up by the respondents as appropriate for the purpose in the different perspectives. An enquiry into the exact reasons for embracing the Baul way of life with the concepts of different ideals reveal that a large number of the respondents (43.66%) have come under this sphere by being impressed by the highly valued way of life. Table 2.10 would highlight this perspective of thinking. The nature of songs and their specialised techniques have attracted many of them (23.14%) to come under the fold of Baul way of life. With them there are other respondents, who have entered into the sphere of Baul life by being unsuccessful in other line of activities (8.29%) and also to satisfy the mere curiosity (6.11 %). After entering matters which pin-point the respective aims. A thorough investigation into the various rends of aims of the Bauls reveals that a large number of them (44.54 %) want to get deep entry into the way of practical *sadhana*, some want to be the full fledged ascetic and, according to them, they get sufficient benefit in the maintenance of the asceticism by being nourished by the Baul line of thinking. It is evident from the Table No. 2.11 that there are distinct aims which are cherished by the different respondents as per their likings. There is the effort to establish own Baul centre (6.11 %), for going abroad to earn fame (6.98 %) to pass the days freely after making detachment with the worldly affairs (6.55 %), to pass the days freely after making detachment whose aim is based on the genuine attempt to inspire the people in this ideal pattern of life.

TABLE 2.8

Different Procedures to propitiate the God

Sl. No.	Particular	Ascetic	Percentage	Domestic	Percentage	Others	Percentage	Total	Percentage
1.	To exert love and respect on the living world ..	2	2.10	4	3.96	1	3.03	7	3.05
2.	To pay respect to the different deities ..	29	30.52	24	23.76	4	12.12	57	24.89
3.	To establish brotherly feeling with the down-trodden people ..	2	2.10	5	4.95	1	3.03	8	3.49
4.	To think about God and His activities ..	32	33.68	33	32.67	18	54.55	83	36.24
5.	To remain in detachment with worldly affairs ..	3	3.15	4	3.96	1	3.03	8	3.49
6.	To keep body and mind free from self-interest ..	3	3.15	4	3.96	1	3.03	8	3.49
7.	To dedicate the life for welfare of the society ..	3	3.20	8	7.92	1	3.03	12	5.27

Table 2.8 (Contd.)

Sl. No.	Particulars		Ascetic	Percentage	Domestic	Percentage	Others	Percentage	Total	Percentage
8.	To honour *Guru*	..	16	16.84	8	7.92	2	6.06	26	11.35
9.	Other Types	..	5	5.26	11	10.90	4	12.12	20	8.73
	Grand Total	..	95	100	101	100	33	100	229	100

TABLE 2.9

Ideal of Baul Life

Sl. No.	Particulars		Ascetic	Percentage	Domestic	Percentage	Others	Percentage	Total	Percentage
1.	To cultivate Vaishnavism	..	20	21.05	18	17.82	4	12.13	42	18.34
2.	To lead honest and mendicant life	..	24	25.26	39	38.61	11	33.33	74	32.31
3.	To love and worship man	..	35	36.84	26	25.74	11	33.33	72	31.44
4.	To follow the path of *Guru*	..	9	9.47	3	2.97	2	6.06	14	6.11
5.	To become free from worldly affairs	..	3	3.15	6	5.94	2	6.06	11	4.80
6.	No clear idea	..	3	3.15	8	7.93	2	6.06	13	5.77
7.	Question is not understandable	..	1	1.08	1	0.99	1	3.03	3	1.41
	Grand Total	..	95	100	101	100	33	100	229	100

TABLE 2.10

Reasons for entering into Baul Life

Sl. No.	*Particulars*	*Ascetic*	*Percentage*	*Domestic*	*Percentage*	*Others*	*Percentage*	*Total*	*Percentage*
1.	Being impressed by the highly valued way of life.	45	47.36	41	40.59	14	42.42	100	43.66
2.	Love and respect for song and dance ..	12	12.63	28	27.72	13	39.40	53	23.14
3.	For satisfying mere curiosity ..	6	6.31	6	5.94	2	6.06	14	6.11
4.	Special liking for vagabond and uncertain life.	24	25.26	9	8.91	1	3.03	34	14.84
5.	Being unable to do anything in other spheres ..	6	6.34	11	10.90	2	6.06	19	8.29
6.	No particular reason ..	2	2.10	3	2.97	1	3.03	6	2.62
7.	By inducement of others ..	0	-	3	2.97	0	-	3	1.34
	Grand Total ..	95	100	101	100	33	100	229	100

TABLE 2.11

Specific Choice in Baul Life

Sl. No.	Particulars	Ascetic	Percentage	Domestic	Percentage	Others	Percentage	Total	Percentage
1.	For getting entry into the way of *sadhana* ..	43	45.26	46	45.46	13	39.39	102	44.54
2.	For accepting full-fledged ascetic life ..	39	41.05	8	7.84	8	24.25	55	24.01
3.	For establishing own centre for cultivating Baul *sadhana* ..	-	-	13	13.60	1	3.03	14	6.11
4.	For inspiring different persons to embrace the Baul way of life ..	-	-	7	6.85	1	3.03	8	3.49
5.	For resisting the irregularities and irrelevances in Baul songs and dances ..	-	-	3	2.81	-	-	3	1.31
6.	For earning fame by going abroad as successful Baul singers ..	-	-	10	9.82	6	18.18	16	6.98

Table 2.11 (Contd.)

Sl. No.	Particulars		Ascetic	Percentage	Domestic	Percentage	Others	Percentage	Total	Percentage
7.	For spending days through complete freedom from worldly attachments	..	8	8.42	4	3.88	3	9.09	15	6.58
8.	No particular aim	..	2	2.10	5	4.87	1	3.03	8	3.49
9.	Not clear	..	3	3.17	5	4.87	0	-	8	3.49
	Grand Total	..	95	100	101	100	33	100	229	100

From the foregoing discussion, as have been revealed from the thorough investigations into the life of the Bauls, it is seen that the Bauls maintain a speciality in their own affairs. But they practically contribute to the idea of establishing reciprocal friendship based on mutual understanding. They think for the people amongst whom they move about and on whom they depend for achieving various ends. The Tables that have been put forward here explore a wide range of happenings attached to the life and activities of the bauls themselves, the people as a whole and the divine as well as natural worlds. These have done a great deal in establishing the traditional views maintained by the Bauls through the ages, though there are a few variations caused by the changes in the value patterns in consequence of the impact of modernism.

3

Bauls in Variegated Thinking Patterns

The Bauls who are found throughout the western part of West Bengal belong principally to two distinct spheres - the *Ascetic Bauls* and the *Domestic Bauls.* The Ascetic Bauls are keen in observing the rules and regulations of the Baul - way of life in a rigid way. They are devoted personalities to maintain the philosophy of the Bauls. But their counterparts in the domestic array do not follow, they do not get any opportunity to abide by the rigid regulations. But it is to be noted that many of them try their level best to follow it, at least the basic instructions of Baul traditions, and any sort of failure in following the regulations is regarded as their utter inability conditioned by their life with so many obligations.

The Ascetic Bauls take initiation in the line of *sannyasa* and they lead the life of ascetic mendicancy. An Ascetic Baul stays in an *ashram* either established by himself or in the *ashram* started by others. These *ashrams* are found mostly in the rural settings. At a solitary place, just at the outskirts of the village and surrounded by green vegetation the *ashram* depicts an ideal place for devotional life and activities. In this *ashram* the Bauls and other ashramites are to maintain their living through *Madhukari* or celebrated begging. The *ashrams* are represented by mud-built and straw-thatched houses which are constructed following the traditional patterns of the rural Bengal village. A visitor to these *ashrams* will be highly impressed by the silence and sanctity of the whole surroundings and also by multi-colour flowers in the carefully grown flower garden in the vicinity of the *ashram.* The Ashram-ites follow a disciplinary way of life all through the time. In the *ashram* there are regular observation of ceremonies relating to the patterns of thinking and path of adoration. Besides these, annual festivals are also observed to celebrate the foundation day of the *ashram,* the birth-day of the founder and the like. These ceremonies are known by the term 'Mahotsab' or great festival. The people belonging to all castes, classes and religions are free to attend these ceremonies and have a close look at the different items of festivals. All are cordially invited to take *prasad* which is to be taken by sitting in a row without maintaining any restriction of caste and creed. The ashram-ites collect contributions mostly in kind from the villagers. Some *ashrams* have got rent-free agricultural lands from the income of which the *Mahotsabs* are arranged.

In these *ashrams* an air of sacred discussions, sometimes of high philosophical level, love and respect for mankind prevail. During leisure hours the villagers mostly agriculturists come to these *ashrams* habitually and have free exchange of talks with the ashram-ites. The villagers possess a reverential attitude towards these *ashrams* and there is a custom in many localities to offer the first *arhi*-full of paddy to the village *ashram* at the time of measuring the harvest in the barn. In addition to this, the villagers are under the obligation to contribute their mite to the *ashram* authorities during the marriage ceremony and other allied social customs performed in their houses. The ashram-ites, in their turn, look into the occasional devotional performances that are held in the individual houses. There are occasions when the villagers seek direct help from the ashram-ites in solving many of their problems, especially related to spiritual spheres. In this way a close link exists between the Baul *ashrams* and the villages and through mutual understanding there develops an amicable background which helps in flourishing the spiritual life of the village in the strict sense of term.

The domestic Bauls do not necessarily live in the *ashrams.* It may be the fact that during their long tour for *Madhukari* or attending any kind of socio-ritual festivals they may take shelter in the *ashrams* but they strictly follow the familial life. They live in the full-fledged life of procreation. Very commonly they call these as *grihastha ashram,* i.e., the family hermitage. Almost all of them are to look after the family and, therefore, regular income is essential for them. They are to haunt for money and other allied materials for the maintenance of their families. It is impossible for them to become mad all through the time in search of the 'Man of the Heart'. Still these Bauls have got full devotion to the cult in their way of life and in no circumstances they neglect to maintain any of the rules that have been imposed on them through the implication of Baul tradition. They are not to blame for maintaining full-fledged families while moving in search of God, rather credit should be given to them for the successful maintenance of the dual roles in these spheres of God and Man. When interrogated, the famous senior Baul, Sudhir Das of Sainthia (Birbhum district), told that these domestic Bauls were always serious in following the two different phases of life - one related to the deep devotion and allied activities towards the Ultimate Being and the other was connected with the familial life like the common people. According to many domestic Bauls the systematic inter-linking pattern of life-philosophy is very much conspicuous in their path of *sadhana* and there is no doubt about the fact that the state of affair is highly troublesome to follow. These domestic Bauls are fit enough to clear their body and mind for dedicating themselves at the feet of the Ultimate Being in spite of their heavy familial ties. On this ground alone the domestic Bauls deserve special credit in the sphere of Baul *sadhana*.

In order to have a clear idea on the family life of the domestic Bauls in addition to their spiritual activities, a detailed person to person enquiry was conducted with some structured schedules covering most of the important aspects of their life and activities. It has been found that 101 domestic Bauls belonged to 14 caste-groups before their coming into the sphere of Baul life. The members of these families follow diverse occupations and maintain regular family life with all sorts of formalities and obligations as are found amongst the common people. The investigation reveals that 32.15% of the families concerned possess their own agricultural lands and in which they regularly cultivate different crops. 69.65% families have their houses on their own residential plots which ranges from 1 *Katha* to 15 *Kathas*. The different Tables put forward in the Appendix will present the categorical nature and extent of the life and behaviour of the domestic Bauls to understand how far they are attached to the worldly affairs and social norms of the locality despite their Baul mode of life.

As regards the different categories of the Bauls, there are so many contradictory ideas amongst the scholars. People living in close association with the Bauls and observing the various behaviour-patterns of the members of this community also differ amongst themselves. In addition to the evaluation of the diverse observations made by the different scholars time to time attempts have been made, in the study, to collect various ideas maintained by the scholars and the common people whose studies are not to be found in any book or journal. In order to have the views of the common but interested people about the different categories of the Bauls a large number of persons have been met with a few short questions. While questioning they were always allowed to talk freely and elaborately on the particular topics. In addition to this a large number of questionnaires had been mailed to the different persons interested in Baul way of life in which there were some pertinent questions of the various categories of the Bauls.

After a long search in the library it has been seen that there is no clear-cut idea behind the categorization of the Bauls. Scholars differ amongst themselves in this state of affair. From our experience it has been seen that all the works done on this principle were based on library works and most of the time the particular aspect in question had been tried to explain through various parallel religious sentiments that grew up during and prior to the advent of the Bauls. There is a tendency amongst the former workers in this line to evaluate Baul philosophy in the perspective of Buddhist thoughts and ideas that developed in this country to a great extent. There is no denying the fact that the Buddhism had once overwhelmed the country as a whole and especially the large tract of the then Bengal became the most dominating figure in the spread of the this religious thoughts and ideas. It is true that Buddhism had exerted tremendous influence on the Bauls and the community in question had assimilated many conspicuous behaviour-patterns of the Buddhism. Similar was the case with other aspects of life of then period. The deep-rooted Buddhist philosophy caused a great deal in creating many new ideas, modes of behaviour and establishing many socio-cultural institutions in this country. It may be the fact that many independent institutions or cultural perspectives that existed during or before the advent of the Buddhism fell into the tremendous influence of that particular religious sentiment and gradually had to adopt some conspicuous view-points.

The Baul philosophy is characterized by full-fledged integration of diverse thoughts, ideas and religious sentiments. It may be called as the melting pot of various cultural perspectives. The Baul sentiment is largely dominated by the Indian folk tradition, rather than any religious perspective. The Baul way of life should be traced in this line. The former scholars in this field tried to trace the origin of the Baul community from the Buddhist philosophical setting. They had made an attmept to throw discernible light on the advent of the Baul philosophy through the gradual development and transformation of Mahayana Buddhism. It attracted large number of people in consequence of its solid foundation in the life and living of the then country. People with diverse thoughts and ideas came under the spell of the Buddhism and were incorporated into it. In course of time there developed a particular community composed of diverse castes and communities, which bore, to a considerable extent, the thoughts and ideas of the Buddhism. When the Buddhism was challenged by Vaishnavism due to the abrupt change over in the political sphere in Bengal, the Baul community adopted many Vaishnavite influences and life-philosophy. It is true that the Baul community is based on a solid ground and its high philosophical features are regarded as unparallel. It may be the fact that this particular community did not emerge from any religious sentiment - it might have got a great antiquity. It may be rooted in the very ancient folk tradition characterized by a particular philosophy based on the love for humanity. This folk tradition might have originated in the hoary past and it assimilated many thoughts and ideas of various socio-religious sentiments during its journey through time. The Buddhist philosophy which once exerted conspicuous influence on the life of Bengal very naturally compelled the folk tradition concerned to assimilate a few concrete thoughts and ideas of the Buddhism. It is due to this reason the Baul way of life reflects many Buddhist beliefs and practices - there are many parallel thinkings, many identical events of life. This does not mean that the Baul life and philosophy had their origin from Buddhist line of thinking. The indigenous traditions were so much influenced and the folk beliefs and ideas were so thoroughly covered up by the Buddhist way of life that the researchers and the investigators of the former period were highly influenced to explore the Baul way of life in the background of the Buddhism. The pre-Buddhist existence of the Baul community has not been explored so far. The indigenous beliefs and mode of behaviour prevailing in the Baul culture provide an indication to the origin and development of this particular pattern of life in the period when the Buddhism did not exert any conspicuous influence in the life of the people as a whole. The indigenous little tradition represented by the Bauls and highly characterized by the integrated thoughts and ideas had its formation in the long time past. At that time Buddhism and other conspicuous religious notions did not emerge and the Baul philosophy was identified as the reflection of the folk mind. That particular tradition, it may be possible, came in direct contact with the great traditions like the Buddhism, the Hinduism and the Islamism, and their different lines of thinking. As a result of this, many great traditional materials have been incorporated into the little tradition which, in course of time, became covered up with the life-philosophy of the great traditions.

During the study and analysis of folk deities in the rural areas of Bengal similar phenomenon is to be met with. The numerous indigenous deities of rural Bengal are found to the veiled with the beliefs and traditions of the Buddhism or similar other religious sentiments. The folklore centring round the genesis of various folk deities are found attired with the different non-folk traditions. These are the concrete example of exertion of influence on the folk traditions by the great traditions. The district of Birbhum is regarded as the centre for the origin and development of Baul way of life in West Bengal and this apprehension is very much supported by concrete facts. It has already been found that the villages in the district of Birbhum are highly characterized by the presence of the Bauls. From time immemorial the Baul *akhras*, that have established in the rural setting, have been and are exerting tremendous influence in the life and activities of the villagers. Various traditional age-old Baul gatherings, that are held annually, take place in many rural settings of Birbhum, the principal types of which are observed at Jaydeva-Kenduli, Kotasur, Vairagitala, Gopalnagar, Dubrajpur, Billamangal, *etc*. Similarly, a folk deity named Dharmaraj is seen to exert his influence in almost each and every village in the district in question. Strictly speaking, Dharmaraj is regarded as the tutelary village deity and during his worship people, especially belonging to the lower rungs of the society, take active part. The nature and extent of the worship of the deity in question reveal the fact that the deity is characteristically of indigenous origin. In the different phases of worship, manners of participation of the people, modes of service and remuneration clear-cut reflection of folk philosophy is observed. Though the analysis of the beliefs and practices, customs and behaviours, as well as the participation of the higher caste groups a clear picture of later incorporation of the different great traditional materials are seen. But a few eminent scholars especially belonging to the Sanskritic literatures, who first of all tried to throw light on the origin and development of the Dharma Cult, were of opinion that the Dharmaraj was basically a Buddhist deity as there were many important Buddhist thoughts and beliefs encircling this deity. With the development of folkloristic study through the adoption of many sociological methods it has been soon realised by a few sociology-oriented reseorachers that there is no reason for assigning Dharmaraj as a deity belonging to the Buddhist pantheon. The Buddhist thoughts and ideas, if this is the case, encircling the worship and nature of the deity might have resulted due to later incorporation of Buddhist ideas during the deity's journey through the period bearing the deep impress of Buddhism. Therefore, it is the clear case of interaction between the little and great traditions. The little traditions of indigenous people of Birbhum villages as exemplified by the Dharmaraj had been heavily influenced by the Buddhism, Hinduism and the like great traditions during the different times and phases of their development in that particular region. It has been established through researches that Dharmaraj flourished as an indigenous village deity during the remote antiquity before the advent of the Buddhism. Therefore, Dharmaraj is basically a folk deity who could maintain his original character in spite of the later full-fledged influence of Buddhism, Hinduism and other perspectives with dominant features of actions.

There is every possibility that like the folk deity Dharmaraj this community composed of folk-meditators like the Bauls have got their origin in the remote past before the advent of the Buddhism and other allied religious thoughts. The Baul philosophy which basically revolve round the love for man and reciprocal understandings, might have originated from the indigenous beliefs and practices. It is high time to turn the eyes of the researchers in this sphere of thinking. But the paucity of adequate data in the establishment of this sort of idea is the basic problem. It is true that the Buddhist thoughts and ideas exerted profound influence on the Baul philosophy and sometimes it is so well-knit and profound that it gives the impression of Buddhism-based line of thinking. A few parallel thinkings in the Buddhism-and Baul way of life have given impetus to the former workers to trace an analogy between the two and then to establish the fact of dominant Buddhist influence on the Baul way of thinking. It ultimately gives rise to the idea of advent of the Baul community from the Buddhist way of life and thinking.

The Bauls, whatever their nature of origin may be, are found to have flourished in multifarious socio-philosophical settings. It is due to this reason there are some basic differences amongst the members of this community. But at the same time it is to be noted that these differences are not acute enough to make the different groups of the Bauls as separate entities. On the basis of these differences in thinking pattern, mode of life and their overall behaviour with others the total community of Bauls can be divided into a few catagories. In the attempt of categorization of the Bauls much stress has been laid on the analytical observations of the general people having special aptitude for close observation on the life and works of the Bauls. As the Bauls are the successful representatives of the rural Bengal and their life and works are altogether processed and conditioned by rural philosophy, so it is worthwhile to evaluate the manner of thinking of the rural people who live in close association with the Bauls. Being the active messengers of folkloric culture and philosophy through the ages, the Baul community throws discernible light on the broad horizon of folk tradition. In consequence of this fact the development of Baul cult can be effectively evaluated if sufficient attention is given to the folkloristic ideas shared and nutured by the rural folk as a whole. In so doing the social history of the region has been studied and the impact of religion and philosophy on the folk mind has been found through the various concrete evidences as illustrated in the numerous rites and rituals of the region concerned.

The categorization of the Bauls as a whole has been attempted the patterns of behaviour, mode of day-to-day life and their approaches to the different aspects of man and society. Generally, the Bauls belong to four different categories - (1) Aul, (2) Baul proper, (3) Sain, and (4) Darbesh, according to many investigators, are related to the four different stages of bodily meditation. At the same time these may mean the four different types of bodily union. It has been accepted by many that the Muslim-originated Bauls are known by the term 'Aul'. The *Gurus* of the Auls are termed as the Aulia, who are highly far-sighted *Sadhakas* of various depths. Aul is regarded as the first stage of the bodily meditation. The meditators belonging to Aul community are the first grade personnel in the domain of Baul theosophy. In the Muslim world there is a word 'Auttal' which means the primary phase of a particular aspect. Therefore, the word 'Aul' indicates the first stage of the overall philosophy centering round Baul way of life. In Arab *Au* means woman and *ula* stands for come down. Therefore, the word that has been formed by these is

Aula, the internal meaning of which is copulation with the woman. In the philosophy relating to *Tantrasar* it has been observed that the world is regarded as the woman and to become in close connection with this woman indicates the sincere effort to know the deep mystery of the world. Also in *Tantra* the word *'Kul'* means the vagina of woman and, therefore, the *Kulachar* or rite relating to *kul* means the observance of rites around woman. In the folk dialect of the related region the use of the word 'Aul' is met with. Sometimes it means the spreading over paddy in the sun or make the paddy turned through the continuous process of upside down and downside up during husking of paddy under husking lever locally known as *Dhenki*. Some say that the word 'Aul' is closely connected with *Akulata* or worried. The person who is worried to have the grace of Almighty is known as *Aul*.

The Bauls come to the second stage. They are of Hindu origin. The Bauls have got similar features as are seen amongst the Auls. The former group is very much devoted to the songs and dances and through these they try to reach the threshold of the 'Man of the Heart'. The Sain is the third stage in the overall sphere of Baul philosophy. They are totally mendicant and wander about in search of God without following any rigid path.

The Darbesh are regarded as the *Gurus* who have reached the ultimate phase of *sadhana*. The Baul-oriented Muslim Fakirs who have performed their meditation deeply and have arrived at the highest step of *sadhana* are known as the Darbesh. But taken as a whole, it is very difficult, at present, to clear out all these differently and separately as there is no line of distinction. During the present period all are popularly known as Baul though there are minor differences in the path of meditation amongst them.

Besides these four types, there are a few other categories which are well worth considering to serve the present purpose of studying the Bauls. An interesting type of this nature is known by the term '*Karta bhaja*' - a community which has got parallel philosophy of the Bauls. This particular community took its origin during the middle of the 18th Century and spread in the district of 24 Parganas, West Bengal. The philosophy of this community is centred round the act of adoration of the *Karta* or head. The folklore that is seen prevalent amongst the people of the related locality reveals the following fact : Chaitannya Mahaprabhu, the great preacher of Vaishnavism in the then Bengal, once became worried about the limited time span in the life of a man for religious preachings. He ultimately became changed and remained in disguise for a time being. One day Chaitannya Deva took the guise of a Muslim Fakir and went to Kanchrapara after crossing the river Ganges at Trivenighat. Thence he proceeded to Ghisepara village where he met Ram Saran Pal belonging to a Sadgop community. The latter lost self-possession on meeting the Fakir and having talk with him. He could not leave the Fakir and expressed his earnest desire to get his sacred company. On seeing this the wife of Ram Saran Pal, "Satima", invited the Fakir to her house and made an arrangement there for his shelter. The Fakir began to stay there and started his religious performances at the said spot. The activities of the Fakir were kept secret and all possible steps were taken by Sri Pal and his wife in this regard. But the Fakir's supernatural activities could not be kept secret and in course of time became known to the public. In consequence of this many people came to the Fakir and thereby became his disciples. Gradually Sri Pal became their *Mohanta* and through the Fakir's instruction he was known as *Kartababa.* On this ground it is accepted that the Fakir-Thakur is the initiator of *Kartabhajan* way of thinking and Ram Saran Pal is *Adi-Guru* or the Primary Preceptor. The personnel belonging to this sect is found to spread over a territory centering round the place of its origin - Ghosepara. To commemorate the sacred happening relating to Fakir and Ram Saran a fair is held at Ghosepara every year on the day of Holi festival. This fair is well attended by a large number of devotees belonging to *Kartabhaja* community. Also the Bauls of different categories visit this fair and celebrate the day and night through their traditional songs and dances.

The *Nerha-Nerhi* community has resulted through the large-scale religious transformation by the Vaishnavite prophets. It is said that through the initiative of Birchandra Deva, the son of Chaitannya Mahaprabhu, a large number of Buddhists came under the domain of Vaishnavism. There is a popular saying that sixteen hundred *Nerha* and sixteen hundred *Nerhi* left Buddhism and took inititation in Vaishnavism through the direct impulse of Birchandra Deva. The Buddhists were shaven-headed which is known by the term 'Nerha' in Bengali and the feminine form of which is 'Nerhi'. The men and women belonging to this community wear loin-cloths and the body is wrapped by white clothes. They decorate their bodies with various sectarian marks by the application of the holy clay of the Ganges. These people are largely seen in the district of Nadia especially centering round Nabadwip.

In the Bengal villages a community known as Vaishnab-Vaishnabi is met with. They take shelter in the *ashram* constructed and dedicated by the villagers. They observe austere life and maintain their livelihood through the singing of devotional songs based on Radha-Krishna philosophy. These persons have great affinity with the Bauls in respect of their way of life and nature of performance of various rites, but differ from the Bauls in the mode of presentation of songs and dances

The Bauls belonging to all these categories are seen to spread throughout the whole region of the western part of West Bengal. But on critical enquiry a kind of regional variation is to be seen. As for instance, the Bauls living in the districts of Burdwan, Birbhum, and Bankura follow a particular trend in their overall way of life which is to some extent different from the Bauls found in Nadia, Murshidabad and other eastern districts. Bhattacharya describes the former type as Rarh-community of Bauls and the second type falls in the category of Nabadwip-community. The latter is also known by the term '*Rasik-Vaishnav*' (1388 B.S.: 370). There are a few differences in the procedure of initiation and also in the manner of conducting *sadhana*.

These Bauls have ultimately come from different castes and in course of their former life, *i.e.*, the life prior to accepting the Baul way of life they have been in close touch with the various feelings of the caste-hierarchical society. Naturally the traditions of the graded society with purity-pollution concept may still be reflected, in whatever form it may be, in the minds of the Bauls even after their total merger in the Baul fold. This continuity of tradition might have affected the overall value system of the Bauls to some extent. In course of investigation the attitudes of the Bauls before and after the acceptance of Baul way of life have been examined through long-term interviews. The Table No. 3.1 will illustrate the different nature of responses of the respondents. It reveals many interesting features. After coming out from the caste-graded society and surrendering themselves in the philosophy of integrated outlook the Bauls are not totally aloof from the influence of the caste-graded society. A large section of them (38.42%) still support the supremacy of the Brahmins and they are regarded as the top-ranking group in the society. 33.72% of the respondents supported the caste hierarchical system

TABLE 3.1

Caste and Class Consciousness

Itmes	*Used to follow the caste-based regulations in former life*				*Supported the caste hierarchical system in former life.*				*Still support the idea that Brahmin is the supreme caste-group.*				*Feel the conspicuous presence of hierarchical patterns amongst the Bauls.*			
	Yes	*No*	*Indiffer-ent*	*Total*	*Yes*	*No*	*Indiffer-ent*	*Total*	*Yes*	*No*	*Indiffer-ent.*	*Total*	*Yes*	*No*	*Indiffer-ent.*	*Total*
Ascetic ..	19	27	49	95	19	26	50	95	24	22	49	95	18	75	2	95
Percentage..	20.00	28.43	51.58	100	20.00	27.36	52.64	100	25.27	23.16	51.57	100	18.94	78.95	2.10	100
Domestic ..	26	41	34	101	41	30	30	101	43	25	33	101	44	50	7	101
Percentage ..	25.75	40.59	33.66	100	40.59	29.70	29.71	100	42.57	24.75	32.68	100	43.57	49.50	6.93	100
Others ..	14	14	5	33	17	10	6	33	21	8	4	33	13	19	1	33
Percentage ..	42.42	42.42	15.16	100	51.51	30.30	18.19	100	63.63	24.25	12.12	100	39.40	57.57	3.03	100
Grand Total ..	59	82	88	229	77	66	86	229	88	55	86	229	75	144	10	229

though 37.55 'of them showed indifference. 25.76. of the respondents were in the habit of following caste oriented regulations in their former life and 35.80% did not follow the same, whereas 38.42% remained indifferent. In this connection, it has been found out that 32.75 % of the respondents feel that there is strong presence of hierarchy amongst the Bauls which is characterized by inequalities.

An attempt has been made here to point out the internal inequalities that exist within this community. The previous pages of this Chapter have been devoted to discuss the various categories of the Bauls that are principally based on sectarian principles and also on regional prerspectives. In the succeeding pages an attempt has been made to point out the different inequalities working internally amongst the Baul community and how they expose themselves by the formation of different class-groups casses that are as follows.

Through observations and enquiries a trend of disintegration is seen among this community though outwardly all of them try to exhibit to close-knit unit. The data so far collected from different regions of the area of study verified by thorough personal enquiries - direct and indirect - reveal that amongst the present Baul community there are four different

Class - A : It embraces Bauls with traditional ascetic way of life. A section of them does not sing or dance, but they engaged themselves in deep meditation. Others practise Baul songs and dances, and these are mostly used during *madhukari* and to show regard to the Man of the Heart. Highly Vaishnavite Bauls sing kirtan songs. They lead austere life in the secluded *ashrams* though many of them have got female consorts known as *sevadasi*. The conjugal life is very much restricted and all of them are to follow strict principles in the day-to-day life. Many of them organise *ashram* - cum - training centres, where the young Bauls may take initiation and go through a long course of severe training for getting entry into the Baul way of life. The representative of this class is very keen and cautious in the observance of rigid regulations of Baul life.

Class - B : It includes Bauls, who live in their own houses and maintain family life. But they keep themselves alert in their every-day life in maintaining the regulated life as directed by the Baul philosophy. They are allowed to perform any kind of activities to maintain their families but it is expected that they should perform *madhukari* for their sustenance. The Baul belonging to this class keep close connection with the people of the locality where they live with their family members. At times they are to share with the joys and sufferings of the people and to join their hands with the efforts made by the people for different affairs of the society. The Bauls under this category are the reputed and popular singers of Baul songs.

Class - C : This class has been resulted through the emergence of the Bauls from Class A and Class B. During recent period some of the Bauls either spontaneously or through the inducement from others have come out of the traditional groups and by contact with outsiders they have been able to go over to different western countries to present their feats of song and dance there. After coming back to the homeland they have become secluded by their changed value-patterns and they have been receiving a renowned position in the minds of the general public. The contact with the outsiders has done a great deal in changing the patterns of thinking of the Bauls and thereby assigning them to a new class. The divine-based indifferrent attitude of the Bauls has been challenged here by the infliction of self-interest-based worldly pleasure.

Class - D : Bauls belonging to this class are popularly known as infiltrated Bauls. The wide publicity of the Baul mode of life effected by the activities of Bauls belonging to the Class C attracted many people with some basic knowledge and ability to sing and dance to come under the purview of the Bauls. They do not bother for any formal recognition for any entry into the realm of the Bauls or they do not receive any basic initiation for their taking up of the Baul way of life. The ordinary persons with melodious voices are readily accepting the Baul way of life exclusively based on the singing of Baul songs only as their mode of livelihood. They utilise these songs for earning some money and not for the propitiation of the Man of the Heart as instructed in the Baul philosophy.

These four categories of Bauls are formal throughout the districts of Birbhum, Burdwan, Murshidabad and Bankura. An internal conflicting attitude is always predominant and in different spheres of the study these features of interactions have been systematically put forward.

The *ashram* ite Bauls nave got specializations of their own. They want to keep all the elements of their life-philosophy secret. These are popularly termed by them as 'Secret Cults'. These ascetic Bauls take initiation in a way as followed by the domestic Bauls mentioned elsewhere in this book. They also depend on four *Gurus - Dikshaguru, Sikshaguru, Sannyasguru and Sangitguru.* But the procedures of initiation are somewhat complicated in comparison with those of the Domestic Bauls. In addition to receiving diverse instructions on the different phases of life the Ascetic Bauls are to embrace rigid procedure in leading their life in the *ashram.* They accept *Sanyasa* and take promise in maintaining self-restraint throughout the life. But it is strange to note that the Ascetic Bauls are free to accept consorts known as *Sevadasis.* The *Sevadasi* acts as a helper of the Baul concerned in proceeding in the long path of devotional practices. They are free to marry provided it takes place under the recognition of the central body of the Ascetic Bauls. The marriage ceremony is a brief affair and it is limited with the exchange of bread necklace together with sandle paste. It is properly known as Kanthi-badal. The conjugal life of the Bauls is very rigid. The Bauls are not allowed to lead free life and to have children. It is regarded as a great offence. But still it happens. In such cases the Baul concerned readily leaves his consort. Sometimes it is seen that a devoted Ascetic Baul takes a *Sevadasi* and begins to lead conjugal life. The Ascetic Bauls are expected to follow sexual continence. But if they fail and the circumstances compel them to have children, the Bauls concerned are to face severe criticism from the main organization of the Ascetic Bauls. A devoted Ascetic Baul, in that case, is free to leave the consort during her pregnancy to save himself from moral degradation, as is believed by them. The female Baul thus deserted may be taken over by any other willing Baul as his consort. The baby in the womb, in this case, would get required recognition from the new entrant concerned. This situation introduce complicacy in the acquaintance of the children in respect of their fathers. It is not unnatural amongst them that the three uterine brothers have got three different fathers. These Bauls always seek opportunities to get new *sevadasi* at very short intervals. Concrete search of *sevadasi* is generally made by them during fair and other Baul assemblages, like *Mahotsab* and allied affairs. During this period the Bauls make fresh contacts with various female Bauls attending the assemblage and try to get into their hearts through song, dance or other allied activities. It is generally seen that the Bauls begin to talk with the desired female Bauls in a very jocular mood and ultimately try to feel their respective mentality. If everything is found all right the Baul concerned forwards his proposal to the female Baul concerned to come by his side for joint *sadhana*. If both the parties are compatible, it is, in most cases, seen that both the male and female Bauls leave the fair silently to meet elsewhere in ceremony. Desertion and acceptance of *sevadasi* by the Bauls are very common phenomena. The deserted female Baul does not feel any sort of embarassment as she is readily accepted with due importance by another Baul. It is seen that the relation which exists between the Baul and his *sevadasi* is not well-knit though a good understanding works between them. The *sevadasi* looks after her male companion, arranges everything during the start of *madhukari* and while going outside for attending *mahotsab* or like gatherings. She sings with him, gossips with him and sometimes smokes *ganja* with him, and all through the time she likes to stay side by side with him. Yet this relation is not rigid. On any minor reason she may go away with her newly engaged male companion or she may be deserted by her male consort on being pregnant.

The Ascetic Bauls are said to perform various secret acts, one of which is the sexual control. The Bauls enjoy sexual life and they consider it essential in the new creation. The world is moving with the silent promise to create more and more. Being part and parcel of the world at large the human being must not keep silent to this clarion call. *Prakriti* and *Purush* should come in close contact to each other to complete the essential phase of life. They are like the two banks of a river - one stays away from the other ; but they unitedly give the form of the river. When rain water rushes and the river bed becomes inundated, the two banks come under a close-knit system. Similarly, *Prakriti* and *Purush* have been giving the shape of the world and both are the inevitable factors. When love inundates in between *Prakriti* and *Purush* like rain water, it bridges the gap between the two factors and then the world flourishes with flowers and fruits. It is the eternal cry of the creation. The Bauls have been able to reach this perspective through their practical *sadhana*. Bodily union of male and female conditioned by love and mutual understanding finalises the ultimate prayer. The Bauls by virtue of their arduous and time-long *sadhna* have been able to support and follow this truth directly but they blaze a new trail which is characteristically of their own. Bodily union of *Prakriti* and *Purush* have been retracked into the yogic association where everything is there but it averts the realistic view points. A close enquiry into this point explores the fact that the Bauls practise various sexo-yogic activities which are of bio-psychic origins. The rigid control of the body and mind or in some cases the control of the physiological functions of various bodily organs have made the Bauls so conspicuous in this regard. Biological union of male and female, according to them, can effectively be channelized into the yogic posture-based activities which give them a thorough controlling factor over the situation. It is very difficult, according to aveteran Baul, who has taken a large number of mates at different times, and to follow this a Baul needs his body and mind completely free and he should pursue the rigidity of the regulations which exist in the perspective of the Baul cult. The number of Bauls, adhering to this principle decreased day by day and at present, according to some Ascetic Bauls, there are so many attractive features of the Bauls and the popularity of this sect is on the increase, yet this particular invaluable bio-psychic character has cut a sorry finger.

A special attempt had been made to throw discernible light on this particular mode of life led by the Ascetic Bauls through the depth-oriented study. The female Bauls following and participating actively, this bio-psychical practice had been approached as per opportunities. A few of them were very much co-operating in presenting their state of mind in the perspective of the sexo-yogic practice - an essential act conducted by the Asectic Bauls. These famale Bauls get practical training in putting forward their physio-psychical co-operation to the respective partners at the remarkable moment of bodily union. In addition to the instructions received directly from the *Guru* at the time of communion of the bodies these female Bauls are to follow a few concrete procedures presented before them theoretically during the period of their initiation and training. It is true that the male ascetic Bauls are to be well-trained in the controlling of the body and minde during the extreme moment of the sexo--yogic practice to enable themselves in the maintenance of the top level philosophy of the sect which signifies the ultimate practice of the union of the souls through mere bodily union. The Baul *sadhana* pinpoints the fact that this particular part of practice centres round the complete control over the sense organs and full command over the breathing system. It consists of the controlling of the courses of the vital wind - *Puraka, Rechaka and Kumbhaka*, as well as the power of controlling of the opening of the urine-cum-semen channel. The Bauls popularly call it as the action of *dama* or the conrolling of the breathing activities. As per instruction of the *Guru* the Bauls practise *Pranayama* or controlling of the breathing. In this practice they inhale air through the left nostril after keeping it for sometime with the body, it is released through the right nostril. This is practised, stage by stage, upto sixty-four times. Through the continuous process of this practice and strength for *Kumbhaka* act is acquired. On this acquisition of this particular power the success of Baul *sadhana* is largely dependent. It is believed that all the nerves become purified and in course of time the 'air' is started to flow towards *Susumna*. It is then the tranquillity of the celebrated 'drop' (*Bindu*) which is established due to the equillibrium maintained in the breathing system. The essence of the Baul *sadhana* is practically based on the act of driving this 'drop' to the upward direction. Bodily union between the male and female Bauls in the perspective of this act is characterized by steady and extremely close union of the earnest feeling of love. Its is the union of the feeling of nature of *Sahaj manus* or Easy Man in Baul thinking. This *Sahaj manus* is regarded as the outcome of sincere and serious activities relating to the cult of the Bauls. This is the state of mind resulted from the entire satisfaction through the union of *Prakriti* and *Purush*. Only the real *Sadhakas* can realise the appearance of this celebrated *Sahaj manus*. They are always alert in getting close association with this *Sahaj manus*. A bit of inattentiveness may be the root cause of his disappearance for ever. Most of the activities of the Bauls are directed to find out the way for searching out the *Sahaj manus*. Sometimes he is known as *Bhaber Manus* or the man of emotion. Many Bauls prefer to call it as *Damer Manus* because of the fact that his presence is felt through the action of breathing or *dama*. It is this man for whom the Ascetic Bauls have fully dedicated themselves.

The domestic Bauls follow the same principles as laid down in the overall Baul philosophy and understanding which the Ascetic Bauls rigidly maintain. It is true that the Domestic Bauls cannot think deeply in respect of high-level *sadhana* as practised by the Ascetic Bauls. Almost all of them are to look after the family and for this reason they need regular earnings for the maintenance of the family concerned. To become mad in search of the Man of the Heart, all through the time, is almost impossible for them. Still these Bauls have got full devotion to their way of life and in no circumstances they neglect to maintain any of the rules that have been imposed on them through the implication of the Baul tradition. They are not to be blamed for maintaining full-fledged families while moving in search of God, rather credit should be given to them for the successful maintenance of the dual roles in these spheres of God and Man. In this connection, the famous senior Domestic Baul of Birbhum, Sri Sudhir Das, has remarked that these Domestic Bauls are always serious in following the two different phases of their life, - one is related to the deep devotion and allied activities towards the Ultimate Being and the other is connected with the familial life like the common people. According to many Domestic Bauls the systematic inter-linking pattern of life-philosophy is very much conspicuous in their path of *sadhana* and there is no doubt about the fact that this state of affair is highly troublesome to follow. These Domestic Bauls are fit enough to clear their body and mind for dedicating themselves at the feet of the Ultimate Being in spite of their complicated familial bindings. On this ground alone the domesticated Bauls deserve special credit in the sphere of Baul *sadhana*. There is no denying of the fact that the Domestic Bauls run parallel to the high level philosophy the Bauls that every activity like swimming, jumping, playing, free moving of arms and legs will be done in the water but the hairs on the head will be carefully kept free from the influence of water. The Bauls say that they will enter into the typical family life like common people but this will not be able to capture their minds to follow only the worldly affairs centred round the problems of family life. The mind of the Baul will be kept free and indifferent from the day-to-day affairs of the family in spite of his commitments in the family concerned. This mind will, for the large part of time, be engaged in the different activities related to the propitiation of the Man of the Heart. Certainly the situation is unique in human society and the Domestic Bauls leave no stone unturned to be in line with this particular state of mind. At the time of investigation into the various mental situations of Domestic Bauls through person to person enquiry it has been gathered that almost all of them make it a point to be indifferent about the worldly affairs, and at the time same time to be alert in relation to the divinely activities in the perspective of the Man of the Heart.

Like the Ascetic Bauls the Domestic Bauls have got their own *Guru* and they dedicate their lives and activities at their feet as usual in convention. They take initiation from the three different *Gurus--Diksha-guru,* (who gives ritualistic initiation), *Sikshaguru (who teaches the principles),* and *Sannyasguru* (who teachs ascetic mendicancy). These *Guru* give the initiators proper training in the maintenance of their life in the midst of diverse complexities relating to familial bondages and obligations. Generally a fourth *Guru*, known as *Sangitguru* (who teaches songs), comes into the picture. All these *Gurus*, jointly participate in the making of a Domestic Baul, who, in addition to his usual family life, would set out in search of the *Maner Manus* after throwing all sorts of worldly matters aside.

The Ascetic and the Domestic Bauls have their origin from the same philosophy and they are to follow the same pattern of thinking though there are some conspicuous differences. These two sections of the Bauls may be called as the two separate branches which have originated from the same stalk. It is true that the Domestic Bauls behave differently from the Ascetic Bauls and in some spheres, the Ascetic Bauls are more rigid and methodical in comparison with their domestic counterparts. But still there is a close resemblance between the lines of movement followed by these two sections. The Ascetic Bauls engage themselves in the divine activities in the perspective of their mendicant life centred round their *ashrams;* whereas the Domestic Bauls do the same thing in the midst of their day-to-day family life established and maintained by themselves. It is true that there are some sorts of the conflicting attitudes between these two sections, but at the same time there is close understanding. There are concrete evidences of free-mixing during any sort of gathering in connection with *mahotsab* or fair. One group fo Baul feels for the other.

But from the behaviour patterns of the Bauls belonging to Class-C, a different picture has been reflected in the total perspective of Baul life. From close enquiry into the patterns of thinking and the way of life led by them it has been observed that these Bauls have been deflected sometimes unconsciously, from the rigid path of the ascetic and domestic Baul way of life. As an emergent group from the ascetic and domestic sections of the Bauls the personnel belonging to this class possess all characteristic features of Baul life. A few of them are the descendants of famous and devoted Ascetic and Domestic Bauls. These people have got the opportunity to present their songs and dances before the appreciating public of world. They have got the opportunity to stage their performance in various western countries and thereby (having received recognition from the western audience) have become secluded from the common stalk at least in their general mode of behaviour. They, by virtue of their recognition and fame, get invitation from various circles to present their highly valued artistic performances at the various public and private stages of worldwide prominence. This has naturally given these Bauls a very wide scope to earn a lot. Most of such Bauls on getting the opportunity have managed to earn money to a considerable extent, and this financial uplift has done a great deal in changing the life pattern of the Bauls concerned. During the course of investigation a number of such financially upgraded Bauls has been met with, who used to earn their living, in their early years through simple begging.

The person to person enquiry into the way of life of the Bauls belonging to this category reveals the following fact. At an opportune moment someone of them had fallen in a favourable good notion of a sympathetic renowned personality, who came across the Baul concerned by chance. With the direct help and co-operation of the appreciator a few Bauls could present themselves in the world perspective. The Baul songs have got some specific appeal - these have got some uniqueness and if these are sung by the efficient singers, a decent atmosphere could be created which would readily win over the hearts of all the audience. The Bauls belonging to this class had got the ability of creating an appreciable atmosphere to charm the audience of all levels of culture. These Bauls had their origin in the traditional Baul families or had their training in the well-organized *ashrams*. As a natural consequence, they were basically qualified in the multifarious performances of Baul songs together with requisite dances. These Bauls added a few special attractive features in the traditional mode of presentation of songs and as because they had a very good control over the tuning and playing of the traditional musical instruments they could not find it difficult to mould the songs and their connected tuning to get equal attraction from all classes of audience. They had developed a changed pattern of dancing which enhanced the rhythmic perspective to the highest level. It was readily accepted by the western audience as one of the most interesting and essential features of the Baul show. In no time those Bauls could exert tremendous influence in the minds of the audience as well as the lovers of folk-songs throughout the world. They received invitation from various corners of the world and ultimately the Baul traditional songs and dances, restricted to some localities of Bengal, became known to the people of the world.

In course of their presentation of song and dance performances the Bauls belonging to that particular category received due honour and prestige as well as they got a good amount of money as their remunerations. This earning of excessive money ultimately caused a great deal in changing the life situation of the Bauls, who went to the foreign countries. These Bauls, though basically initiated in the Baul way of life, centred round the philosophy of mutual love and freeness from worldly pleasure, based on self-interest and earning of excessive money, began to go forward for getting worldly fame and fortune. In due course they have consciously and unconsciously deviated from the central theme of the Baul way of life. A few of them have been able to accumulate enough of wealth. They have migrated to the urban areas after constructing new houses with modern amenities. Though they do not forget to maintain a very weak link with their village homes or *ashrams* especially during ceremonial occasions, yet they fail to honour their former pattern of life on which all the activities of them are categorically based.

This particular situation has brought a stirring effect in the community of the Bauls. At the moment it has been seen that most of the Domestic Bauls especially belonging to the younger generation are hankering after going abroad. They always think in terms of this. They are of opinion that if anybody gets a chance to present his songs in the foreign countries, he would be readily accepted by the people of this country. It would be easier for that particular Baul to get frequent invitations from the public organized recitals as well as from the *Akasvani* and *Doordarshan Kendras* for the presentation of his songs. It would give him due honour and prestige but also his financial position would necessarily be raised to a considerable extent. The Bauls of the present day want this and in order to get a chance for going abroad a Baul can do anything which may go against his devoted line of thinking. The worldly fame, that has been established in the minds of the general public in the midst of whom the Bauls live and perform their activities, of the foreign returned Bauls, as well as their sudden and thoroughly improved financial situation have allured them to follow their path. It has, no doubt, brought a challenge to the Baul life natured by the agriculture-based rural society.

A recent development to this effect has been categorically felt in course of investigation into the present trend of Baul life. A section of urban agents has become very much active in tracing out the young Bauls in the almost inaccessible rural area with promising tune controlling qualities. These agents, I am told, are the admirer of songs sung by the Bauls and they mix with the Bauls very closely through their frequent visits. In course of this intimacy these agents select the prospective rural singers and make arrangements for their going abroad. In this work of selection they sometimes take the help of local Baul-lovers who pay due respect to the indigenous songs and dances of the Bauls. After selection the agents make all the arrangements for the travel and transport of the Bauls and they are accompanied by the experts appointed by these agents. It is informed that they have got some international arrangements through which they are able to organize the Baul song recitals in the different renowned stages of the world.

The Bauls, thus selected, start for the western countries and present the songs according to the arrangements made by the agents. They collect money from the box offices prior to which they give proper publicity of the Baul song and the singers. At times the Bauls are made to present the songs even before the road-side gatherings. During this sort of performances the agents become alert in collecting money from the road-side listeners. In this way huge amount of money is raised by the agents and the Bauls concerned receive a nominal portion of it. All that they receive is the opportunity for extensive travel through the western countries and listeners abroad. Most of the Bauls who have visited the foreign countries through the activities of these agents feel embarrassed and they are of the opinion that they are being exploited by these "fortune seekers", who are excessively eager to draw some practical benefit at the cost of their tradition-bound qualities. These Bauls after their return from the foreign countries face difficult situation in adjusting themselves with the traditional society of the Bauls. After their return they see that they have been diverted from the original path of the Baul way of life. It is very difficult for them to bridge up the gap thus created through the new achievements made by them. They receive due prestige from the general people owing to their tour through the foreign countries but they are to face criticism from the devoted Bauls of the ascetic and domestic nature because of the distortion of the Baul songs and dances made by them at the time of presentation in the public gatherings of India and abroad. There are some Bauls who directly appreciate the move taken up by these Bauls by breaking through the barriers to present their feats in the world perspective. They have given the Baul song *vis-a-vis* the Baul culture a conspicuous position in the world's intellectual sphere and thereby they have received due recognition. Some of the Bauls are of opinion that they have done a very good work and their activities should necessarily be appreciated.

But there are some ascetic Bauls who go against this move. They are deadly against the activities of those Bauls who have been trying to present their songs and dances in the various renowned stages of the world. The main point of their opposition is that the Bauls concerned deviate themselves from the basic philosophy of the sect. They are of opinion that the Bauls, whatever category they belong, must follow the basic principles of Baul life, failing which they would lose the very ambition of life. It is not desirable for the interest of the whole Baul community. These orthodox ascetic Bauls do not recognise the renowned Baul singers who have exerted their influence on the different parts of the world, as sincere and serious members of the Baul community. They are good as singers of Baul songs, no doubt, but, according to them, melodious tone and rhythmic dances are not the only characteristics of the Bauls. The Bauls are provided with a spiritual understanding since the time of their initiation through rigid methodical procedures. It is essential that each and every member of the Baul community must abide by these basic rules and regulations and any sort of distraction is regarded as offensive. The Bauls going abroad and to present their songs and dances are charged by these orthodox Bauls owing to the former's laxity in following the rigidity of the Baul life.

It cannot be denied that these accused Bauls have done a great deal in popularizing the Baul songs in the world and also to raise the status of the Baul way of life in general. They have not the credit of placing the Baul thinking and tradition - bound songs and dances in front of the world audience. It is, no doubt a remarkable contribution. Of late, the Baul songs and dances have found a prominent place in the minds of the general public in our country. The sophisticated public of the present day have taken much interest in these songs and dances and it is the immediate result of world recognition that has been effected by the untiring zeal of a section of the Baul singers.

In order to get a clear idea on the nature and extent of intra group conflict based on the behaviour of the international Baul singers a group discussion was conducted at Kotasur *ashram*, during the celebrated Baul conference held from 1st to 3rd September, 1983. The group discussion was conducted amongst the orthodox ascetic Bauls, the domestic Bauls and the members of the research team, which was headed by the present author. The organiser of the Kotasur *ashram*, who himself was a Baul by initiation, also took active participation in the discussion and he was all along alert in questioning and counter-questioning. The following Bauls participated in the discussion :

1. *Rupdasi* - A female Baul popularly known as *Gosain-Ma.* She belongs to a very ancient Baul family in Birbhum district. As a *Sadhika* (female ascetic), she is renowned and she has gone through a long proces of secret and devoted activities assigned to the Bauls. She is regarded as the administrative authority of the Baul community. Rupdasi is the issuer of ruling at the time of any irregular phenomenon seen amongst the Bauls of any category. She comes from Chandrahat *ashram.*

2. *Madananda Mohanta* - A well-known ascetic and a successful Baul devotee. He has conducted a number of *ashrams* and many Bauls are especially indebted to him for his able guidance in the line of *sadhana.* He plays the role of advisor in many problematic situations relating to the life and works of the Bauls. He has got the credit of analysing the different aspects of Baul life and has met and consulted many Bauls during life-long *sadhana.* He belongs to Sahapur *ashram.*

3. *Bhabananda Das Vairagi* - As an ascetic he is reputed and in course of his following rigid Baul way of life he has developed an eminent personality. He has applied this sort of personality in establishing and running a few ashram-cum-training centres of the Bauls. He has got a very good command over the existing regulations of the Baul community. He observes all the concerned regulations with deep devotion. He comes from Marugram *ashram* in Birbhum.

4. *Biswanath Das Baul* - A devoted and reputed Baul singer. He is the possessor of a very sweet voice and he has got the credit of setting to music a large number of Baul songs belonging to different categories. He is well-versed in the basic structural patterns and grammar of diverse songs. He used to broadcast Baul songs from the Calcutta centre of *Akasvani* regularly. At present Sri Das has given up the practice of singing songs and has directed his total attention to the line of *sadhna.*

5. *Gour Das Baul* - He is popularly known as Gour *Kshepa.* Gour Das is the possessor of an attractive voice and when he sings with the accompaniment of dance the audience are sure to become spellbound. He has travelled extensively throughout European

countries and has presented Baul songs at various international centres. Sri Das has got the special characteristics of spontaneous tuning of Baul songs and making them presentable within few minutes. He is a regular singer in the performances organized by the *Akasvani* and *Doordarshan.*

6. *Shyamsundar Das Mohanta* - An orthodox ascetic Baul. He does not sing or dance. He tries to reach the goal through deep-rooted meditation. Sri Das leads an austere life in the strict sense of the term. He is directly related to various administrative perspectives of Baul way of life. He is interested in silent meditation, and therefore, he does not like to talk fluently with others. He helps everybody in finding out the path for salvation. His silent mode of *sadhna* is of a very high order and it signifies the high philosophical background of the Baul life and activities.

7. *Santu Sengupta* - He is an initiated Baul. He comes of a traditional Baul family and at present he is in charge of the Baul *ashram* at Kotasur. Sri Sengupta is a teacher by profession and he edits a weekly newspaper *Didibhai* published from the *ashram.* He is very much interested in the maintenance of the traditional Baul culture conditioned by the love for humanity. Every year he organizes an assemblage of the Bauls on the auspicious day of the foundation of the *ashram.* It is attended by a large number of genuine Bauls who come here through invitation from the *ashram.* He arranges for a very good exposition of Baul philosophy through various concrete attempts during the conference.

With the above-mentioned notable personalities from the Baul community the group discussions on different basic points started in the *Natmandir* of the *ashram* during the dead hours of a night. First of all, Rupdasi, the administrative authority of the Baul cult, was asked various questions on the anomaly of the Baul sect. It was observed that during recent period many persons had been taking shelter in the Baul way of life, they sang Baul songs and approached the public for help. Some of them could secure a conspicuous position in the sphere of the presentation of Baul song. After the establishment of general pupularity of the Bauls in the minds of the public effected by the international sanction through the vigorous efforts of some Bauls, as indicated earlier, these newly introduced Bauls could find a fertile ground to spread their positive influence amongst the people and thereby to earn something. Rupdasi was of opinion that this sort of infiltration of the ordinary singers into the Baul sphere of life was harmful to the particular cult. They felt it seriously and various discussions had been made amongst them. But it could not have been checked. These people, though outwardly showed high devotion to the Baul way of living, were far from being Bauls. There were many persons who had not even taken initiation from the authorized *Gurus* not to speak of following the rigid Baul regulations. When asked how this sort of infiltration of unwanted persons could be put an end to or at least minimized, Rupdasi paused for a moment and replied in pessimistic tone. As per instruction of the Baul cult various persons should be inspired to come under the perspective of it and thereby to set them in the path of love for humanity. But as per tradition the Baul administration should not, rather must not discourage or blame for coming under the direct influence of the Baul way of life. Naturally the present Baul administration had nothing to stop and take a stern step in resisting the incoming of various persons under the Baul way of living. Madananda Mohanta opined that they, in no circumstances, could be called Bauls - they had nothing by the ability to sing Baul songs. At the same time it should be noted that singing of songs in popular Baul tune alone could not serve the purpose. It has a devotional side too. The Baul songs are not ordinary songs : those are the medium of offerings to the Ultimate Being. Naturally, a Baul singer should have the ability to perform properly with due respect to it. But amongst the infilteators it had just became the medium of earning money. Bhabananda Das Vairagi said in a very eloquent manner that those infiltrators, can hardly be termed Bauls, they have given a severe blow to the basic structure of the age-old Baul cult that had developed after the selfless and life-long spiritual activities of many devoted Bauls. Until and unless this unhealthy development is nipped in the bud, the Baul cult would be very much affected. Shyamsundar Das Mohanta went to the extent of saying that the actual Bauls are rare. He explained the term 'Baul' etymologically and showed that the Bauls should pass their life always in deep devotion to the Almighty and try their level best to make themselves free from all wordly affairs. If it was seen that any Baul had been attracted by personal comfort or self-centred activity, then it should be taken for granted that the Baul concerned had missed his mission. Missionless activities of the Bauls were utter offensive affairs, which, in the long run, spoiled the traditional background of Baul culture. When Biswanath Das Baul of international fame was interviewed with, the question of the presentation of the Baul songs in the way that was being done by the infiltrators, he pointed out a different set of principles which he was pledged to follow in his life. He opinod, the singing of songs in a melodious tone maintaining all the basic regulations of music was nothing but the paying of homage to the Man of the Heart in the preliminary stage of meditation. When the meditator goes high up in the line of his *sadhana,* he may approach the Man of the Heart through direct communion of his deep holy acts. Sri Das informed that he gave up the practice of singing of Baul song though he was the possessor of a melodious voice, as well as a successful composer and tuner. He felt that by giving up the singing habit he could find out ample time in his possession to engage in devotion to him.

But Gour Das Baul, rather Gour *Kshepa*, opposed the view-point raised by Biswanath Das. He was of opinion that the very pattern of songs and dances followed and nurtured by the Bauls had got the uniqueness about them which have no parallel. The songs accompanied by dances must be regarded as the basic element of Baul culture and each and every Baul had got the prime duty to nourish and develop these artistic activities for his maintenance as well as for the flourishing of the Baul cult as a whole. Gour *Kshepa* was very much active during the interview and he first of all elaborated the personal experiences gained by him in course of his tour throughout Europe. He placed it with self-confidence that it was the unique patterns of the Baul songs which exerted a great role in placing the Baul cult in the international sphere. Therefore, the songs should never be ignored and, he thought, there was no other element in the Baul way of life which could replace the songs and dances. The *Maner Manus* of the Bauls was practically constituted by the deep devotion of the Baul ascetics which was encircled by the halo of songs and dances. Therefore, according to Gour *Kshepa,* the exclusion of songs and dances meant some sorts of distortion of the Baul cult.

Sri Santu Sengupta raised a point regarding the status of the international Baul singers in the traditional Baul setting which was being nurtured and protected by the orthodox Baul administrative authorities. He opined that these people should be congratulated for giving the Baul songs not only an international value, but they did a great deal in attracting the people of our country to become what was called Baul-minded. It had rather become a fashion amongst the sophisticated people to enjoy Baul songs - the cultural heritage of the country. The point was readily picked up by Rupdasi, who was all along silent after her initial conversation. She was of opinion that these international Baul singers were like her sons and as mother she must congratulate them and accept whole-heartedly their untiring effort in placing the Baul cult in the limelight. But when they sat together closely to analyse the nature and extent of these activities, she could not but be worried. The philosophy of Baul sect is centered round the particular idea in which a Baul concerned must remain aloof from worldly affairs. He must not hanker after any fame or he should not extend his hands to get recognition from others. The pertinent question was that who was the giver of recognition? The Baul songs and other allied activities had already been recognised at the feet of the Man of the Heart and, therefore, what was the necessity of any worldly recognition ? The Baul *Sadhika* remarked that the very attempt was ridiculous. There must be sincere attempt to follow the recognised pattern of Baul songs and other features of Baul life and which was, according to her, the correct and deserving attempt to show regard to the Baul way of life. Biswanath Das, then came forward with his observation that the Bauls presenting their songs and dances in the international spheres did not follow the basic principles of the art so sincerely developed by the ascetics through the ages. Most of the songs had been twisted and made use of to please the foreigners according to their liking and the immediate effect of it was injurious to the interest of the Baul cult.

Gour *Kshepa* was then requested to say something on the point. He readily accepted the grievance put forward by Biswanath Das Baul. He acknowledged the point whole-heartedly that some Bauls with melodious voice and good knowledge of dance recital could win over the hearts of many foreign audience and critics, and in return, they received worldly fame and easy money to improve their economic standard readily. These Bauls by virtue of their international reputation, thus acquired, continued to earn fame and money after returning from foreign countries. In course of time, it was seen that they went off the track which was evident through the changed behaviour-pattern in their every-day life. Still they remained in the minds of the general public and sometimes they claimed a very high status because of the western recognition. There were some Bauls, who, in course of their wanderings, fell in a trap organized by some persons or groups. They went with the agencies concerned and staged various programmes on Baul songs and dance before various public gatherings in western countries. After returning homeland they had to face a difficult problem in estbalishing themselves in the original cultural matrix of Baul community. On getting unexpected honour and glorious stand, the Baul concerned became over whelmed and on coming home he could not become free as before and failed to go out for *madhukari* - the basic feature of Baul life. As a necessary consequence, these Bauls were gradually turning into professional Bauls moulding their activities as per demand of the public. This situation very naturally dissociated them from the original Baul way of life. It has been felt from close observations on the movements and universal patterns of the Bauls belonging to different categories that a conspicuous trend of clash has been working amongst the Bauls though they sit, gossip, sing and eat together in the celebrated gatherings.

The infiltrated Bauls forming the Class D are always taken as the outsiders by the members of the other three classes. Owing to gradual popularization of Baul songs and their re-evaluation in the perspective of the cultural heritage of the society by the urban educated people with modernized understandings the number of the infiltrated Bauls is on the increase day by day. These folk-singers come from the different spheres. There are good many of them who are employed in different organizations, some of them have got their own business units; others are just vagabonds. Many unemployed young men with melodious voices have become professional Baul singers. These singers adopt all the outward characteristic features of the Baul community. They dress themselves perfectly as the Bauls and behave in the way as the Bauls do. They do not go to any *guru* or perform any sort of sacred activity assigned to the Bauls. What they do is the copying of the outward movements of the Bauls to impress the public for satisfying their need. These infiltrated Bauls carefully imitate the trend of presentation of songs as followed by the established Bauls in the international field. They sing the hit songs sung by the established Bauls belonging to the Class C and try to catch attention of the public. The songs are utilized by these singers to earn money. They have become Baul singers only to earn their livelihood. They present their songs in a melodious way in the running trains and buses, in the roadside tea stalls, in bus stands, at the fairs and festivals. They are expert enough in attracting a large number of audience within a very short time. These singers are in the habit of presenting the songs before the public in a very light mood so that the outward meaning of the Baul songs allures the general public. The songs are accompanied by free movements of the body, in dancing mood and the peculiar tuning of the *gabgubi.* These outward features of actions of the body as well as the musical instrument becomes very much enjoyable to the common people with limited or no formal education, and having no sense of understanding of the inner meaning of the songs presented by them. The outward meaning is very simple and it is closely connected with their day-to-day work and behaviour patterns amongst the near and distant relations.

The Bauls belonging to this class roam about the different places and present their songs whenever they find an opportunity. They sing other types of folk-songs. Sometimes the popular film songs are also sung by them. When they attend the Baul fairs during different times of the year, they become full-fledged Bauls not only in the outward make-up but also in the mode of presentation of songs. It cannot be denied that these infiltrated Bauls exert considerable influence on the minds of the public as they are very close to them.

During Baul fair at Jaydeva-Kenduli the number of these Bauls tops the list. A large number of such infiltrated Bauls visit this fair every year and through their active participation they enhance the importance of the place. There is no doubt about it. Many of them come under the sphere of Baul way of life only for the three or four days, that is, so long as the fair in question continues. For the rest of the year they perform other activities outside this particular sphere of life. A large section of them work in the near about Durgapur Steel Project and during Jaydeva-*mela* they make themselves prepared for accepting the temporary Baul life. After close enquiry it has been gathered that most of them are related to the villages of East Bengal, now in Bengladesh. From the very early days of their life they had been getting the direct influence of folk songs and mainly of Baul-oriented songs which naturally had exerted conspicuous influence on the life and living of the immigrated people. This particular feature is being handed down through generations. It is because of this the younger folk, who have taken their birth long after the immigration of the elderly persons, have developed a special mental aptitude for the Baul songs, as well as the Baul way of life.

The Bauls belonging to the Classes A, B, and C do not generally allow these infiltrated Bauls to present their performance in close association with them. A considerable gap exists between A, B, C and D Classes. The personnel belonging to the last class are not regarded as Bauls in the strict sense of the term. Some ascetic Bauls are very much vocal about the evil activities done by these people. According to them these so-called Bauls have been exploiting the tradition-bound Baul way of life by misusing the songs of devotional nature. These are not to be sung in a haphazard manner, nor to be presented for cheap entertainment of the public. These have got a ritualistic and philosophical appeal rooted to the kindness of the Ultimate Being and naturally these are to be used by those people who have got proper qualities and requisite rights to employ these with due sincerity and devotion. In the opinion of the eminent ascetic Bauls, these people with profound cheap popularity in respect of presenting Baul songs should be given proper resistance so that their misdoings may be effectively checked.

This sort of large scale infiltration into the Baul community has brought an immediate effect. At present a question is generally put forward as regards the genuineness of the Bauls. The influence of the Bauls belonging to the Class D has been so extensive that the whole Baul community is going to be overlapped by the former. They are always hankering after cheap popularity; they try to get a chance of going abroad and want to have an opportunity to broadcast their songs through *Akasvani* or telecast their performances through television programmes. The serious appreciators of the Bauls have become embarrassed in view of this state of affairs. They fail to make differentiation between the genuine Bauls and the fake Bauls. The activities of the latter type of Bauls have become so broad and effective in the various age-old Baul-*mela* that the genuine Bauls become reluctant to attend these only to avoid the large scale misdeeds of the fake Bauls. Thus the four distinct classes of the Bauls have been grouped into two separate categories - *genuine* and *fake*. Sometimes it is noticed that the Bauls from Class C are slowly entering the sphere of fake Bauls owing to their gross aversion to follow the sanctified rules and regulations of the Baul way of life. It has naturally become an unfortunate situation. The result of this has been an unending conflict between these two categories of Bauls.

Despite all sorts of differences and inequalities, the Bauls of all the categories are to follow some rigid principles as per convention, and everybody tries, even the personnel belonging to the Class D, to maintain it as far as they can. The rigid rules and regulations are mostly respected by the individual Baul as he thinks that these are the only means to maintain the proper standard of the community and to keep up its prestige and power. But sometimes these rigid rules and regulations become very much difficult for some Bauls to follow according to the actual patterns. Sometimes it becomes practically impossible for many reasons, yet the Bauls cannot support this inability mentally. Being processed through the systematic procedures of aims and objectives of Baul life as well as of the esteem of *sadhana*, the Bauls automatically develop a particular mental situation which always attach much value to the basic principles of Baul way of life. Therefore, any sort of conscious and unconscious avoidance to these or intentional circumstantial neglect brings positive effect on the mind of the Baul. Table No. 3.2 indicates that 80.35% of the respondents have put forward negative replies when they are asked whether they feel any discomfort in following the strict principles of Baul life. Only 11.79 % give positive response while 3.49 % is indifferent. A large number of the respondents (38.42) feel embarrassed if the rigid rules are not mainained. 22.71 % of the respondents do not have any such embarrassing attitude, whereas 20.09 % them remain indifferent. The matter is not clear to 18.77% of the respondents.

The Bauls have embraced the mendicant life characterized by so many events of sacrifices and rigidity of regulations. They are seen to perform all the basic formalities and to try for meeting required condition of basic philosophical principles. There are definite aims in Baul way of life which the members belonging to this community try their level best to achieve. There are various stages of satisfaction in following the principles of Baul life with which somebody is very much conscious whereas others are indifferent. An enquiry into the trend of satisfaction and pleasure in Baul life has been made and it will be seen from the Table No. 3.3, that most of the respondents (82.96%) feel satisfied with the particular way of life they have been leading. 3.93 % of the respondents are partially satisfied whereas 8.29% of them are not satisfied with the Baul way of life. 4.80 % of the respondents fail to understand the very line of satisfaction. But a large section of them (55.02 %) feel that they have not been able to achieve the real aim of Baul life. 21.83 % of the respondents have possessed the idea that they have reached the aim partially whereas a small number of respondents (4.80 %) feel that they have been able to arrive at the goal of Baul *sadhana*. To 18.34 % of the respondents the particular question is not at all clear. Thus the Bauls belonging to all those categories have a feeling of satisfaction in following the Baul way of life but most of them are highly conscious about the actual aim of this highly esteemed life and many of them hardly claim the successful reaching of the goal in their continuous journey through the long way of *sadhana*.

TABLE NO. 3.2

Different Feeling in connection with Rigidity in Baul Life

	Feeling of discomfort in following the strict principles of Baul LIfe					Feeling of Embarrassment if the rigidity of Baul Life is not maintained				
Types	Positive feeling	Negative feeling	Indifferent feeling	Not clear	Total	Positive feeling	Negative feeling	Indifferent feeling	Not Clear	Total
Ascetic ..	4	86	2	3	95	25	21	26	23	95
Percentage ..	4.21	90.53	2.10	3.16	100	26.32	22.10	27.36	24.21	100
Domestic ..	19	73	4	5	101	52	18	15	16	101
Percentage ..	18.81	72.28	3.96	4.95	100	51.48	17.83	14.85	15.84	100
Others ..	4	25	2	2	33	11	13	5	4	33
Percentage ..	12.12	75.76	6.06	6.06	100	33.33	39.40	15.15	12.12	100
Grand Total ..	27	184	8	10	229	88	52	46	43	229
Percentage ..	11.79	80.35	3.49	4.37	100	38.42	22.71	20.09	18.78	100

TABLE NO. 3.3

Nature of Satisfaction and Achievement of Aim of Baul Life

Particulars	*Satisfaction in Baul LIfe in all respects*					*Achievement of the Real Aim of Baul Life*				
(Types)	***Yes***	*No*	*Partial*	*Not Clear*	*Total*	*Yes*	*No*	*Partial*	*Not Clear*	*Total*
Ascetic ..	85	4	3	3	95	9	38	34	24	95
Percentage ..	89.47	4.21	3.16	3.16	100	9.47	40.01	25.26	25.25	100
Domestic ..	59	11	5	6	101	2	63	21	15	101
Percentage ..	78.21	10.89	4.95	5.95	100	1.98	62.37	20.79	14.86	100
Others ..	26	4	1	2	33	1	25	5	3	33
Percentage ..	78.79	12.12	3.04	6.06	100	-	75.75	15.16	9.09	100
Grand Total ..	190	19	9	11	229	11	126	50	42	229
Percentage ..	82.96	8.29	3.94	4.81	100	4.81	55.03	21.84	18.34	100

4

Bauls in the Congregations

The Bauls offer themselves in the *mahotsabs* or great festivals that are arranged at different places throughout the year. Most of the *mahotsabs* are associated with fairs which have their own age-old traditions. These fairs are attended by large number of common people who enjoy these gatherings to their hearts' content. These satisfy the dual motives of the common people--one belongs to the ritualistic as well as philosophical perspectives, and the other is connected with the day-to-day materialistic necessities. In these *mahotsabs* and connected fairs the Baul-way of life is seen to be fully flourished. The Bauls are to be found here in their natural mood - they behave freely during this time. During *mahotsab* they are to follow various rigid rules and regulations. Various customary rites are performed to regularise different irregular activities done by the Bauls, consciously or unconsciously. Therefore, the Bauls can be seen at close quarters and their underlying activities can be understood through regular visits to these *mahotsabs* and fairs.

The *mahotsabs* are held in different *akhras* or centres where the Bauls stay and engage in their spiritual *sadhana*. These *akhras* have been established either by an individual Baul *Guru* or these have been started through the joint enterprise of a number of Bauls. Sometimes the villagers of a village of the number of villages establish *akhras* and these are dedicated to the Baul especially belonging to the ascetic section. The *akhras* play the essential role in the development and spread of the Baul culture and most of the time these attract many devotees to this Baul line of thinking. The *akhras* work as the places of connection between the ascetic and the domestic Bauls. These also work as the platforms where the interested people can come in direct touch with the Bauls. In other words these are called the living temples of the living God centred round the Man of the Heart. There are a number of important *akhras* where the Bauls assemble regularly and exchange their thoughts and ideas. Sometimes they get the opportunity for communicating new ideas discovered and developed by themselves. In this investigation a number of *akhras* have been studied and the *mahotsabs* and fairs have carefully been noted to understand the nature and extent of the Baul culture and its adjustment with the socio-philosophical set-up of the country as well as its linkage with the people belonging to various castes and creeds.

The Baul-Mela at Jaydeva-Kenduli

Jaydeva-Kenduli, in the district of Birbhum, is regarded as the renowned Baul developing centre throughout West Bengal. This particular place, now a dilapidated tiny village on the northern bank of the river Ajay, is characterized by some basic principles which do a great deal in flourishing the Baul-way of life. The internal connection of the Bauls with this particular place is so great that an individual Baul feels it an offence to keep himself away from attending this place during a particular time of the year.

The *akhra* at Jaydeva-Kenduli village deserves mention in this regard. This particular *akhra* is constituted of eight mud-built straw-thatched houses under a big banyan tree. By the side of this *akhra* there is an old *tamal* tree and due to which this *akhra* has been named as *Tamaltala akhra*. This *akhra* is inhabited by 10-12 Bauls permanently and in addition to this the floating members occasionally visit this spot and stay here for a short duration. The *akhra* in question has a special characteristic of its own. The village Jaydeva-Kenduli, where the *akhra* is situated, is characterized by a traditional cultural history as it is the birth place as well as the place of work of the famous poet Jaydeva. Jaydeva flourished during the second half of the 12th Century A.D., and he was the Court Poet of Lakshmana Sen, the last Hindu King of Bengal. The capital of Lakshmana Sen was not far from the native village of Jaydeva. He composed the famous book *Gita Govinda* in a melodious language which was characterized by the sincere and devoted presentation of the divine love between Radha and Krishna of the great Vaishnava tradition. Jaydeva attempted to get himself acquainted with the God through the medium of love. His consort, Padmavati, who was thought none but the part of Radha herself, was highly devoted to the path followed by Jaydeva. The story of Padmavati and Jaydeva woven round the famous Lyric *Gita Govinda* has been penetrated into the inner recess of the heart of the people especially belonging to the Vaishnava sect and the persons interested in the Vaishnava literature.

The village Jaydeva-Kenduli is situated on a small tract of land just by the northern side of the Ajay river. This village is inhabited by six different castes and the Brahmin caste is the dominant one among them. The village, though economically depressed presents a well-knit picture of various sacred centres belonging to the Vaishnavas as well as folk traditions. The famous temple of Radha-Madhava is situated just on the bank of the river Ajay. The temple is decorated with different types of terracotta figurines which depict the various phases of the love affairs of Vaishnava tradition. It is said that Jaydeva himself used to worship the deity Radha-Madhava. Padmavati was always engaged in making various arrangements for the Puja including cleaning of the temple premises. At present the devotees have installed the stone-images of Jaydeva and Padmavati inside the temple. The *ashram* established by the Vaishnava Sadhus belonging to the Nimbark Community is a special attraction of this sacred place. It has a remarkable history and it is run by a well-organised unit constituted exclusively of the Sadhus of the said community. This community feels glorified to think of themselves as relatives of the poet Jaydeva as the latter belonged to the religious sect. Originally these Sadhus belonged to Vrindaban. Long ago one Radharaman Vrajabasi - a Sannyasi of Nimbark community - came to Kenduli with a *Saligram Shila* (a black stone worshipped as the symbol of Vishnu), named Rajrajeswari, on getting an instruction through dream. Radharaman got the direct assistance and financial help from the then Maharaja of Burdwan, who was pleased to donate requisite land at Kenduli under his zamindari to set up *ashram* and to build temples. Ultimately the Sadhus could establish a well-organised *ashram* here and they were able to win over the hearts of the local people through various benevolent activities. The organisation took it as one of the main responsibilities to protect the valuable memory of Jaydeva and to publicise the great poet's life and activities. The *ashram* authorities claim that the place of the poet's original residence is within the boundary of the *ashram.* It is supported by the famous Vaishnava Pandit Late Harekrishna Mukhopadhyay. Prof. Suniti Kumar Chattopadhyay also refers to the strong belief of the locality relating to the birth place of the poet Jaydeva. This *ashram* is a flourishing centre for Vaishnava belief and ideas.

Just at the eastern corner of the village the famous Kuseswar temple stands on the bank of the river Ajay. At this sacred place Jaydeva attained the divine grace through mediation. Kadam-Khandi Ghat--a traditional landing-stair for taking bath in the river Ajay - is another important sacred spot which is believed to be blessed with Jaydeva's direct connection. At this landing-stair Jaydeva used to take bath and here in the shallow water of the river he got the image of Radha-Binode. The *Maha Smasan* attached to this *ghat* is also a famous place of sacred importance. The temple of Radhaballava indicates remote antiquity. At present it stands in the midst of old vestiges of ruined temples, fragments of sculptures and remnants of old residences of the Mukherjee family which is regarded as the original settlers of the village. Under a big banyan tree at the western side of the village there is a sacred spot known by the term 'Vaishnav Gosain'. On a raised platform a number of wooden sandles and a few burnt clay horses act as the symbol of the deity. This spot lies just by the side of the Bauls *akhra.* Besides these Jaydeva-Kenduli village is provided with other important sacred centres like the *ashrams* of Khotorey Baba, Kangal Kshepa, Monohar Kshepa, Gangamata, Nagababa, Brahmacharibaba, Ramkripa Sanghram, Katyayani and Kali temple are also remarkable in this sphere. There is an important folk religious centre in the midst of the houses of the Bagdis who are lower caste people. This deity has been commanding tremendous influence in the locality irrespective of castes, classes and communities.

The *akhra* of the Bauls, being situated in the heart of these sacred centres, is directly and indirectly influenced by the thoughts and ideas of these holy units. Attempts have been made here to study the detailed organisation and workings of the *akhra* in the perspective of these sacred centres and the age-old annual fair commonly known as Baul Mela, which is held in January. At present the Bauls staying in this *akhra* have been interrogated individually and their day-to-day activities, trend of inter-personal relations, their attitude towards the locality and *akhra* organisation have been studied through enquiries and observations in the village and also by close conversations with the Bauls concerned.

The *akhra* is maintained by one Baul, named Sudhir Das. He is regarded as the leader of the Baul community in Jaydeva-Kenduli. He was born at Tikarbeta village about 2 kilometres from Jaydeva-Kenduli. From his childhood days he used to visit this Baul concentrated village and became inspired by this particular way of life. He, in course of time, came in touch with the then famous Baul Halababa and began to live in his company. He took his initiation from Kangal Baul of Nabasar village and received various other instructions to lead Baul life from Halababa. Sudhir Das is the follower of the Vaishnava Sahajiya Baul Sect. The Bauls belonging to this particular region strictly follow this particular way. On person-to - person enquiry it has been revealed that owing to the tremendous influence of Vaishnava religious teachers, poet and devotees throughout the district in question and especially in this very region encircling Jaydeva-Kenduli the Bauls showed strong leanings to this Vaishnava philosophy.

The word '*Sahaja*' means esay. According to this philosophy, the formalities of religion and observance of various ceremonial matters stand in the way of attaining God's grace. On this ground, they defy all types of formalities and various ritualistic paraphernalia. In this system of maintaining life, emphasis is laid on the psychological aspect of the Yogic practices. In this system the human love is raised morally to the sublime level and the divine being is comprehended to be in the human body. The eternal love between Radha and Krishna is the basic philosophy of this way of thinking.

The Bauls in this *akhra* follow this principle strictly and they always praise in the name of Radha and Krishna. They lead conjugal life and feel themselves as parts of this divine couple. It has been gathered from direct investigation that all types of matrimonial relations are performed through Vaishnavite principle. They have taken consorts through the traditional way of exchange of "mala-chandan" and through the performance of other allied Vaishnava rites. The Bauls, in this *akhra*, are highly devoted to the various perspectives of *Gita Govinda* composed by the poet Jaydeva. They are highly influenced by teachings of Sri Chaitannya Deva who spread Vaishnava faith and ideas widely throughout Bengal during the critical period of religious feuds and large-scale conversion into different religions, especially Islam.

In this *akhra* varied informations have been gathered to focus the trend of interactions of the Bauls with the Vaishnava faith and traditional folk beliefs that have been flourished in different sacred centres since very old times. It has been seen that the Baul way of life is highly influenced by the life and philosophy of the locality. At the first instance it has been seen that the Bauls in this centre establish the portraits of Radha-Krishna, Sri Chaitannya in the special altars to pay homage to them. These Bauls are extensively influenced by the life and activities of the poet Jaydeva. They feel themselves closely associated with him. The Bauls, living in other places do not possess this particular idea. In order to find out other specialised features amongst the Bauls in this *akhra*, special emphasis has been laid on the study of the minute details of the workings of the various sacred centres at Jaydeva-Kenduli.

There is a regular convention amongst the villagers in this locality to visit the sacred centres at Jaydeva-Kenduli during different occasions throughout the years. During this visit it is regarded as an indispensable affair to have a look at the Baul Centre and listen the melodious songs composed and sung by the Bauls. The Bauls lead conjugal life yet they remain aloof from all sorts of worldly matters. They love and respect themselves and both of them possess equal status in the day-to-day life. They hate the social inequality, artificial hierarchy of castes, classes and religion. Their principal attitude is to believe man and to show proper respect to him irrespective of his caste, class and creed. All these matters are communicated through the songs presented by them in the finest manner, and also through their practical behaviour-pattern. The Bauls play the most important part in the observance of social harmony and they function so intellectually that the people in general do not understand and cannot capture the actual theme of their workings.

The Bauls have been performing the most essential national duty of social integration which is the main topic of discussion in the present day India. Their songs on different perspectives touch the inner recess of the hearts of the people. It had been observed during field work that the Baul songs presented at *Vaishnava Gosain tala* at Jaydeva-Kenduli moved the general listeners coming from different villages. Most of them gladly confessed that during the song performance they felt an upward thrust in their mind and they could feel that they were much risen from the insignificant worldly affairs for the time being. It is certainly not an easy task. Therefore, the Bauls act as the social teachers and their workings and movements focus that sphere of thinking which is highly valued by the present National Government.

The village, Jaydeva-Kenduli, has no special attraction. It is like any other village in this region having common problems of rural life. But on the specialised days the village concerned takes thoroughly changed condition of life. The total background of the grossly backward village changes as if in a magical way and the whole village becomes a sanctified unit for the spread of love and respect amongst each other. The Bauls take the dominant role in driving their philosophical understanding.

On the day of *makar-sankranti* which falls on the last day of the Bengali month *Pous* (December-January) the great festival starts and it lasts three days. The highlight of this event is that the Bauls in their thousands attend and actively participate in the fair that is held in honour of the great poet Jaydeva. The principal features of this assemblage are as follows:-

(1) A fair is held with thoroughly agriculture-based nature of economy.

(2) The items of amusements that are arranged in the fair are mainly meant for the rural people.

(3) Various Vaishnavite temples and religious centres work as the special pilgrimage for the aged persons.

(4) Special altars that are raised temporarily for the roaring folk deities here exert tremendous influence of regional folk cults on the participants.

(5) A number of ritualistic feeding centres, organized by the different *akhras* which function for the three festive days, arrange for serving meals to the people irrespective of castes, classes and religions.

(6) These temporary *akhras* make special arrangements for providing shelters to the public as well as to the Bauls. In addition to these all the *akhras* prepare special platforms for the presentation of Baul songs. These are provided with microphones.

(7) Bauls in large number begin to reach the fair on the previous day of *makar-sankranti*. They take shelter at the different *akhras*. The domestic Bauls come along with their families. They come in so large a number that the particular fair take the character of *Baul-mela* or fair of the Bauls.

The main characteristic of the *Baul-mela* is that it is essentially a spontaneous assemblage of the Bauls. There is no formal invitation or sending of message to the community of the Bauls. The fair is also a spontaneous gathering of all people mostly drawn from the different villages. The place is especially characterized by being the birth place of the great Bengali poet Jaydeva and everything is based on popular sayings. The different religious texts though try to recognise the place as the place of birth and activities of the poet yet there is no definite historical and archaeological proof in favour of this. The folk-lore of the region is highly rich and it accommodates the different activities of the poet Jaydeva and his consort Padmavati in this village. It is so elaborate and deep-rooted that this particular folk-lore dominates everything in this fair. Various places or remains of activities of this village, that had direct connection with the poet Jaydeva, become the main centres of attraction of the devoted groups of people who visit the fair to meet religious formalities. The fair is considered by the Vaishnavites sacred to the highest degree and it comes next to Vrindaban which is especially characterized by the celebrated activities of Radha and Krishna. Padmanvati and Jaydeva are considered by the Vaishnavites the parts of Radha and Krishna. It is because of this fact that this place is popularly known as the *Rarher Vrindaban* or Vrindaban of Rarh. The natives who cannot arrange to have a celebrated visit to Vrindaban and also to come in direct touch with the dust particles of the celebrated paths of Vrindaban consider it a special privilege to visit Jaydeva-Kenduli during the three-day long festive occasion. According to them, the visit runs parallel to the act of visiting the holy Vrindaban. Thus it becomes the special pilgrimage for the rural Vaishnavites.

The connection between the Baul community and the holy place of Jaydeva's birth and divine activities is very difficult to trace. It has been gathered that the Bauls have been coming to this village since a long time and they themselves cannot shed any light in connection with this particular point. They admit without any hesitation that they feel violent excitement in them for coming over here and offer themselves to honour the celebrated day of Jaydeva's birth anniversary. Some are of the opinion that it is the day of Jaydeva's great departure from this world. The Nimbark community at *Mohanta Asthal* arranges for the ceremonial funeral rite on that particular day in the memory of the great poet Jaydeva. Whatever may be the actual incident, it is seen that the people belonging to all classes and creed flock to this dilapidated village materially and economically but extremely rich in ritualistic philosophy, and offer there homage from the core of their hearts, to the great Vaishnava Poet and Philosopher. This particular fair is highly characterized by the sincere attempts for cultivation of the traditional culture. Since long time past the Jaydeva-Kenduli fair has been the celebrated pilgrimage for the eminent personalities in the sphere of Sanskrit and Bengali languages and literateurs. In this fair a number of organizations with literary appeal arrange for literary conferences. A number of renowned poets and litterateurs; from the different parts of India, especially from Santiniketan and Calcutta pay regular visits to this fair and by their different literary activities here pay their homage to the poet Jaydeva. The renowned Sanskrit scholar Mahamahopadhyay Haraprasad Shastri and the eminent poet-philosopher Rabindra Nath Tagore visited the place many a time during the festive occasion in search of the Bauls and their spontaneous activities. Besides these the scholars like Kshitimohan Sen Shastri, Harekrishna Mukhopadhyaya, Upendranath Bhattacharya, used to go there at different times for having a close look at the life and activities of the Bauls. Jaydeva-Kenduli fair is the paradise for the lovers of song and music. The Bauls present the songs of diverse nature throughout the day and night continuously and the listeners become overwhelemed with the systematic presentation of songs. The total atmosphere of the village as well as the region faces a thorough and abrupt change owing to these activities of high literary and musical value.

The Jaydeva-Kenduli fair is regarded as the celebrated seat for the exposition and exhibition of various feats of the Bauls. The Bauls believe that this particular place has got the special appeal which instigates the Bauls of all categories to exhaust their all mental excitements to the Man of the Heart. The unique features of this place is that the continuity of the traditional Baul culture is still prominently visible in all respects in spite of various prominent changes. The Bauls stay here for three full days during which they take shelter at different *ashrams*. Most of the time they spend the days side by side with the common people. The Bauls present their songs and dances one by one in the different platforms, especially constructed for this purpose. The audience belonging to all classes sit down encircling the platforms and neglecting the chilly winter nights they establish an inseparable unity with the singers. The close link connects the devoted singers and the appreciating listeners is the main factor which plays a great role in making the performance living in its totality. The Bauls sing songs here which range from high philosophical thinking to the light socio--economic understandings. Sometimes the day-to-day family life like the interactions between husband and wife, between mother-in-law and daughter -in-law and between the two co-wives become the central themes of many songs which are sung in a very humorous way. The common illiterate people enjoy these songs fully through their various wordings by wordings. But these songs have got an internal appeal which depicts the deep-rooted philosophical understanding. These are for those persons who have got the training and ability in going to the depth of importance. But these are also enjoyable for the listeners, who cannot penetrate through the very wordings of the songs. Here lies the uniqueness of the Baul songs. These songs readily unite all classes of listeners-illiterates and highly educated, rural agriculturists and most sophisticated urban people, young and old as well as the fun-loving and highly religious-minded persons. In the different *akhras* and Baul *manchas* of Jaydeva-Kenduli fair this particular situation is highly illustrative. The illiterate rural listeners sit side by side with the sophisticated lovers of songs from urban setting. The total atmosphere as well as the traditional surroundings become highly congenial for lifting all the cultural barriers amongst the different classes and grades of people. It is nowhere to be found. It is this congenial atmosphere which has given the Bauls a favourable background to impress their thoughts and ideas upon the minds of the people through their songs.

It is customary that the Bauls should visit the different *Akhras* during the night and present their songs on the special platforms. It is highly characterized by an attitude of healthy competition. Sometimes two Bauls start putting questions and forwarding replies through the songs. When it reaches the maximum point, it becomes a highly intellectual fight. It is enjoyable as well as thought provoking situation. There are times when the preceptor or *Guru* starts this sort of intellectual combat with the disciple or *Siswa*. Both of them put questions and forward ready-made answers through the instantaneous composition of songs. These songs are composed then and there and made to tuning immediately after this. This particular state of affairs not only needs the special aptitude for the composition of lyrics as well as very good command over the technique of tuning but also an overall knowledge over the religious text and mythological perspectives as most of the questions are put in connection with these perspectives. The performances are mainly done by the Ascetic Bauls though the Domestic Bauls with conspicuous personalities take part in these. The infiltrated Bauls also become very much active in the presentation of songs at the different *akhras* and though they do not have thorough understanding of Baul philosophy they apply all sorts of sincerity and seriousness in the presentation of the songs. These songs are admired by them very much and for which they have come, of course temporarily, under the sphere of Baul way of life.

The Bauls of all the categories stay in different *akhras* all through the time but they spend the day-time in gossiping amongst themselves. The Domestic Bauls are found to be busy with their family members. The infiltrated Bauls roam about here and there for getting various advantages. The Bauls are very much addicted to smoking of hemp to a large extent. Some of the Bauls are continuous smokers of hemp and a few of them make such forceful puff that it attracts many people. Sometimes it becomes the enjoyable affairs. This addiction to hemp smoking has been increasing day by day amongst the Bauls and it is seen that many common people especially the younger generations from the urban settings make contact with the Bauls for the regular smoking of hemp. The senior Bauls are of the opinion that hemp-smoking helps them in freeing the body and mind for spontaneous activities relating to the singing of songs that are used for the purpose of paying homage to the Man of the Heart. The smoke of hemp lifts the body on a particular height and this disconnects the worldly feelings of the body facilitating the person concerned to offer his clear mind at the feet of the Ultimate Being for which the Bauls have been wandering about. But the fact of the matter is that these days the smoking of hemp is practised principally for amusement and especially amongst the younger section of the Bauls it is very common. The hemp - smoking is, no doubt, an essential happening in Baul life. The Bauls greet one another, when they meet for the first time, in the name of *Guru*. They utter the word 'Jai-Guru' and which is followed by the offering of hemp for smoking. But this courteous approach is being degenerated into excessive use of hemp for seeking pleasure. This foul practice should be checked to some extent to save the Bauls from gradual doom. It has been observed during thorough investigations that many of the reputed Bauls have been going astray and their health has been spoiled due to the excessive inhalation of smoke emitted from hemp.

During Baul song performance through the night it has been categorically observed that a few Bauls have become addicted to drinking liquor to a considerable extent. The poets, litterateurs and lover of music visit the fair every year and through personal contact they arrange for their shelters in the Baul *akhras* and live there freely. Most of them drink liquor profusely, smoke hemp in a wild manner and thereby pass the leisure periods through merry-making. These intellectuals spend sufficient amount of money for the arrangement of the *akhras* and other allied affairs and through all these tricky practices they can easily win over the hearts of the Bauls. Some of the Bauls who stay very close to these intellectuals for this period become very much addicted to drinking which goes against the Baul way of life. In the Tamaltala *akhras* it is observed that during song and dance performance a number of young 'appreciators' of the Bauis and the Baul songs, I came out one by one in an unbalanced state caused by excessive drinking. A few Bauls also went along the same way and naturally they could not present their songs owing to their unsteady state of body and mind. It is a no doubt a trickly situation and the Bauls have been facing this. It is matter to be looked into with unbiased outlook and definite measures must be adopted to help the Bauls for coming out of this vicious circle of receiving worldly pleasure and instantaneous amusement through the drinking of liquor and the smoking of hemp.

Jaydeva-Kenduli fair, that is spontaneously held in the sacred memory of the poet Jaydeva, was started long ago. Formerly, it used to be held on the bank of the river Ajay, beside the famous *Kadamkhandi Ghat*. It is said to be blessed with the coming of the river Ganges during the dawn of *Pous Sankranti*. Owing to Jaydeva's heartfelt prayer and great devotion the river Ganges became highly pleased and in order to lessen the labour of Jaydeva the Ganges herself reached the celebrated *Kadamkhandi Ghat* of the river Ajay, where Jaydeva used to take his bath. It is said that on the dawn of *Pous Sankranti* the water current in the river Ajay takes the reverse course *i.e.* downward stream moves in upward direction. This situation has been firmly established in the minds of the local people, who till today gather in large number to have a sacred dip in the sanctified water. The Bauls also subscribe to this local belief that has been and is being handed down through generations. They sing songs in the praise of the glorified water and its salubrious effect on the body and mind of the bath-takers. After taking bath in the early morning the people distribute alms to the poor and the disabled who take shelter just on the two sides of the path leading to the bathing *ghat*. Then they bow down before the leading folk deities placed on the especially prepared raised platform just at the entrance of the *ghat*. These folk deities have got close link with the surrounding villages and the villagers by traditions. The pilgrims then pay visits to the different temples and connected religious centres provided with deep-rooted beliefs and faiths. It is taken by all as the pious activity to have a look into workings of the *akhras*, especially during the distribution of the cooked *prasad* to the devotees and the common people sitting in a row without any caste and class discrimination. They also sit very often in the row and take *prasad*. These *akhras*, most of which start their temporary activities here for the three days of the fair, are organised by the pious personalities, the *Sadhus* or the ex-zamindars. On the eve of the fair all the organisers arrange for temporary sheds made of bamboo poles, jute cloth, tarpaulin and straws at particular sites that have been especially demarcated and maintained by traditions. The organisers then make special provisions for cooking the huge quantity of *prasad* to be served from morning till evening to the pilgrims, devotees, beggars and any person who likes to have it. Naturally, a tremendous preparation is needed with provisions for huge quantity of rice, vegetables and other allied cooking materials in addition to a large number of working and managerial personnel for giving proper shape to the celebrated and responsible promise made by the families or organisations concerned for the charitable supply of food to the attending persons during the three-day period of Jaydeva-mela. The organisers of these *akhras* make ceremonial installation of the family deity or the deities they particularly worship at the especially prepared alter. The cooked food items are ceremonially dedicated to the deity or deities concerned for converting these as *prasad*. The *Sadhus* generally install the image of their respective *Gurus* in the special altars of the *akhra*. The family-organised *akhras* are maintained by the individual family contributions. Most of them have got *Debottar* land from the income of which the whole programme for charitable supply of food can be implemented. The *Sadhus* receive contributions from their disciples and devotees for the proper implementation of the programme in question. The internal organisation is highly characterised by the unique appeal. All the persons wishing to have *prasad* are cordially received by the organisers through highly submissive posture and with folded hands. The items are served to them very carefully and in a dignified way after throwing aside all the rigidities of the caste barriers and untouchability-oriented outlook for taking and serving of cooked food. The persons taking food in the *akhras* are not allowed to lift their used leaf-plates. The organisers take it as their sacred duty to lift these themselves as the honourable guests should be treated in this manner. The dining ground is washed and cleaned by the organisers themselves. It is somewhat unbelievable to point out that how the rigidity of the caste barriers, class consciousness and the Brahmin-dominated purity-pollution concept disappear for this three-day period. It is nothing but a miracle and which is tradition-bound. This miracle takes the proper form through the attitude of inartificial love for people and profound respect for people and profound respect for humanity. The love-oriented philosophy of Jaydeva works as the dominating factor in the overall establishment of love and respect for man irrespective of castes, classes and religions. The love lyrics written by the poet Jaydeva have got penetrated well into the recesses of the hearts of the common people and that is why the people of the locality are able to readily contribute to the idea of love and respect governing the organisational patterns of the *akhras*.

The Bauls, as a natural consequence, get here a fertile field for their basic activities centering round a particular philosophy of love for all and feeling for oneness in the midst of various diversities of life as a whole. It is for this reason the Bauls find here very conducive atmosphere for their *sadhana* through the various performance of songs. They are glad to have in this village blessed with the birth and activities of the worshipper of love, the devoted audience whose mental attitudes have become fully receptive to accept and assimilate both the external and internal feature of the Baul songs. It makes the Baul very easy to express himself. The barriers of man-made human society fall flat on the ground as if automatically and he finds the golden opportunity to exert his influence in a proper manner. It is because of this situation the Baul assemblage here becomes so fascinating. The Baul feels the clarion call of *Jaydeva-Kenduli* in the inner recess of his heart and he cannot help coming over here to bow down at the feet of the Man of the Heart, which is so full of life and vigour in this traditional village of Birbhum district.

The Bauls though they are the part and parcel of Jaydeva-*Mela* keep themselves away from the traditional beliefs and practices of the fair. The

Bauls do not like to pay any visit to the temples or to take purificatory bath in the river Ajay. They do not like to roam about in the fair to have a look at various merchandise that have been put up for sale. But they are keen and interested enough to find out the different incidents of love, features of oneness, fusion in beliefs and practices of diverse nature for putting these events in their different songs. Some scholars have expressed their inability to understand the connecting link between poet Jaydeva and the Bauls. In the Jaydeva literature no detailed reference of the Bauls is met with which is worth mentioning. The Bauls, on the other hand, cannot definitely explain the cause of the binding force between them and Jaydeva's activities. Jaydeva used to worship Radha and Krishna and he, in close association with his wife Padmavati, could find out the proper perspective of love for which Radha and Krishna became celebrated. Jaydeva and Padmavati were successful in exploring the path of love to reach the Ultimate Being represented by Radha and Krishna. The Bauls also been able, through their long-term *sadhana*, to search out the Ultimate Being after proceeding through the path of love. The Bauls appreciate the close knit love between Radha and Krishna and it is the love which the Bauls pay due respect. Padamavati and Jaydeva are regarded as the true representatives of Radha and Krishna and they are the real exponents of love-philosophy which the Bauls propitiate from the core of their hearts. The Bauls show profound respect to these exponents of love, Padmavati and Jayeva, and only for this they rush to the holy place of their appearance and activities on the auspicious day characterized by Jaydeva's remarkable achievements for the people, *i.e.*, bringing of the Ganges through the up-stream of the Ajay. After thorough enquiry into the different events that occur at the *Jaydeva-Kenduli* and having liberal talks with the Bauls as well as the Vaishnava Prophets and *Mohantas* living there it has been observed that the basic principle of the *sadhana* of the Bauls and do the propitiation pattern of Jaydeva is the same. It is based on profound love which the worshipper or the *Sadhaka* must acquire from the inner recess of their hearts. This particular perspective unites the Bauls with Jaydeva, and it is so rigid and inartificial that after the travel through centuries it has remained unchanged in spite of abrupt changes that have exerted deep effect on the human cultural perspectives and value-attitude system.

The Baul assemblage that starts at *Jaydeva-Kenduli* fair on a particular day of the month of *Pous* does not end suddenly but it continues through the different *akhras* of the region. On the third day of

Baul assemblage of *Jaydeva-Kenduli* fair a ceremonial finale is held. It is known as *Dhulot* or the ceremonial wallowing in the dust with the joint singing of devotional songs accompanied by dance. After this ceremony the Bauls attend in large number in the shrine of Villamangal Thakur situated in a village named Villamangal-Viluria, about three kilometres west Jaydeva-Kenduli. An observer of the *Kenduli-mela* on the third day will be astonished to see that the Bauls, Fakirs and common pilgrims are walking in a row over the narrow path-way by the bank of the river Ajay. They all have determined their destination at the famous religious centre that has developed in the sacred memory of another Vaishnavite poet and philosopher, Villamangal, whose *sadhana* was mainly based on the principle of love to humanity. It is very difficult to trace the information about the early years of life Villamangal Thakur. In later years he became famous by writing the book, *Sree Krishnakarunamrita.* He established his *Sadhanashram* or hermitage for meditation at Viluria village on the north bank of the Ajay. There is a popular folk-saying in this locality about the total moulding of life of Villamangal Thakur. He was deeply attached to a village woman named Chintamani in his youth. The attachment was so deep that one night after completing the funeral rites of his father Villamangal Thakur set out for the residence of his beloved. It was a stormy night and associated with heavy downpour. The river Ajay was in flood. Villamangal Thakur was then overwhelmed with the outburst of passion. He took hold of a floating corpse and with the help of which he crossed the turbulent river. It was dead hours of night: Chintamani was asleep and the door of her bed-room was closed from inside. Villamangal Thakur began to shout from the top of his voice but to no effect. Nobody responded to his call. He then tried to leap over the wall and at that time he saw a long rope hanging from the wall. He caught hold of that rope and entered into the room of Chintamani. A hanging snake on the wall was mistaken by him as a rope. When Chintamani knew everything about the risk and endeavour taken by Villamangal Thakur, she became furious. She began to rebuke Villamangal Thakur by saying that if he could offer half of this love to the feet of God, his life would have been significiant. Being rebuked by Chintamani, Villamangal Thakur Came to proper sense. He realised the remarks put forward by Chintamani and from then on he began to offer his heart full of love at the feet of Radha-Krishna. He went to Vrindaban and after long-term meditation there he became a devotee of Radhha-Krishna.

The village Villuria is regarded as the native place of Villamangal Thakur. He stayed here till his great departure from this world. The whole area gradually engulfed by jungles and nothing remarkable was there excepting the pile of ruins. A dilapidated temple is still standing here and at the central part of which there is a raised platform. It is recognised as the lying-in room Villamangal Thakur. At the courtyard of the temple there is a paired *tamal* tree which is identified as the representatives of the divine pair as exemplified by Radha and Krishna united together by the bond of love. By the side of this there is one *Akshay Bot* or the immortal Banyan tree.

On the third day of the Bengali month *Magh* (January-February) every year the annual festival is held here in commemoration of the poet Villamangal. It is organised by one Vaishnavite *Sadhu* who came here long time ago; he cleared the jungle and established one *akhra* here to facilitate to temporary stay of the devotees and the Bauls. A *mahotsab* is held on the 3rd day of *Magh* when all the Bauls take active part in the presentation of song and dance in honour of Villamangal and Chintamani. The charitable supply of cooked food is arranged for the day when all the devotees and piligrims sit down side by side to take food. The attending Bauls make some special arrangement to offer heart felt honour to Villamangal Thakur for his love-seeking path of worshipping God. It has been found that during various song and dance recitals the Bauls have become fused with the common people-the artificial discrimination has been vanished.

A section of the Bauls hurriedly start for the Darbesh *Ashram* at Dubrajpur to attend the *mahotsab* which starts on the 3rd day of *Magh* and continues for two days. Many Bauls go direct to Dubrajpur from Jaydeva-Kenduli fair. The Darbesh *Ashram* is situated at a very picturesque place just by the side of the famous Pahareswar hillock at the outskirts of Dubrajpur town. There is a permanent Baul *ashram* here and it is at present run by Sri Gangadhar Das. He is an initiated domestic Baul. The Darbesh *ashram* is characterized by the presence of the temple of Darbeshji, a prophet in the sphere of Bauls *Sadhana*. The *Guru* of this *ashram* was Atal Behari Darbesh, who came here from a distant place and made his centre of meditation in a temple dedicated to Darbeshji, who was the initiator of this *ashram*. At that time the whole area was totally covered by jungles and the people could not go beyond the Pahareswar hillocks Darbeshji started his activities there and in course of time he came in touch with the locality. A few local people were attracted towards his amiable nature as well as miraculous activities. He incidentally came in touch with the Raj family of Hetampur Rajbati and was able to make the Raja convinced by his divinely activities. Raja was pleased with him and permitted him to establish a full-fledged *ashram* at the place where he settled down temporarily. When Darbeshji approached the Raja for the donation of land to be utilised for *ashram,* the Raja asked him to dig out a spadeful of earth from that land and then spread these as far as he could. Darbeshji did it and he could spread over that spadeful of loose earth over nine acres of land. As per the word given to him by the Raja, the nine acres of land was donated to Darbeshji for his *ashram.*

Once the Raja of Hetampur sent his personnel to collect wood from the jungle. The workers started the work of felling the dried up trees in the jungle and its vicinity. In course of their work, a few workmen came nearer to the *ashram* site and seeing a dried up tree there, they went to fell it. Darbeshji resisted the attempt on saying that he took rest under the tree. Moreover, the tree was within the jurisdiction of his *ashram* and so they had no right to cut it down. But the workers did not pay any heed to it and during the brief absence of Darbeshji they tried to fell it down. But it was surprising that during the operation of felling the said tree, the workers began to vomit blood. On his return Darbeshji saw the incident and began to admonish the workers. Darbeshji then sprinkled water from his *Kamandalu* and, it was surprising enough that the tree became full of life again. There is a popular belief that the particular tree is still standing in full vigour by the side of the temple of Darbeshji. Derbeshji became well known to the locality by performing these types of miracles and gradually people belonging to all levels began to come to him for getting his kindness and advice to solve various problems of their life. In due course, Darbeshji got many active disciples and sincere devotees to help him in the constructional activities of the *ashram.* The *ashram* had been dedicated to the wandering Bauls. Still today the Bauls and all other religious mendicants may take temporary shelter in this *ashram* in course of their wanderings through the region.

The annual festival or *mahotsab* is held every year following the closure of the Jaydeva-Kenduli *mahotsab* and it is popularly known as *Rahi machchab* or the festival of road. While going away from the famous Jaydeva-Kenduli *mahotsab* the travelling Bauls and other religious mendicants stop here for a day or two and participate in the *mahotsab* of Darbesh *ashram.* The organizers of the *ashram* make arrangements to send formal invitation to the different *akhras* of Jaydeva-Kenduli for attending the *mahotsab* at Darbesh *Ashram.* They also send invitation to the influential and devoted people in and around Dubrajpur. A temporary arrangement for providing shelter to the attending Bauls is made by erecting bamboo poles and covering these with the help of jute clothes and tarpaulin. There is a spacious *Natmandir* here which provides room for many persons. A special platform is erected for the Baul singers who dance and sing there throughout the night. The inauguration ceremony of the *mahotsab* is held on the 3rd day of *Magh* in the evening. It is known as *agamani.* A few Bauls and other Vaishnavite mendicants sing *Kirtan* and devotional songs to the accompaniment of *kartal, khol, dubki, khanjani* and *ektara.* It is followed by *mahotsab* next day. Formerly the expenditures for the great festival was borne by the Raja of Hetampur. But after the abolition of zamindari right it has been stopped. Still in order to maintain the custom a few performances are held in this connection. Just on the eve of *mahotsab* a devotional party consisting mainly of Bauls pay ceremonial visit to the *Rajbati.* There they pay homage to the temple deity of Radhaballabh. After this they receive ceremonial donation in the form of rice, pulses, vegetables together with some money to be used in the *mahotsab.* The descendants of the Raja provide *mukhamachchab* or feeding of sweets to attending Bauls and their associates. Hundreds of Bauls then start village begging singing devotional songs in chorus. Most of the housewives offer rice, pulses, vegetables and few coins to the party and bow down before the devoted gathering. Then the party returns to Darbesh *ashram* and after this the *anna-chhatra* or the charitable supply of rice starts ceremonially.

In addition to village begging the organizers very often approach the local traders and to well-to-do devotees to contribute towards the celebrated serving to the religious mendicants. Recently one belonging to Dhanpota village in 24 Parganas district of West Bengal person having strong leanings towards Baul philosophy and interested in the Baul way of life has taken the full charge of this three-day long well-known festival. His name is Sri Tapan Das Sain. He is above eighty years and is always assisted by his *Sevadasi* in these religio-philosophical activities. He is a graduate. After conducting the *mahotsab* at Jaydeva-Kenduli he comes with his party and all necessary materials to Darbesh *ashram* and arranges for everything. It is due to this fact it has become easier for the organizers of this *ashram* to run the festivals smoothly.

In this *mahotsab* the Bauls themselves prepare their food. The *Sevadasis* of different Bauls assist in the different stages of cooking. Very often the people of the locality come forward to help the Bauls in different stages of their work. After the preparation of food materials all are ceremonially dedicated to the deity in the temple of Darbeshji. It is respectfully offered by Sri Gangadhar Das. It follows the *mahotsab*. The Bauls sit down in different rows in front of the temple premises. But one distinction is maintained here. The Ascetic Bauls popularly known as *Bhekdhari* Bauls take their seats away from the others. If anybody fails to follow this principle he is reminded by the *ashram* authorities or the person concerned, who is in charge of inspecting the rows. The persons besides Bauls are not allowed to take *prasad* in those rows, in any case. On taking their seats in two separate units the leaf-plates were spread before them one by one. From the very beginning special care was taken to maintain all sorts of regulations. It was reported by one of the organisers that in the event of occurrence of even the slightest irregularity the Bauls, especially the ascetic group, would stop taking food and would leave the *ashram* immediately. To serve these mendicant was a very difficult task and it needed a mental attitude of deep devotion and selfless service. It was seen that *Sainbaba* (Sri Tapan Das Sain) and his consort were very much concerned from the very outset as regards maintenance of the ritual order. A few Bauls started singing of devotional songs in the praise of the *Guru* to the accompaniment of *kartal* and *gabgubi*. The singing troupe began to go round the place where the Bauls were sitting for having meals. Then the food items were brought to be served by the Bauls themselves. First of all, the rice was served, and then followed the other items. But the sitting Bauls did not touch these. All of them were engaged in reciting the verses that were composed in the praise of *Guru*. Some were composed to depict the importance of having that *mahaprasad*. It went on uninterrupted. The *Sevadasi* of *Sainbaba* then offered lighted incense sticks to each of the Bauls which they stuck to the ground by the side of their leaf-plates. Then the taking of food started but it was not done silently. All along they were engaged in reciting verses of various kinds and all the attending Bauls, participated with it in delightful attitude.

A large number ot devotees and curious visitors from the common people crowded before the place of *mahotsab* to have a pious look at the feeding of the Bauls. Most of the time they lent their voices in the loud call in the name of *Hari* like "*Hari Hari Bol*". At the end of the feeding ceremony the Bauls waited for sometime when the *ashram* mother came forward and asking permission from the sitting Bauls, she picked up one boiled rice from the residues in the leaf-plates of each of the Bauls collected in a metal plate. These were then mixed up and served amongst the attending people as *mahaprasad*. First of all, the organizers of the *ashram* took it ceremonially. There is a general belief in the locality that this *mahaprasad* has a tremendous effect in controlling the body and mind, and inspiring them to follow the right path.

At night the total atmosphere of the *ashram*, as well as its surroundings underwent a total change due to the systematic presentation of Baul songs of diverse nature in melodious tone. People from far and near attended the performance of song and dance. The traditional songs of rural Bengal sung by the experienced singers and enjoyed by the devoted listeners in that solitary part of the country left an earnest appeal in the dead hours of wintry night.

The *mahotsab* at Darbesh *ashram* closed with the performance of *Dhulot* and it was done by the Bauls under the direct sponsorship of the organizers of the *mahotsab*. The people of the locality took active part and at the time of performance of *Dhulot* there was no distinction between the Bauls and the common people. The latter lent their voices in the chorus sung by the Bauls. In this way a close link was forged between the Bauls and the common people.

At the end of the ceremony most of the Bauls go to Banamalipur *ashram* in the district of Burdwan. It has flourished in the midst of coal industrial complex. This particular village has a long history behind it and it is blessed with the occurrence of a renowned Vaishnavite fair. There is a temple of Mahaprabhu here. It is said that the village in question is glorified by the ceremonial visit of Mahaprabhu himself in the distant past. However, the Bauls consider it their sacred duty to pay their homage during the observance of annual festival at Banamalipur *ashram*. The Bauls here felt the sweet memory of Mahaprabhu - the living exponent of love for humanity on which the Baul philosophy is founded. The fair is largely attended by the workers from the collieries during the present period and naturally it takes an industrialized colour. A large number of tribal people are the regular visitors to the spot during festive occasion. They belong to the Chhotanagpur region but came to this part of the country for working in the collieries. The Baul songs presented by the attending Bauls leave an indelible impression on the minds of the tribal people as well as other minors who think differently throughout the seasons. On completion of the festival the Bauls depart at different directions.

The Baul-Mela at Santiniketan

The Baul gathering at Santiniketan is held more or less three weeks before Jaydeva-*Mela*. A fair with rural characteristics is held every year at the *ashram* premises of Santiniketan on the 7th day of the Bengali month *Pous* (December -January) to commemorate the foundation day of Santiniketan. On that particular day father of the poet Rabindra Nath Tagore, Maharshi Devendranath, established a miniature *ashram* for the cultivation of the celebrated Vedas and related Vadic performances. Rabindranath, in later years, gave proper shape to that *ashram* and ultimately he made the place a full-fledged institution of variegated learning that brought it international fame. Gradually the place could receive All-India importance through the continuous efforts made by Rabindranath. People from different parts of India came here for getting themselves enlightened with the knowledge in different perspectives of life. These efforts received requisite recognition from all over the world and Rabindranath was able to establish here the international seat of learning under the name of Visva Bharati.

During the period of his stay and work over here Rabindranath came in close touch with the Bauls of Birbhum. He had some solid background of Bauls, talked with them and enjoyed their songs and dances from close quarters. In Birbhum he was overwhelmed with the basic philosophy of these rural mendicants and spent a greater part of his time in composing songs based on Baul philosophy and life-style. He used to invite some of the eminent Bauls at Santiniketan when he behaved with them in a very hospitable mood. This tradition is still being maintained here. It is for this reason the Baul song and exposition of Baul culture find a prominent place during the three-day long fair at Santiniketan popularly known as *Pousmela*.

In the *mela* premises a temporary *Pandal* is erected for the shelter of the Bauls who come here through proper invitation from the *mela* committee. The *mela* committee reserves the right for inviting a particular Baul. Generally a list preserved here and by following which the formal invitations are forwarded at least two weeks before the actual date of starting of the *Pousmela.* On reaching the fair the Bauls take their shelter inside the *Pandal.* Along with the Bauls a number of Fakirs following sufistic way of life come here who stay inside the same *Pandal* but they reserve a corner side for their temporary living. The Bauls are not the centre of attraction in the *Pousmela* as is seen in other fairs of Birbhum and Bankura. They are regarded as a part of the whole gathering. Their identity here is actually established by invitation and official recognition. A few Bauls have been met with here who have attended the fair uninvited formally and naturally they are not recognised by the *mela* committee. They attend the fair due to the inartificial mental impulse and take delight in being associated with the celebrated Baul gathering. But the thing is that this impulsion readily receive a severe shock when these Bauls are treated otherwise. They are not allowed to present their songs in the *Sangit-Mancha* especially prepared by the *Mela* committee. Only the invited Bauls are allowed to present their songs before the audience according to the time schedules prepared by the *mela* committee. There is no other arrangement where the uninvited Bauls, especially belonging to the younger sections can get the opportunity to offer their songs. There is no other alternative but to sing their songs inside the short space of the *Pandal.* Many audience attend these performance but due to shortage of space everybody feels embarrassed. Moreover, the singing of songs at three or four places in this short space creates a chaotic condition. There is no traditional pattern of *mahotsab* here and none get any opportunity for the celebrated charitable supply of food. The invited Bauls and the Fakirs are supplied with lunch and tiffin coupons by the production of which they receive the required dishes from the scheduled shop. The uninvited Bauls are to face a troublesome situation in respect of procuring food. They spend the small amount of money that they collect from the audience by singing songs for having food.

Pousmela has got different appeals in the minds of the people. It has got no religious background and naturally the rural sentiment does not enter into the very recess of it. The Bauls do not come here spontaneously with an urgent appeal for paying their homage to any Baul *Guru* or renowned ascetic in this line. People attending the fair do not look at the Bauls with deep devotion and as an essential part of the fair. They enjoy Baul songs side by side with other miscellaneous folk songs, as well as sophisticated songs, dances and other performances. All through their stay in the *Pandal* organised by the *Mela* Committee, the students of the song and dance sections become, to some extent interested with the Bauls, individually or in small groups, and have some essential discussion with them. A few sophisticated people are very often seen to make contact with the Bauls and in this a choice is most often seen. They are interested only with the renowned Bauls. Some of them are called in their individual houses for singing of songs in a homely atmosphere. The singers receive remuneration for this; but it is restricted to the eminent singers only.

In *Pousmela* the audience are not mentally equipped to enjoy the Baul songs presented by various Bauls and evaluate these on their very nature of presentation. The audience here are conscious about the fame and reputation of the Baul singers and they are well-known to them on basis of their personalities. There is no scope here to judge the nature of presentation of songs without knowing anything about the singer. Therefore, in *Pousmela* no spontaneous character is to be observed in the coming of the Bauls, their behaviour-patterns, their presentation of songs and other allied activities. The whole affair is conditioned by many artificial barriers and the mental appeal fail to rise above these obstacles.

In *Pousmela* the Bauls find themselves in the distinct categories,-- the favoured Bauls and the neglected Bauls. The favoured Bauls also face different inconvenient situations in *mela* due to partiality of the organizers. It has been reported that favoured Bauls belonging to the top level category receive a good remuneration in comparison with those of the second grade quality. The Bauls do not whole-heartedly support it and naturally most of them do not feel easy in the premises of the *Pousmela.*

The Baul Gathering At Kotasur

Looking into the nature and extent of the Baul centre at Kotasur, popularly known as *ashram,* it is felt that it is unique in itself. It has a tradition of its own which has been traversed by many ups and downs. Kotasur is small but very ancient village situated nearly 12 km. from Sainthia - the main business centre of Birbhum. Being developed by the side of the Muyurakshi river this *akhra* is regularly visited by the travelling Bauls throughout the year. Besides the annual gathering of huge number of Bauls with diverse characteristic features, which is held on the 15th of the Bengali month of Bhadra (August - September), many occasional assemblages of the Bauls take place here when the interactions of various thoughts and ideas as followed by this community with variegated life-style are clearly highlighted.

From time immemorial the Kotasur *akhra* has been playing great role in the shaping and patterning of the Bauls. One Kshepa Chand Gosain, a devoted Baul, was probably the founder. He became Brahmachari at the tender age of twelve and left home to roam about here and there in search of the truth. During his journey through the country, he came to this spot which was jungle infested at that time. He was a very good organizer and he could shape this spot as an ideal Baul *akhra* where the intending persons were only initiated in the Baul way of life, but also they were trained up in the idealistic perspective of Baul culture. There are numerous oral tales depicting Kshepa Chand's life and activities moulded by supernatural power. Kshepa Chand was a very good composer of Baul songs and he had the credit of presenting a large number of songs with high philosophical standpoint. His consort, Kshepa-Ma was a very powerful ascetic and she devoted her life to make the Kotasur *ashram* an ideal one. Kshepa-Ma is still a remarkable figure in the minds of the Bauls in this locality. She tried continuously to establish different ideal *akhras* of the Bauls and she could set up as many as 22 *akhras* in the district of Birbhum. Kshepa-Ma took departure from this mortal world in the year 1260 B.S. (corresponding to 1853 A.D.) Her disciple, Srimat Motidayal Goswami took the charge of this *ashram*. He was a devoted Vaishnava and wrote a few books (in manuscript form) on Vaishnava and Baul philosophy. Besides this, he composed a few beautiful Baul songs and left a glorious past which is still pulsating in the day-to-day life and activities of the *ashram*. The day of his disappearance from this mortal world - 15th to the Bengali month, Bhadra (August-September) - is observed as the day for Baul festival. The befitting successor of Motidayal Goswami was Ragaranjan popularly known as Ragbaba. He used to lead an ideal Baul life and made his level best to bring various prosperity to the *ashram*. He was not only a good composer of Baul songs but he also showed proper eligibility in playing various musical instruments and presenting different types of *Kirtan*. At present this *ashram* is being organized and maintained by the successors of Ragbaba and they have shown profound interest in devoting the *ashram* in the development and maintenance of the traditional Baul *culture*.

The annual *mahotsab* of Kotasur is tradition-bound. A large number of Bauls from the different districts of West Bengal attend the *mahotsab* through formal invitation. The Bauls start coming here during early hours of the 15th day of Bhadra which is the day of *Agamani*. The Bauls take shelter in the temple premises as well as in the specially erected tents with the help of bamboo poles, jute clothes and tarpaulins. The ascetic Bauls prefer to stay in the temple premises. In Kotasur *mahotsab* a number of eminent ascetic Bauls regularly attend to pay their homage to the *atan* of different devoted workers in the line of Baul way of thinking. This *ashram* is a self-dependent unit. It has sufficient area of agricultural land and through the income of which the expenditures in the observance of the *mahotsab* is met with. Moreover, a few devoted persons in the locality, some businessmen with ritualistic outlook very often contribute as far as they can. The organizers of this *ashram* belong to a highly prestigious family. They have earned fame through different philanthropic works done inside and outside the district of Birbhum. The present organizer, Sri Santu Sengupta, is very much interested in journalism and has got very good knack in the literary works. A weekly news-magazine, entitled *Didibhai* is brought out from here. A printing press has also been started inside the *ashram*. Thus in addition to the religious activities the *ashram* has been provided with literary and intellectual activities. In the perspective of this, many intellectuals are also invited to attend the *mahotsab*. Most of the time a few conferences are held where in-depth discussions on Baul philosophy are made. Thus a fertile field is created here through the coming of two groups of personalities - the Bauls and the intellectuals, who, in course of their reciprocal conversations, may explore various spheres of knowledge and general understanding.

On the day of *mahotsab* the Bauls belonging to different categories began to sing devotional songs to the accompaniment of *khol, kartal, gabgubi* and *ektara*. The organizational part of the *mahotsab* was completely controlled by the owners of the *ashram* and though the Bauls were engaged to do their own activities yet their were conspicuous restrictions. The ascetic Bauls only were allowed to take part in the cooking and distribution of food materials. The preparational activities were principally done by the inmates of the *ashrams*.

At about 12 o'clock the Bauls took their seats in different rows for taking *prasad*. It was decided by the Organizer-in-Charge to make separate arrangements for the Ascetic and the Domestic Bauls. But all of them Join their voices in the inaugural song sung in chorus. Many of the Bauls loudly recited the rhymes composed in he praise of *Guru*, as well as of Hari. The Bauls took their meals in the sal leaf-plates. A few of the Ascetic Bauls used their own characteristic utensils made out of hard skin of pumpkin and coconut shell. The ceremonial feeding of the Bauls were attentively observed by many people of the village including the invitees who came to participate in the conferences. The taking of food started after recitation of rhymes glorifying the grace of *Guru* in the life of the Bauls. The main organizer of the *ashram* referred to the complicated rules and regulations which they were to abide by rigidly during the feeding ceremony of the Bauls. A number of Ascetic Bauls in the surrounding area who hold the administrative sphere of the Bauls and organize a few ideal Baul *ashrams* are regular visitors to this *ashram*. During the annual festival they come forward to resolve many complicated issues facing the community of the Bauls. Many cases of socio-ritual conflicts and tensions that exist in the community in consequence of violation of norms by any individual Baul are seriously dealt with. Any Baul detected as such is not allowed to sit in line with the other Bauls. His supporters, if any, also receive the same kind of treatment. It was reported by the main organizer that a few years ago a critical case was detected. The *Sevadasi* of a particular Ascetic Baul became pregnant, which was a very sinful affair as well as derogatory on the part of the Ascetic Bauls. Both of them attended the *mahotsab* at Kotasur *ashram* and stayed inside the temple premises. A few eminent Ascetic Bauls who could understand the situation became furious. They declared that there was no other alternative for them but to refuse food here as the sinful activities had been neglected here. It went against the organizer of the *ashram* who readily expressed his total ignorance about the said fact and requested the leading Ascetic Bauls to manage the situation so that the spirit of the age-old *mahotsab* can be retained. It mean for the Bauls and naturally it was the sacred duty of the Bauls to honour it. At that earnest request the leading Ascetic Bauls discussed among themselves and thereby arranged for short-term ceremony in which the Baul concerned was compelled to appear before all and confers his misdeed. He was then forced to divorce his consort ceremonially and live separately. At that very conference a young Baul was requested to accept the *Sevadasi* of the offending Baul as his consort through a short ceremony sponsored by the attending Bauls.

This sort of *mahotsab* is regarded as a favourable place for seeking befitting consorts for the Bauls. A large number of Ascetic and Domestic

Bauls, accompanied by the female Bauls are the regular participants in the *mahotsab*. Naturally, the Bauls seeking for their consorts come to this place with a mind to get a suitable consort through personal contact. It was reported that last year an aged and renowned Ascetic Baul, Shyam Sundar Das Mohanta, came to this *ashram* with a mind to find out one young *sevadasi* for serving him in different affairs of his *sadhana* as well as daily mode of living. For a long time he had been living alone though he was in charge of a reputed *ashram* at Aduri village in the district of Birbhum. But he had to return empty-handed as he did not get any opportunity to come across any solitary *sadhika* or female Baul there. It is also the place where the separation between the Baul and his *sevadasi* is effected owing to gross inability of the *sadhika* to assist the Baul *sadhaka* in his way of *sadhana*, the *sadhika* is left formally. Sometimes the lack of mental understanding between the *sadhaka* and the *sadhika* lead to their separation. Often this formal separation is immediately followed by taking of a consort by another Baul. The deserted *sevadasi* may unhesitatingly accept another solitary Baul as her companion and after living together for sometime they perform formal ceremony in respect of *sadhaka-sadhika* union based on selfless love and mutual respect. This *ashram* is characteristically suited to these secret as well as personal activities of the Bauls because of the following reasons:-

(1) This *ashram* is started by *Kshepa Ma* or the blessed mad mother, the legendary Baul with versatile qualities for conducting Baul *sadhana*. The Bauls believe that her immortal soul is still roaming about within the four boundaries of the *ashram*.

(2) The *Bakul* tree that exists with full vigour and which has been in full blossom all the year round is regarded as the most auspicious and pulsated in spiritual life in the sphere of Baul *sadhana*. Under the shade of the tree the great Baul *Sadhika Kshepa-Ma* used to conduct *sadhana* and it was her celebrated seat.

(3) The temple premises of the *ashram* accommodate a number of *samadhis* (burials) of the Baul *Gurus* which are regularly propitiated by the extremities. It is firmly believed by the Bauls that the immortal souls of them move about in the air within the jurisdiction of the *ashram*, and these have been keeping vigilant eyes on the activities of the Bauls.

(4) This *ashram* is always blessed with the presence of the top level Ascetic Bauls who not only control the various activities of the Baul community but also suggest various means to help solving different problematic situations faced by the community in question. During annual *mahotsab* many of them come over here and stay side by side for at least three days.

On *Mahotsab* day a song recital is held in a special *Pandal* erected outside the *ashram* building but within the jurisdiction of the *ashram*. It is easily accessible to all persons and a large number of audience from far and near attend the recital. It is characterized by the presentation of deep-thinking songs that are sung in a sombre and devoted mood. There are some scholasitc Bauls who do not generally sing publicly come forward to offer songs in deep devotion to the celebrated founder of the *ashram*. Following this all the ordinary singers present their songs one by one and audience enjoy these to their hearts' content all through the night. The organizers of the *ashram* sometimes make arrangements for the competition of the Baul singers. A larger number of eminent singers take part in it and they try to show their all sorts of techniques and skill in music and tuning. It becomes very much enjoyable as well as thought-provoking performance. The judges appointed on behalf of the organizers select the competent singers and honour them with prizes.

On the last day the essential feature of this festival is held which is known as *Madhukari*. From the very early morning the preparation for *Mudhukari* is made. A huge quantity of *bhog* is prepared which consists of different types of fruits, *luchi*, curry, sweets, and rice-porridge. Besides these, bucketfuls of beverage made of pulped *bhang* are prepared. The Bauls are heavily supplied with hemp for smoking. Hundreds of Bauls accompanied by large number of villagers and attending persons to the *mahotsab* then start for *Madhukari*. They sing a special type of song with the accompaniment of *khol, kartal, ektara, gabgubi, etc*., and make round over the extensive area. All the participants start wild dancing as if all of them have gone mad in the search of the celebrated Great Mad or the Man of the Heart. When the *Madhukari* party passes through the village path all the persons from each and every household come out to pay due respect to the Bauls. They bow down in honour of the *Baul-Guru*. All of them then come back to the *ashram* after the lapse of four to five hours. On their return the *Dhulot* is held when all the participants smear mutually the mud and dust of the courtyard of the *ashram* signifying the end of the festival.

The Baul-Mela At Sonamukhi

The *mahotsab* at Sonamukhi in the district of Bankura deserves mention in many respects. The Baul assemblage in the different *akhras* of this village presents various interesting facets which are to be assessed properly to unfold the different perspectives of the Bauls. Sonamukhi is a very old village and it is of a very large type having as many as eighteen wards. It is inhabited by 24 caste-groups and a large section of these still follow the traditional callings. The village has been named after Swarnamukhi Thakur-the village tutelary deity. The temple of this deity is seen in the village and there is a stone image inside it. Besides this there are many temples, which are seen here and there in this village. A newcomer to this village will readily identify it as the village of temples. Sonamukhi village is famous for the presence of large number of tanks have got supernatural stories behind each of them. The village is mainly based on agricultural economy and most of the caste-groups adhere to this economic perspective even today. Recently, the village is on the verge of the change due to the urban impact and in consequence of which the basic socio-economic pattern of the village has been facing conspicuous alterations.

On the *Ramnavami* day of every year a Baul assemblage is held commemorating the sacred birth anniversary of Sri Manohar Das, the worthy disciple on Mohan Chand - the great *Guru*. Hundreds of Bauls of different categories, Vaishnava saints and prophets of other religious sects visit this village spontaneously to pay their homage to the great Baul at his ancestral residence. No fair or any such aspect is held during this assemblage. The Bauls, first of all, go to the Manohartala, where a temple is seen. In this temple there are images of the Lord Nityananda, popularly known as "Gour-Nitai". On a special altar beneath these images the photograph of Manohar Das is placed and by the side of which the wooden sandal and the *kolkey*, *i.e.*, the earthen bowl for smoking hemp used by him are carefully preserved. A large number of devotees belong to this village and surrounding villages are seen to offer *pujas* to the temple deity, as well as to Manohar Das. On both sides of the path leading to the temple, there are a number of temporary shops which provide sweets and other allied materials for worship. Many Bauls and *Sadhus* are seen to take their shelter in the spacious *Natmandir* at Manohartala. They have formed different groups and engaged in discussions of various topics, simple and light gossiping or in singing song with *ektara* and *khanjani*.

The Baul *mahotsab* in this village continues for three days starting from *Ramnavami*. Manohartala is the central unit of the *mahotsab* and everything is controlled from here. But the Baul *mahotsab* comes into full swing and vigour in a particular part of the village known as Ratanganj. There are altogether 12 different *akhras* here. These are known as *Bara akhra* or Manohartala *akhra*, *Chota akhra*, *Babur Pukur akhra*, Herekristo *akhra*, *Bharat akhra*, Bomsankar *akhra*, Behal Gosain's *akhra*, Swarnamoyee *akhra*, Anuragi Gosain's *akhra*, Sain *akhra*, Natun *akhra*, Gostha Das's *akhra*. In all these *akhras mahotsab* is held for three consecutive days and the Bauls dance and sing in the different *akhras* all through the night. People transcending barriers of castes and classes take *prasad* from these *akhras* along with the Bauls and they find ample opportunities to come very close to the Baul community which facilitates the understanding of their specific life-pattern to some extent. The Bauls of different categories sing various songs so spontaneously and the people feel so delighted that Sonamukhi *mahotsab* is popularly known as *Mini* Jaydeva or Jaydeva *mahotsab* in miniature form. Whatever may be the fact, the Sonamukhi *mahotsab* differs from that of Jaydeva one in some fundamental aspects which have been discovered from close observations. The most prominent differences are as follows:-

(a) In Sonamukhi the Bauls attend the shrine of Manohar Das through properly identifying him as the Baul *Guru*. The Bauls think themselves as part and parcel of Manohar Das, the Great Baul. They visit the temple and offer direct homage to him.

In Jaydeva-Kenduli the Bauls do not recognise the poet Jaydeva as the Baul *Guru*. They do not find any direct connection with him. They also do not visit the temple of Jaydeva or pay any attention to the sacred geography related to Jaydeva.

(b) In Sonamukhi the Bauls visit the different *akhras* throughout the night and present their songs. There is no fixed *akhra* where a Baul can present whole of his offering of songs. The audience move from one *akhra* to another for enjoying songs. Here the *akhras* are loosely arranged.

In Jaydeva-Kenduli the Bauls do not move so rapidly from *akhra* to *akhra*. The audience also take their seats more or less permanently in an *akhra* and enjoy the songs. The *akhras* are strictly arranged here.

(c) In Sonamukhi the organizers of the *akhra* invite the Bauls formally, sometimes in writing for presenting their songs.

In Jaydeva-Kenduli nobody invites the Bauls. They come spontaneously and sing various songs according to their choice.

(d) In Sonamukhi the audience is not so well-knitted. They come freely to enjoy the Baul songs for the night and then they go back to their homes, The crowd is not tied up in a common understanding and they do not live, of course temporarily, side by side neglecting all unfavourable situations.

The audience of Jaydeva-Kenduli is not only well-knitted but also they have prepared mental situation to accept the deep philosophy of Baul songs. Amongst the audience there is a close fellow-feeling as all of them share a common interest in a common perspective. In Jaydeva-Kenduli there is no question for the audience to go back to their homes-because the *akhras* have become sweet homes for almost all the audience.

(e) As fair is not associated with the *mahotsab* at Sonamukhi, the *akhras* become almost deserted when the song is over temporarily. Here the people do not find any other opportunity for refreshing themselves in the midest of enjoying songs consecutively.

The fair is of special importance in Jaydeva-Kenduli. All the *akhras* become packed up with audience all through the time. There are many other opportunities to get themselves refreshed with other items in the fair as per choice and taste. So, the audience never feel bored.

The *mahotsab* is arranged by the local festival committee which is constituted of the young men of Sonamukhi. The focal point of this festival is lying with the *Bara Akhra.* It is at present organised by Sri Premananda Das. But he does not stay here all through the time. The *mahotsab* of Sonamukhi ceremonially starts from the day of *Baruni* bath which is held 12 days before *Ramnavami.* The local festival committee takes the initiative to bring Sri Premananda Das through invitation and he was given full charge of the festival. As per his instruction the Bauls and other devoted personnel are invited, and the local committee makes the effort for the collection of rice, pulses, vegetables and cash donations from the village and other neighbouring areas.

In this *akhra* the Baul song is held on a permanent *Natmandir* at the one side of which the burial tomb of Mohan Chand Darbesh the great Baul *Guru,* is situated. Many eminent Bauls reaching Sonamukhi, first of all, present their songs before Darbeshji and from there they move about the different *akhra*. This *akhra* is well-organized and the volunteers are all along alert in maintaining order of the *akhra* during the presentation of songs by the renowned Bauls.

The other *akhras* are organized by the founders themselves. In all the *akhras* there are arrangements for taking of *prasad,* though there are some restrictions. The doors of most of the *akhras* are kept open for staying of the outsiders. In all the *akhras* the portrait of respective *Gurus* are kept in specially made seats and are decorated with garlands and incense-sticks. The Bauls and other devotees residing in the *akhras* are paying their homage to the *Gurus* after taking bath in the morning.

All the *akhras* make definite arrangements for the presentation of songs by the invited Bauls. The *mancha* or platforms have been erected with a canopy of cloth or tarpaulin. There are arrangements for electric light and microphones. The Bauls move with their musical instruments from one *akhra* to another. Sometimes the distance between the *akhras* becomes too much and in the dead hours of night the audience are to cover the whole distance walking on foot. The roads leading to the *akhras* are not smooth and not well-lighted. In most of the *akhras* there is no proper sitting arrangements and most of the time the attending people are to enjoy the song in standing position.

During our visit to these *akhras* and observance of various activities many characteristic features were observed. It was seen that though the people contribute as per their ability to the general funds of the *akhras*, yet they are not so interested in coming over to the place where *mahotsabs* were being held. Some of the people preferred formal invitations from the organizers of the *akhras* for taking *prasad* there. At the time of taking meals consisting of rice, pulses and vegetables, it was seen that somewhat clear-cut distinction of caste and rank was maintained, people belonging to higher classes felt hesitation to sit along with the Bauls and other nomadic saints for obtaining *prasad* in leaf-plates. The audience in the different *akhras* could not whole-heartedly become part and parcel of the song recital. Many people lack proper patience to hear the in-depth songs sung by the Bauls. A section of audience was very much active there and which was constituted of the young men of the locality most of whom were the workers in various industrial settings. They did not bother for any philosophical understanding. They had no time, rather patience to hear the serious songs sung by the Bauls. They were fond of listening to light songs placed in a very light mood with perverted body movements. They were reaching the *akhras* in large numbers and tried to enjoy the songs standing inside the *akhra*. In order to satisfy this class of audience some of the Bauls were tempted to present very light song in a very light mood. The audience belonging to the class mentioned was very much pleased and all began to encourage the singers for a repeat performance. Therefore, owing to influence of this class of audience every thing in Sonamukhi went in a different way. The serious and devoted audience did not feel happy with this, rather they were embarrassed. Sometimes it went to the extent of throwing obscene remarks at the time of singing of even devotional songs. The organizers also felt embarrassed in these states of affairs. All felt that in Sonamukhi the general nature of audience was going to be decreased day by day. A few sections of audience belonging to the younger generations had become problematic. It was seen that they were reaching the different *akhras* suddenly and creating troubles to the singers and the general audience by various means. On reaching the Babur Pukur *akhra* in early hours of night it was seen that the performance of Baul song was totally stopped there though the elaborate arrangements were made and a very spacious stage was constructed. On enquiry it was known from the organizers that from the evening that particular centre became very much attractive as many eminent Baul singers attend it and which became crowded with all categories of audience. But all of a sudden a group of young audience reached there and to the utter surprise of everybody they cried aloud with the words "snake, snake". It created a puzzling condition to the general audience enjoying various types of Baul songs, and immediately they took to their heels for safety. Readily it was discovered that the youngsters came here with the bad intention of breaking away the rigid assembly of the singers and audience. The organizers of the said *akhra,* Sri Ananta Das, became very much disgusted at the evil activities of the youngsters. He felt ashamed of their behaviour and it was really a matter of disgrace especially before the respectable persons who came from outside. But in the *Bara akhra* all possible care was taken by the volunteers there to resist any sort of evil activity. However, it was seen that the nature of audience in Sonamukhi was not so devoted and serious as was found in Jaydeva-Kenduli. Mention must be made that in all the *akhras* efforts were made to create a serious atmosphere by displaying the photographs of the *Guru* and his worldly belongings in the shrine and continuously singing of devotional songs. A number of *Sadhus* from different places of India was seen to attend some of the *akhras like Bomshankar akhra* and Anuragi Gosain's *akhra.* In the day time most of the *akhras* became the centres of thoughtful discussions between the ascetics and the interested common people. On the last day of festival the *dhulot* is held when the Bauls, other religious personnel, people of the locality and the persons coming from outside dance and sing in wild manner dividing in many groups. These groups go in a procession to the Manohartala at the other side of the village. It is witnessed by a large number of people of different caste-groups who consider it as a pious activity.

Some Baul Assemblages Around Sonamukhi

Sonamukhi *mahotsab* is followed by the mahotsab at Nabasan *akhra.* Here the festival starts on the full-moon day following the *Ramnavami.* This *akhra* is situated in Chandar village near Beliatore of Bankura district. It is Vaishnavite *ashram* and organized by the Baul *Guru,* Sri Haripada Gosai. A fair is held on the Full-moon day and where a Baul shelter is prepared to accommodate hundreds of attending Bauls. A *mahotsab* for the Bauls and other allied persons is arranged which continued for three consecutive days. The *ashram* has got some landed property, from the product of which the expenditure for the *mahotsab* is partially met. The deficit is offset by the contribution raised from the villagers.

A few other *akhras* around Sonamukhi arrange *mahotsab* just after the renowned Sonamukhi festival. These are Khayerbuni Banrujje *ashram*, Chawdhuri *ashram* of Radhamohanpur, Madhyam *ashram* and Jagatbandhu *ashram* of Khayarbuni, Narayan Das *ashram* of Dhulai and Birchandrapur *ashram*. All these *ashram* have been functioning for more than 50 years. The organizers of these *ashrams* follow the similar pattern of festival of the Bauls as is maintained at Sonamukhi. Most of the Bauls from Sonamukhi visit these *ashram* one after another as per date schedule of observance of *mahotsab*, and continuous closeness with the Bauls and their activities, no doubt, exert tremendous influence on the life of the villagers as a whole.

The Baul Gathering at Ghosepara

A different nature of Baul gathering is seen at Ghosepara in the district of Nadia. This particular place is regarded as the pilgrimage of the Kartabhaja sect of the Bauls. A large number of Ascetic and Domestic Bauls visit the place of festival which is held on the *Dolpurnima*. Many family members, who are the followers of this sect, begin to reach the place for different parts of the country. Generally the people used to go to Ghosepara from Kanchrapara Railway Station by bus. There are regular bus services from Kanchrapara. But during the festive occasion a large number of special buses regularly play for three days. In recent years owing to the construction of the new Railway track and opening of the Kalyani-Ghosepara Railway Station people find it very easy to reach the spot of festival. Right from the previous night of *Doljatra* the pilgrims and the Bauls along with other religious personnel begin to assemble here and with the time the crowd becomes solidified.

In Ghosepara there is no temple or idol. The residence of Karta Ram Saran Pal is regarded as the highly sacred place for all classes of pilgrims. In this residence there is a spacious courtyard, and at the corner of which there is a pomegranate tree. Under this particular tree Satima, the consort of Ram Saran Pal, attained divine grace through austere religious practice. After crossing decades of stress and strains the pomegranate tree is still standing with full vigour. There is a popular belief that this tree is pulsated with spiritual life and people pay their homage to it from the core of their hearts. The priests stand in front of the tree. The pilgrim come with the materials for worship as per ability and hand over these to the priests. Huge quantity of sweets, fruits, clothes and even vegetables from fields are seen to accumulate her. The pilgrims stand in row for hours together to have the chance for offering *puja*. Sometimes the pilgrims tie up stones or burnt clay horses in the branches of the celebrated tree with the help of strings. During this tying operation, they express their mental wishes within themselves. On having the desired result they come to untie these stones or clay horses and offer required *pujas* to the celebrated tree. There is a strong belief that by offering *pujas* to Satima with due honour and sincerity the people can solve many critical problems in their life. The blind can get power of sight, patients suffering from incurable diseases may be fully recovered.

This courtyard leads to another courtyard inside where there are living rooms used by Ram Saran Pal and other *Kartas* in the later years. All the furniture, beds, clothes and wooden sandles used by each of them are preserved in their respective rooms. There are large-sized oil paintings depicting the *Kartas* separately. By the side of these rooms the special room for Satima is seen. All the materials used by Satima are preserved in this room. At the back of these living rooms there is a large tank known as Himsagar. It is a very large-sized tank with high embankments on four sides, on one side there are steps made on cement concrete which leads to the bottom level of the tank. The pilgrims believe that this tank has got some spiritual power. During ceremonial occasion a holy dip into it has got miraculous effect. There is a widespread belief that through taking of a bath in it, the dumb persons are readily blessed with the power of articulation, the sterile woman may acquire the ability of producing children. The persons suffering from incurable diseases may get relief from the hazards of diseases if they take holy dip into it with full devotion to *Guru*. It is for this reason the pilgrims rush to the tank from the early morning of the Full-moon day and thousands of them are seen to take bath there. The disabled children especially the deaf and dumb ones are brought here to take bath and at that time sincere efforts are made to observe the effect of taking bath. In distant past a dumb person readily gained the power of speech just after taking bath in this tank. It was done unconsciously. This incident is still pulsating in the minds of the people of the locality and amongst the large section of the disciples and devotees of Aulchand. In order to share the grace of Satima people of all castes and communities, take bath in the tank and cover the path from the tank to the shrine by making *dandi*.

The pilgrims come mostly with the member of their family to pay their homage to the *Karta*. During this visit they stay here in family groups. It is seen that each family takes shelter under a particular mango tree in vast open field. These trees have been planted by the different families in the name of their *Karta*. These trees are well-demarcated according to the different families. These are considered the family tree and occasional care is taken for their safety. The family concerned cooks beneath the tree and they also make some offerings to the tree and it is considered to be possessed of a living force. If the particular tree is uprooted or if it is found to be dead, then another sapling is planted here. In this way a huge mango garden has been grown here in course of time. The festival is associated with a large fair in which various merchandise from all over the district of Nadia as well as from Calcutta are presented for sale by the traders. The fair takes the All-Bengal character with multifarious arrangements for fun and fieasts.

Ghosepara is regarded as the great pilgrimage for the Vaishnavas. It is the holy place for the people belonging to the *Kartabhaja* sect. During fair a number of Bauls, Fakirs and other religious mendicants visit the place and enjoy three days here through the performance of various ritualistic activities. The Bauls take shelter in the different *akhras* organized by the disciples of Satima. Most of these *akhras* provide food for the Bauls and other such mendicants. But generally there is no provision for taking charitable supply of food for the public as a whole. The families belonging to the *kartabhaja* sect are to prepare their own food there. In order to do this they purchase new earthen-ware vessels, wooden faggots for fuel, and raw food materials. The cooking is performed by themselves. A few *akhras* organized by the well-to-do disciples of Satima make some arrangements for *annachhatra* or charitables supply of food irrespective of caste and creed. The followers of *Karta* do not support the differences between individual human being; they go against the caste discrimination. This attitude is conspicuously maintained by them when they are out of their homes and especially on the pilgrimage. But they are not so rigid in maintaining this norm of the sect they follow while they are inside the family.

The Bauls indulge in songs and dances during the night. Inside each of the *akhras* arrangements are made to accommodate the audience. Sometimes the open field is selected for the performance of Baul songs. In the moonlit night this open-air song recital takes a unique look. The audience are charmed by both the environmental situation as well as the mellifluous songs of the Bauls. The Bauls coming to Ghosepara mostly belong to eastern districts of West Bengal and most of them have got their origin in the then East Bengal. In their songs the life and living pattern on both sides of the river Padma, the love and fierceness of this turbulent river as well as the philosophy of the East Bengal villages are found to form the central core. In Ghosepara fair "Sri Chaitannya Mahaprabhu Baul Sangha" conducts a very large type of *akhra*. It is organized by its present Supervisor-Baul, Narottam Das. Originally, he belonged to the then East Bengal. His father was an inhabitant of a village in the District of Jessore. But when Narottam Das was three years old he was brought by his parents from there to Kalyani where he settled permanently. Narottam Das's father and grand-father were Bauls. He is purely a domestic Baul and earns his living through *Mahdukari*. He maintains this large type of *akhra* only with the help of others. He is proud of his disciples and devotees who come forward every year to extend their help and co-operation in organizing this *akhra* at Ghosepara. There is a very good accommodation for the Bauls who come from faraway places. He also provides some Bauls with food. In this *akhra* a very good arrangement is made for the presentation of Baul songs throughout the night. The audience find here a very suitable atmosphere for the enjoyment of Baul songs. Some eminent Bauls from the western part of West Bengal, especially from Birbhum and Bankura visit Ghosepara during the ceremony in question. Purna Das of Birbhum has a separate *akhra* of his own at Ghosepara fair.

The Baul *akhra* belonging to Sri Chaitannya Mahaprabhu Baul *akhra* becomes the main centre of attraction of the audience and the devotees. In the morning of *Doljatra* day a brief ceremony is held here in front of the portrait of Sri Chaitannya. Devotional songs are sung by many singing groups and then the playing with *abir* starts. First of all, the *mohanta* of the *akhra* offers *abir* and sweets to Sri Chaitannya which follows the distribution of *prasad* and smearing of *abir* on the foreheads of the eminent personalities. All types of singers including the Bauls conduct devotional songs all through the time. All the pilgrims and other visitors to this fair engage themselves in the playing with *abir*. The characteristic feature of the *Holi* festival of Ghosepara is that no liquid colour is used. Only *abir* is allowed here. In this revelry with *abir* ceremony a close bond is established between the Bauls and the pilgrims as also the ordinary visitors.

Different movements and behaviour-patterns of the people belonging to various categories in the Ghosepara fair is centralised on the particular theme as established by Aul Chand - the celebrated founder of the *Kartabhaja* philosophy. It expresses that God is the Creator of the Universe and *Guru* or *Karta* is the direct representative of God. The people belonging to the community have deep faith in the supernatural power of the *Karta.* The *Karta* may have got disciples from both the Hindu and the Muslim communities. The disciples belonging to different castes and communities does not make any distinction amongst them. Owing to this sort of philosophy and understanding the Ghosepara Baul *mela* becomes a unique centre for reciprocal friendship amongst different classes and grades of people.

The Baul Gathering at Agradwip

The ceremony of Ghosepara is followed by another fair at Agradwip in the district of Burdwan popularly known as Ghose Thakurer *mela.* In the Ganges there is a small island like landmass where the fair is held on the last *Ekadasi* day in the month of Falgun (February-March). The real name of Ghose Thakur was Govinda Ghose. Once the son of Govinda Ghose went to offer food to their family deity Sri Gopinath and at that particular time he died. Govinda Ghose became very much shocked at that incidence. But in due course he received the blessings of Gopinath who ordered through dream that after the death of Govinda Ghose his soul would be offered food and drink through ceremonial rite. According to this arrangement the annual funeral rite is held on the day of his death. On this occasion a *mahotsab* is held lasting three days. On the first day *Chinra-machchab* is performed, *i.e.,* flattened rice, curd and fruits are given to the attending persons. *Anna-machchab* is held on the second day of the festival when the attending devotees are supplied with boiled rice, pulses, and vegetables. This function is associated with a large type of fair. Nearly two hundred *akhras* are functioning here. In these *akhras* a large number of Bauls, Fakirs and other religious mendicants take shelter. Most of the *akhras* become living centres for presentation of Baul songs. All types of audience enjoy these songs that are sung by the Bauls spontaneously. The Bauls occupy a dominant position here. The worship of Gopinath is based on love philosophy of the Vaishnavas. The continuous festival for three days persons together and make this place a centre for friendship and mutual understanding.

This fair was originally administrated by the Mallick family, ex-zamíndar of the island. The island is mainly populated by the Yadav families, the principal economy of whom is milk trading. They contribute a lumpsum amount for the organization of the *annachchatra* in the *akhras*. At present this fair is organized by the local committee in collaboration with the Block Development Office.

The Baul Gathering at Mahesh

A somewhat full-fledged assemblage of the Bauls is held at Mahesh during the well-known *Rathajatra* festival. Mahesh is very old village in the district of Hooghly. The river Bhagirathi flows by this village. The village is glorified by having the traditional temple of Jagannatha. Long long ago one Dhrubananda Vaishnav established a small temple of Jagannath and began to propitiate regularly. It is said that Dhrubananda once went to Srikshetra for paying visit to Lord Jagannath. He got an instruction through dream that on returning to Mahesh he would be blessed with the visit of Lord Jagannatha Himself. According to that dream he came back to Mahesh and got that idol of Jagannatha Deva on the bank of Bhagirathi. A temple was constructed immediately at Mahesh and arrangement for daily worship was made accordingly. Dhrubananda breathed his last in 1553 A.D. and after which his disciples sincerely continued the work of propitiation through generations. Then the responsibility was transferred to Kamalakar Pipplai, the close associate of Sri Gourangadeva. From that period the organization of worship of Jagannatha Deva has been conducted by the members of the family of Sri Pippalai through the ages. In course of time the fame of Jagannatha Temple at Mahesh became wide spread and ultimately it could gain popularity with all sections of pilgrims. The *Rathajatra* of Mahesh gradually became famous and got recognition and popularity like that of Puri. The then zamindars of the region contributed tremendously for the development and organizational activities of the Jagannatha Temple of Mahesh.

A large-sized iron Chariot of Jagannatha Deva is brought out at Mahesh during *Rathajatra* festival. This particular Chariot was prepared in 1292. A.D. and it was donated by one Krishna Chandra Basu. Earlier, the Chariot made of wood. The Chariot is drawn through the G.T. Road running through Mahesh when a large number of devotees assemble for a devoted *darshan* of Lord Jagannatha Deva on the Chariot. The temple premises become overcrowded. On both the sides of the G.T. Road a number of stalls is set up selling various merchandise to the visitors to the *Rathajatra* festival. This festival is the biggest of its kind in West Bengal and ranks next to the *Rathajatra* festival at Puri. The *Rathajatra* fair offers an opportunity of get-together for many people. A large number of Bauls and Vaishnava mendicants attend the *Rathajatra* festival. The Bauls take their shelter in the temple premises. There are a few closed and open verandahs inside the temple premises, where they arrange for their shelter. The Bauls sing throughout the night. A large number of audience come to the temple premises to have a look at the Bauls and to listen to their songs. The Bauls do not go out with the *Ratha* and they do not engage themselves for pulling the rope of the Chariot which is considered a holy act. The Bauls sing the glory of the pious act of pulling the rope and also to get a *darshan* of the deity on the Chariot. But they do not like to interfere into it. The Bauls visit the temple regularly during the *Rathajatra* festival, sing and dance throwing light on the past story of development of the temple, pay homage to the Lord Jagannatha and then go away. There is no arrangement for any *annachchatra* here. Nobody looks after the Bauls. They come spontaneously, stay there with full delight cook their own food here and go away after the festive occasion is over. Still the pilgrims and the common visitors to the temple, come in direct influence with the Bauls, who stay in the temple premises and sing varieties of songs all through the time.

5

Bauls in Relation to 'Sufis'

The 'Sufi' view of life rejects all the religious dogmas and the rigid formalities of religious practices. According to their belief, religious formalities are the obstacles in the closest union between man and God. God is regarded as the Absolute and the universe represents the manifested attributes of God. The Absolute can be realised only through love, and "in order to love and know God, Sufi must lose himself in the love and knowledge of God" (Nicholson, 1976 : 13). The task of annihilation of infinite distance between God and man can be perfectly done by God.

Sufism has its own characteristic features. "Sufism is the spirituality or the mysticism of the religion of Islam" (Stoddart, 1976 : 19). It is regarded as the central point constituting the Revelation of Islam. Some assert it as the most powerful current of the particular total wave which constitutes the Revelation of islam. (Lings, 1975 : 15). The word 'sufi' has been derived from the Arabian word 'Safa' which means sacredness. Those, who are free from worldly self-centred activities and are pure in body and mind, are regarded as the 'Sufi'. According to another theory, the word 'Sufi' has been derived from the base word 'Saf' which means Class. Those people, who have been able to secure the highest class before God by virtue of their devotion to the God, proceed in the line of spiritualism and religious activities, are regarded as 'Saf'. But there are a few scholars who believe that the word 'Sufi' has its origin from the word 'Sub', which means wool. According to them, the Sufi saints and followers used to wear coarse woollen clothes and it ultimately became their fashion. At that time those people who gave up organised family life, and became ascetics very commonly wore wollen garments. Thus these mendicants wearing woollen garments became popularly known by the term 'Sufi'. The sufistic idea is based on the idea of love and "he that is purified by love is pure (Safi) and he who is purified by the Beloved is a *Sufi*" (Schimmel, 1975 : 16). The particular person is completely absorbed in the Divine Beloved and he always thinks in terms of Him and thereby he attains the proper rank of a Sufi. Sufis believe that the human being is the manifestation of the Absolute and the love is regarded as the main motive force to realise the Absolute. The Absolute is the Supreme Bliss and it is also regarded as the Personal God. It is intense love which can bring God nearer to the human being. It is firmly believed that the God is the only Truth in the Universe. He is not only the Truth, but He also represents infinite love. It is the ultimate aim of man to get the love of God. The Sufis are eager for the complete union with God (*tawhid)*. The soul is being separated from its Maker and becomes lost in the utter bewilderment of the world which must take all possible steps to reunite with Him. It is the principal aim of the life of the Sufis and they have been conducting this particular practice with all seriousness. The Sufis are always on a journey to God. This journey is marked by the awakening of the particular concept that the phenomenon world is working as the veil which covers the Divine. The Sufis must begin the quest through the removal of the veil in question. In so doing they should understand that the veil and the Divine are one and the same thing. When a veil is seen a reflection of the Divine is characteristically marked. There are two principal aims of Sufism. One is the total annihilation of the individual existence which is known as *Fana*, and the other is the existence in the attributes of the God, called by the term *Baka*. Sufism ushered in India in the concrete form during the eleventh Century A.D.. In this first stage of Sufi infiltration some eminent apostles, *viz.*, Rumi, Sayed Nather Shah and Makhdum Sayed Ali Uluvvi'al Huzurri exerted tremendous influence. But Sufism began to spread amogst the people of India in the latter half of the Twelfth Century A.D.. During this time Sufism could enter into the very recess of the hearts of the people. The Chisti and the Suhrawardi orders of the Sufism found sufficient ground in this country at that time. It was evidenced by the coming and setting down of the eminent apostle Khwajah Mu'inud-din Chisti in Delhi in 1193. He was regarded as the founder of the Chisti order in India. The other order, *i.e.*, Suhrawardi was founded by Shyak Baha' Ud-din Dhakriya Multani.

These two Orders of the Sufi could attract a large number of persons in India under their fold. During the latter part of the 15th Century A.D. another Sufistic Order, the Naqshabandi Order was founded in India by Khwajah Muhammad Bakri Billah.

Sufism found a receptive ground in India just after its entrance owing to the Pantheistic mysticism of the Upanishads, the mysticism rooted in love and devotion in the Vaishnavite way of thinking and the Sahajiya background of the Buddhism. Starting from the 12th Century onward the social history of India had been highly characterized by the multifarious interactional patterns in the fields of politics and religion. In that international perspective a trend of compromise was very much effective. Sufism did a great deal in establishing the compromising trend amongst the people of India facing diverse conflicts from various angles. As a natural consequence Sufism in India found a very favourable condition in its spread through the length and breadth of the country.

The Sufis who came to India followed a particular life-style which was against the traditional, orthodox thinking. In India the Sufis belonging to the Chisti Order became dominant. A few of them became the *Gurus* or preceptors of the contemporary *Badshahs* and *Amirs*. There are still so many *Samadhis* of these Sufi preceptors which draw a large number of devotees all through the time. But innumerable number of the *samadhis* of the unknown Sufi saints are to be seen throughout the different parts of India. Most of these have been lying neglected. Some of these have been dilapidated and are gradually being engulfed by the overgrown jungles and bushes. It is to be noted that in India the *Samadhis* of the Sufi saints are comparatively large in number than in other parts of the world. It has been so because of the fact that in India the Sufis did not receive any resistance and they were free from oppression. The endurance of the public of India and the philosophy of co-operation gave the Sufis protected shelters here. Whereas in Muslim countries the Sufis did not receive such treatement, rather they had to face tortures.

In Bengal there are a large number of Sufi centres in the different urban and rural areas. These have been developed round the *Samadhis* of the eminent Sufi saints. People of all castes and communities regularly pay visit to these centres and offer their homage. In some cases annual fairs are held on the occasion of the death anniversaries or other important events of life of these saints. These fairs are characterized not only by the active participation of the people belonging to all the communities but also, there develops a particular atmosphere of religious integration where the people belonging to diverse socio-religious perspectives find a spontaneous feeling of oneness.

The close study amongst the Sufis and the Bauls signifies the fact that there are remarkable resemblances between these two groups of mendicants. The mendicants coming from Islam community and following the Sufistic ideas are termed as fakirs. These fakirs possess some distinguished features which come in parallel to those of the Bauls. In spite of their close resemblance in the thinking and general behaviour patterns some scholars do not like to draw any parallel between the two. Bhattacharya (1388 B.S. : 483) believes that the similarity in the Baul and Sufi ideas in only extrinsic, but there is no resemblance between the inner philosophy and method of *sadhana.* He goes to the extent of saying that only in three spheres the Sufis are closely related to the Bauls. These are summarized in the following way : -

(1) The presence of *Paramatma* or *Allah* in the body of man and man is the reflection of the Absolute ;

(2) The *Sadhana* in both the cases is based on self-realization. The Sufis want to achieve the condition of *Fana or* passing away of consciousness in mystic union with God. The Bauls want to make realization of the *Maner Manus* by the Acquisition of the ecstatic state through the conjugal union of the *Prakriti* and *Purusha ;* and

(3) Total avoidance of the rites and rituals.

It has been seen through the continuous observations on the general behaviour patterns as well as the process of *sadhana* that the Sufis come very close to the Bauls. Sometimes it is so closely linked that it seems the Bauls have got their origin from the Sufistic mentality or at least the Bauls have been moulded heavily by the Sufi way of life in course of their developemnt through the ages. Some scholars put forward the idea that the Bauls are the final products of assimilation of the Sahajiya and the Sufistic ideas. It is ascertained that "the Sufistic ideas, that were thus introduced, were soon assimilated with the preavalent Sahajiya ideas and the result of this amalgam has been the Bauls of Bengal". (Dasgupta; 1940:1941).

On a point by point analysis of the different characteristic features followed and maintained by the Bauls and the Sufis, it is seen that there is a very close resemblance between the thinking patterns of these two spheres. Firstly, the Sufis are engaged in joint singing and dancing. They present songs and dances based on the theme of their deep-rooted *sadhana*. It is known as *Sama*. Through these songs and dances the Sufi Fakirs try to attain *Fana*. The Bauls are always in the lively mood of presenting songs and dances. These are the media for their propitiation of the Man of the Heart. They sing songs of diverse nature for self-expression. After the appearance of Sri Chaitannyadeva the then Bengal became suffered with the atmosphere of music activities represented by the *kirtans* related to the Vaishnava Padavali. Owing to this a special idea had developed in the minds of the public that music took active part in the proper explanation of any idea related to religion.

Secondly, the Sufi philosophy bears deep influence of *Guruvada*. They need the direct help and support of the *Guru*, who is known as *Murshid, Pir* or *Sheikh*. The disciple is known as *Murid*. Before taking initiation the disciple is to go through a period of apprenticeship, the time period of which is generally three years. During this period the suitability of the disciple concerned is verified through his various activities. In the first year, of the apprenticeship the disciple is to devote himself in the service of the people. During this time he should think that all are superior to him, all are his masters and he is their servant. In the second year, he will be engaged in the service of God. He must adore the God after winding over all sorts of personal interests as well as worries and anxieties. The third year will have to be devoted for the service of the self. He must take all possible steps to improve the mental situation. It is the time for warding off all sorts of worldly thinking and to direct all attention to the God. After the successful completion of the three-year apprenticeship, the *Murshid* or *Guru* initiates the person concerned to accept the life of Sufi. He is offered a dress with multi-coloured patches, which is known as *Khirpa* by the *Murshid*. In the line of *Guruvada* the Bauls strike parallel to the Sufis. In the Baul *Sadhna* the *Guru* is held in highest esteem. No *sadhana* of the Bauls can be performed without the direct help of *Guru*. The person seeking entry into the Baul way of life, must prove himself worthy of the initiation. The *Guru* observes the activities in the spiritual spheres as well as in the general behaviour patterns of the disciple from close quarters. If the *Guru* is satisfied on the apprentice-disciple, he allows him to be initiated. During this period apprentice-disciple has to show some concrete evidences of his trend of dedication in the overall Baul philosophy based on the principle of love and respect to all. The journey of the Bauls is aimed at realising the Truth which transcends all sorts of wisdom, intellectual persuasion and speculative discourse. Therefore, the direct guidance and concrete instruction of the *Guru* is essential to lead an individual Baul into the realm of Truth. The *Guru* is the person who can show the light to illuminate the darkness of ignorance. The Baul philosophy is centralised on the idea that a man must take all possible measures in his life to win over the dark phases of ignorance through the infliction of the light of knowledge. This light of knowledge can properly be obtained if he gets the kindness of *Guru.* Thus both the Sufis and the Bauls are directly dependent on their respective *Guru*, and in this Guru-based philosophy both the mendicant groups are influenced by the same basic principles.

Thirdly, the Sufis and the Bauls are especially noted for the heterodoxy. Both the mendicant groups equally go against the prevalent customs and traditions of the society. They do not accept the institutionalized attitudes maintained by various religious communities. They disagree with the artificial barriers of human communities--they discourage the attempt of classification based on caste and creed. The philosophies of the Sufis as well as the Bauls teach the truth that man is the highest order in this Universe. The ultimate amelioration of the creation is the man and this man gets his full and successful form when he becomes full-man. The God himself takes his seat in the full-man. Therefore, in order to understand this man all sorts of barriers as sponsored and maintained through customs, rites and rituals must be overthrown.

Fourthly, the Bauls do not stop after placing man in the highest esteem in the creation. In man he tries to find the principles of his life-long *sadhana.* What he finds in the Universe in which he lives and works, he traces the ultimate reflection of these in the body of man. The human body is regarded as the micrcosm of the Universe. The body of man is thought to be the little Universe - a natural phenomenon. The Ultimate Reality resides within the body of man and to understand it, one is to explore the underlying mysteries of the body of man. The Bauls have been continuously searching out this Ultimate Reality who remains in the body in the form of man or *manus.* The Bauls popularly sing that which are found in the Universe are seen to be packed up with in the little Universe, *i.e.*, the body of man. The Sufis also run parallel to these thinkings in their *sadhana*. They consider human body as the sacred shelter for the Beloved. It is futile to go on a pilgrimage that are found to flourished in the different parts of the world, neglecting the depth of treasures in the human body. The Sufis believe that a really devoted person will get everything from his love for humanity because of the fact that the body of man is the sacred seat for all senses, consciousness and truth.

Fifthly, in the idea of the Man of the Heart, the Bauls come very close to the Sufis, The Bauls believe all through the time that the Ultimate Reality resides in the inner recess of the heart of man in the form of *manus*. The ultimate Reality is not to be regarded as an abstraction. Also it is not the mystic expression of the metaphysical Being or a philosophical conception of Divine Entity. It is nothing but a concrete reality. This concrete reality, or 'Man', or the Divine Self inhabits in each human body. So, this Man is closest to every person. This Divine Self is not conceived of even if there is His close connection by anybody without proper initiation. The imperfect knowledge and uninitiated mind keeps him far off. The Sufis contribute to this idea. The famous Sufi Saint Siraj Sain opines, "The 'Man' lives in this man. A good many of saints and mendicants search Him through the ages. The moon is seen reflected in the calm water of the tanks and rivers, but it is not possible to catch it. So is He, Who resides in the body of man". In the Baul and Sufi philosophies this Man is addressed by various names besides *maner manus*. He is called as *adhar manus* (Man uncatchable), *ajana manus* (Man unknown), *sahaja manus* (Man absolute), *sonar manus* (Man of gold), *bhaber manus* (Man of devotion), *atal manus* (Man unflinching), *raser manus* (Man beloved), *achin manus* (Man unknown), and so on. There are some other terms depicting this Man of the Heart which are populariy known as *Gosain, Murshid, Navi* or *Rasul*. At times the Absolute Reality is described as Nur or the divine light. These diverse nomenclatures are centralized at one point, *i.e.*, the human being feels the existence of unknown bird or *Achin pakhi* which flits in and out of the cage cosntituted by the body itself. The Sufis and the Bauls have got identical ideas on the Man of the Heart, and for whose search and propitiation they have been moving about from time immemorial. In this particular conception of the Man of the Heart a systematic and time-long mixing of different ideas is propounded by many scholars. Some go to the extent of saying that in this motion of thinking there is "a happy mixture of the conception of the *Paramatman* of the Upanishad, the Sahaja of Sahajiyas and the Sufistic conception of the Beloved" (Dasgupta ; 1940 : 207).

Sixthly, in the Sufi and the Baul thinking there is much stress laid on, love for humanity. There are a great many philosophical features and actions which influence the overall perspectives of these two religious thoughts. But it is the love philosophy which has made these two spheres distinctive in the world perspective. The Sufi's message is : "love all by forgetting the self-consciousness. While doing good to others, the individuality of the man concerned should be forgotten" (Ikbal, Muhammad S.; 1943 : 105). The Baul also spends much of his time in the search of Man through the infliction of love and respect to the community of man. He has learnt the ideal love between Radha and Krishna and fully utilises the teachings of this divine love in his propitiation of man. Love is the central theme of his songs, dance patterns and talk with the people.

From the above discussions it will be readily clear that the Sufis and the Bauls run in parallel ways in respect of their journey to follow the road leading to *sadhana*. Coming from the two different religious faiths these two groups of mendicants very naturally possess some basic differences in the mode of *sadhana* but in most of their behaviour - patterns they have been fused with each other. In songs and dances the Sufis resemble the Bauls. Both the groups sing songs based on each other's religion and philosophy. The Sufi-influenced mendicants unhesitatingly sing the devotional songs based on the love philosophy of Radha-Krishna. They do not hesitate in singing the songs that have been composed on the theme of the love feelings of Chaitannyadeva. On the other hand, the Bauls characteristically sing the *murshid* songs in which "we find a mixture of the Indian spirit with the spirit of Sufism". (Dasgupta; 1940 : 194). The *Guruvad* is highly effective in the songs of both these groups of mendicants. During the presentation of songs and dances they equally depend on the *Gurus* and before starting the song recital all the singers express formal respect to their respective *Gurus* and sing the rhymes in the praise of the *Guru*. They ask for the solution of different problems and want to get themseleves acquainted with the reasons of diverse irregularities found in the surroundings. These two groups of mendicants are equally heterodox, they keep themselves aloof from any formalities or religion. They are against the different institutions of society created by man. They present peculiarities in dress, in general make-up and in the mode of talking to the people. They are accessible to the people belonging to all castes, classes and religions. Both of the groups believe in the theory of getting the grace of God through the unveiling of the truth. The eternal truth is the sacred seat of God. When a man is free from all sorts of worldly anxieties and can ward off his self-interest, he is eligible to proceed through the path of *sadhana*. If this *sadhana* is pursued in a right way, one can feel the heavenly pleasure for feeling the existence of the Man of the Heart in the body of man as both the mendicant groups believe that human body is the seat of everything and a *sadhak* is expected to get all he desires from the body of man. But the approach to the Man of the Heart should be made through the love for humanity after breaking through all the customary barriers that have been imposed by the society of man. As they have originated from two groups of differnt religious faiths, so they may possess a few and significant dissimilarities in the mode of *sadhana* but on deeper enquiry it is observed that the basic principles of their ways of *sadhana*, the innate philosophy of their behaviour-patterns are centred round the same ideas.

The Fakirs in this country are the carriers of the tradition of the Sufis. They wander about through the villages of Bengal and pay regular visits to the *majars* or holy *burials* of the Sufi Saints or *Pirs*. They have got Islam origin but have firmly embraced the Sufistic mentality of keeping themselves aloof from cutomary rites and rituals. They consider man as the Supreme Being and his propitiation is in essence the worship of the God. These Fakirs sing songs in the praise of man and they ask these men to get the lesson of love which tops all attempts to receive the grace of God. Like Baul fairs, there are few fairs of the Fakirs which are held in honour of the eminent Saints, *Pirs*, or *Gurus* of the Fakir community. These fairs are equally attended by the Bauls and they participate actively in the different stages. People belonging to all the religious spheres. *viz;*, the Islam and the Hindus, not only attend the fairs of the Fakirs, but also they pay their homage for asking the grace of the Sufi Saints. In the following pages the analytical descriptions of a few Fakir fairs are given to understand the basic nature of these assemblages.

A small village named Patharchapuri by the side of the Suri - Rajnagar Road in the district of Birbhum secures international fame for a few days in the month of Chaitra (March - April) owing to holding of a fair in memory of a Sufi Saint, Data Saheb. The village Patharchapuri is a thinly populated village in which Muslim Community and a few lower caste groups of the Hindu community inhabit. The village is belived to be blessed with the glorious birth of an esteemed Sufi Saint, Data Saheb, previously known as Mehbub Shah. He did not belong to this particular region - he came here from western India. In course of his wanderings for the proper performance of his *sadhana* Mehbub Shah reached the vicinity of the village in question. There he was attracted by the shady village caused by the growth of numerous trees. He selected one of the trees there and under the shade of which he started his meditation. In due course he reached the goal and then he came very near to the people. He had profound love for the people amongst whom he performed his *sadhana.* As a Sufi Saint, Mehbub Shah was free from all sorts of wordly desires and he could win over the self-interests in the strict sense of the term. When his fame as a *siddha purusha* s pread throughout the country, people belonging to all spheres began to spproach him with various material offerings of high monetary value. Mehbub Shah loved all those people who came to him but he did not put any attention towards the material offering made to him. He immediately distributed all those materials to the poor and needy persons. He was a self-abnegating saint and due to his frequent gift-givings to the people he was popularly known as Data Saheb, *i.e.*, a personality with munificent nature.

A few are of the opinion that Data Saheb was a Brahmin. He left his home when he was young and incidentally came in touch with a Sufi family. The husband and wife constituting the particular family was issueless and they regardily accepted him through parental affection. In course of time that Brahmin young man became highly influenced by Sufistic mentality and he accepted the Sufi way of life. As he came from the Hindu community and later he embraced the Sufi-influenced sphere of life, Data Saheb had been similarly approached by the people belonging to both the Muslim and Hindu communities. Still to-day the *majar* of Data Saheb in Patharchapuri village is visited by all people without any distinction of castes, classs and religious groups. In the region under study there are so many stories depicting the spiritual power and supernatural activities of Data Saheb. He is well-known to each and every body of this locality. His existence is to be conspicuously found in the folklore and traditions of the region. Data Saheb is still a legendory insure in the hearts of the people. But the information on Data Saheb and his activities are not varified by historical records. It is very strange that the events which have taken place in the historical periods cannot be evaluated in the absence place in the historical periods cannot be evaluated in the absence of historical data. But the behaviour-patterns of the people and rich store of folklore materials centering round Data Saheb reveal the fact that Data Saheb's personality reached the corners of all the houses over the vast region of the country.

Data Saheb departed from this mortal world in the Bengali year 1298 and the date was the 10th of Chaitra (March-April). In this particular day people not only from this region but also from all parts of India, especially people belonging to the Islam community are hurried to this tiny village to pay their homage to the Sufi Saint. The villalge suddenly becomes thickly populated by influx of people and it took an illuminating look owing to the large fair that is held in connection with the observance of the *Urs* of Data Saheb. A considerable number of pilgrims from bangladesh and other adjacent Muslim countries visit the *majar* of Dat Saheb during this and due to which the most ordinary village like Patharchapuri receives an international importance. Patharchapuri becomes a sea of people and as the people belong to the diverse religious beliefs and multifarious spheres of activities it is highly characterized by the distinct picture of great union of *Mahamilan* in this *Sadhanbhumi* or the land of great meditation.

The sacred centre of Data Saheb is situated at one corner of the village. The *majar* is seen at the central part of it and by the side of this the living room of Data Saheb is seen. On the Western side of the *majar* there is a mosque and the spacious chowk is seen on the eastern side of it. The fair is held inside the village and on both sides of the road. A large number of shops of different nature is seen on the chowk as well as in the attached mango garden. Special buses regularly ply from different Railway stations, like Bolpur, Sainthia, Suri and Dubrajpur for carrying the huge number of pilgrims. In addition to this numerous buses from distant palces both inside and outside the district maintain close and direct connection with the village. Hundreds of reserved buses are parked at the entrance of the village which changes the total atmosphere of this insgnificant village. The fair starts just at the entrance of the village and multifarious commodities of daily consumption are brought for sale amongst the rural people. From the bus stand to the entrance of the village proper a number of disabled beggars take temporary shelters on both sides of the road. They perform various means and sometimes make bodily tortures to attract the kindness of the pilgrims. The pilgrims after reaching the fair site take shelters in the temporary tents prepared by the *mela* committee in the private houses or in open verandah, in the shade of the trees and falling which they do not hesitate to stay under the open sky. The fair is highly characterized by the coming of huge number of Fakirs and Vaishnava Bauls. The Fakirs take shelter in the vicinity of the *major*. They stay in groups or individually. The Vaishnava Bauls also are seen to stay here along with the Fakirs. The large number of pilgrims pay homage to the *majar* of the renowned Sufi Saint. There is a custom of offering *chadar* with musical procession illuminated by coloured lights. The *chadar* is held stretched by a number of devotees over their heads and it is then placed on the majar of Data Saheb. The *chadars* are of different colours and some of which are ornamented with minute work of *jari* (thread of silver). The building accommodating the *majar* bears an inscription in Bengali which reads as "Dargah Sarif, Hazrat Data Mehbub Shah Oli Ret". It means the place of pilgrimage, Hazrat Data Mehbub Shah a great personality blessed with the God's grace. Besides the offering of *chadar* the pilgrims offer *sinni* and flowers with sweets or dedicate castrated goats or fowl to the Sufi Saint. The inner room of the *majar* is always characterized by the fragrance of the smoke emitted from the incense burner and the total atmosphere takes a gracious outlook. At one corner of the main building stands Data Saheb's personal room. The used wooden sandles, the large tongs and a wooden snake are kept on a wooden platform to exhibit these amongst the pilgrims. The pilgrims consider this a pious act to have a sacred look at these personal belongings of the great saint. The Khadim places these materials on the heads of a pilgrims on request and the token money is being collected in a collection box. It is not a compulsion. The snake made of wood has a history, rather a folk belief of its own. Once a python in the neighbouring forest chased Data Saheb, who asked the snake not to proceed further. But the snake did not pay any heed to it and the result was that the snake became transformed into wood through the curse of Data Saheb. There is a centre for offering sacred ashes and amulets to the who desire it pilgrims. The ashes are collected from the sacred fire burnt before the *majar* and the amulets are prepared from the small pices of the *chadars* that are offered on the *majar*. The pilgrims from the different communities collect these ashes and amulets for their welfare. There is a belief that taking of a small quantity of ashes of Data Baba cures all sorts of abdominal diseases. The amulets have got a protective effect against all types of misfortunes.

In the *majar* of data Saheb a *mahotsab* is held in which all the attending Fakirs and Bauls are provided with charitable supply of food. A huge number of goats and fowls are dedicated every day. Out of these four castrated goats and twenty-five fowls are kept apart for the *mahotsab*. The *prasad* is prepared by mixing rice, pulses, potato and the flesh of goats and fowls together. It is served to all the attending persons belonging to the Fakir community and other devotees. The Bauls are provided with uncooked rice, pulses and vegetables. Most of these Bauls take shelter in a nearby *Ashram* known as Basir Baba's *Ashram*. As the Bauls, attending the Patharchapuri *mela*, mostly belong to the Vaishnavite section, they do not entertain the non-vegetarian meals.

The *mela* committee is constituted by some eminent personalities, who belong to Suri. The Muslim gentlemen generally take the different offices and there are a few Government officials in the committee. Former Data Saheb. They still organise the whole *majar* throughout the year excepting the *Urs* festival. It has been taken over by the elected *mela* Committee and sponsored by the Government of West Bengal from the hands of the Khadims following a clash amongst themselves and a tremendous mismanagement. Thousands of *chadars* are offered to the *majar* on the festival days and thousands of castrated goats and fowls are offered. These animals are collected and sold to the interested parties through auctions. Through this system a huge amount of money is collected and in the year 1983 more or less Rs. 1,06,000 - 00 were received by the Committee besides the amount got from the collection box. The money is kept in the Bank and a sufficient amount is spent for the organization and supervision of the fair.

The pilgrims coming from outside take shelter in the guest-house of the *majar* on payment of nominal contribution. A large number of pilgrims, from the neighbouring regions, are poor and they take shelter in the open places. A number of family-units grow here and there. They are to prepare their own food after erecting temporary hearths. Owing to this practice the *mela* premises become dirty with the extracted liquefied starch from boiled rice and remain of other food materials thrown out here and there. But the strange thing is that no fly or like insect is seen here for the three days. The people believe that flies, mosquitos and ants go out of this village during the period of festivities owing to Data Saheb's pious activities and his profound love for the devotees. Many people still belive that the heaps of dirts and refuges that accumulate during these periods are blown away by the heavy storm that regularly occurs after the completion of the ceremony. During recent period the *mala* committee arranges for temporary electric supply to illuminate the *majar* and the *mela* premises. The *majar* building is highly illuminated with colourful lights. Arrangements for clearance of the roads and the premises of the *majar* are made by the mela committee. A large number of volunteers belonging to both Hindu and Muslim communities work day and night to serve the people. The members of the mela committee keep vigilance watch with the help of the police to maintain peace and order of the fair. But the insufficient water supply causes acute problems to the people. In this driest part of the region and during the dry season many devotees feel helpless due to want of drinking water.

The Bauls attend this fair in large number. They sing songs throughout the night. The speciality of this fair is that the Vaishnavaite Bauls and Muslim Fakirs sing songs in a common sitting. In these singing performances various songs are sung, the themes of which are centred round both the Hindu and Islam religious ideas. In the *ashram* of Basir Baba a *kirtan* song highlighting the Vaishnava love and affection was being sung in which there were a few Fakirs besides a large number of Vaishnava Bauls and other Hindu devotees. It is surprising that the performance was being held spontaneously. Inside the premises of the *majar* a platform is raised for the song-recital in which the Bauls and the Fakirs sing individual and joint songs and thereby pay homage to the Sufi Saint. Throughout the day the Bauls present their songs in the traditional mood at the different places of fair and sometimes they are seen to sing songs under the shade of a solitary tree in the open field.

The Fakirs are the special attraction in this fair. They arrange separate singing performance at their temporary shelters within the *majar* premises. At the main *ashram* in the majar a group of Fakirs coming from distant places of India take shelter and there they arranged for various discussions and presentation of songs. They are the followers of Chistiji and Abu Hasan. It had been seen during investigation that with the Fakirs a few Vaishnavite mendicants also were engaged in religious discussion. During dancing and singing of the Fakirs all the people, irrespective of castes and communities were enjoying fully. The Fakirs principally sing a particular kind of song which are akin to the *Dehatatwa* songs of the Bauls. The themes of these songs are based on similar principle and the lines of approach are the same but the mode of presentation and tuning are different. The Fakirs sing songs to the accompaniment with some characteristic musical instruments, like *Dotara, Dubki, Khamak, Dugi* and large tongs. Sometimes a *tintara* type of instrument is also used. The Fakirs in their songs, sung within the premises of the *majar*, pay homage to Datababa and in some songs his multifarious qualities and spiritual activities are broadly depicted. His live for common people are people's all-round regard to him, most of the time, form the subject-matters of songs. In these songs the Bauls also participate and this participation is sometimes direct and at other times indirect.

Unlike Bauls the Fakirs wear black coloured garments of loose type known as *alkhalla*. Sometimes this loose and long gown is made of small pieces of multicoloured clothes. A few Fakirs wear white *Pyjama* and coloured coat. Their heads are always covered by caps of different colours but most of the time these are decorated with silver threads (*jari*). They invariably wear bead necklaces round their necks. These beads are of different colours. Sometimes they use the necklace made of *rudraksha*. A few female mendicants of Fakir group are also seen in the fair. They wear black or white coloured *sari*. Sometimes *alkhalla* type of dress is also seen. Different types of bead necklaces are found to be hung around their necks. They are very much fond of wearing coloured glass bangles.

During the fair of Patharchapuri the Fakirs are seen to stay in different groupwise temporary settlements. These groups are generally formed by the disciple Fakirs of the same Precepts ; or Fakirs coming from particular palce form a group. It is seen that even in the driest and hottest period of the season the Fakirs sit before the fire of *dhuni*. *Dhuni* is also seen to be kindled at the *ashram* premises of Basirbaba, - an *ashram* situtated at the south-western corner of the *majar*, established by a Saint. There is no close relation between these two centres, yet during *mela* period the *ashram* of Basirbaba makes an arrangement for *mahotsab* for a few days. In this *ashram* most of the Bauls take shelter. They also actively participate here in the preparation of food. Both male and female Bauls and other Vaishnavite mendicants take active part in it. A huge *pandal* is erected with the help of bamboos and tarpaulin in front of the *ashram*, where the Bauls and the Fakirs songs are sung side by side. it becomes the ideal centre for the joint enterprise of these two groups of mendicants with different religious backgrounds. A close co-ordination is always seen and both the groups try to throw discernible light on the oneness of the lines of meditations by the Bauls and the Fakirs.

The general public attending the fair mostly belong to the Muslim community. The shop-holders especially the sweetmeat and the stationery shops belong to the Hindu community. A considerable section of the people attending the fair are the Hindus and they represent different low caste groups. The people belonging to these communities come to this fair with a common intention to pay homage to the Sufi Saint. It is true that the Hindus do not offer *chadar* to the *majar* like the Muslims but they offer *sinni* and other materials in honour of the great saint. During the night people belonging to both the communities sit side by side to enjoy the various songs presented by the Fakirs and the Bauls. Most of the time they sing jointly. Thus amongst both the singers as well as the listeners of Fakiri and Baul songs the artificial distinction of religion and faith disappears owing to the freeness of mind caused by the teachings and modes of behaviour of the great Saint in whose sacred memory the fair is being held.

On the concluding day of the ceremony it is customary that the organisers of the festival, both the khadims and the personnel of the present *mela* committee, make personal visit to the temporary shelters of the Fakirs and the Bauls. In this formal visit deepest thanks are given to all of them for making this religious fair pulsate with lively activities through their songs and dances. At the concluding phase of the ceremony the presentation of a *chadar* takes place. It is seen that during these days thousands of *chadars* are deposited at the *majar*. These are collected by the organizers and the Bauls and the Fakirs are invited formally to take the presentation of *chadars* for their personal dress during the presentation of songs and dances. A list is prepared for this and the Bauls are seen to top the list and they are called first of all to receive the customary presentation. Then comes the turn of the Fakirs. On the closing phase of the ceremony a great *mahotsab* is held at the *ashram* of Basirbaba and to organise this raw food materials together with dedicated goats and fowls are sent to the said ashram by the *mela* committee.

The *majar* of Alam Shah - a Sufistic Saint of wide fame, is also a centre fo active assimilation of the people having diverse religious beliefs and traditions. The graveyard in question is situated under a big banyan tree just beside the Andal-Sainthia Railway track of the Eastern Railway. It is about 1.5 Km. north of Dubrajpur Railway station. Long ago one Dayaram Shah, a Fakir having sufistic leanings,. reached this spot which was heavily dotted by dense forest. He was then travelling throughout the country for conveying to the people the message relating to the love for humanity. As a proper Sufi, he had given up all sorts of personal thinking. He came here from his holy visit to the Data Saheb's *majar* at Patharchapuri. On his visit to this particular solitary spot, Dayaram Shah became very much overwhelmed and he felt that this place was provided with a sort of divine grace. He could feel it through his spiritual power. He spent the night there and though there were a number of ferocious animals in the forest he did not care that situation. He was the messenger of love and naturally he was not afraid of any cruelty coming from any quarter. During night Dayaram Shah got a divine instruction through dream that the particular spot where he slept was provided with sacred qualities for performing time-long *sadhana* here. Dayaram made up his mind to conduct his *sadhana* here, and in the morning he arranged a spot under a big tree of the jungle to stay and meditate without any interruption. In course of his *sadhana* Dayaram could perform miraculous activities. He was very sympathetic to the ailing humanity and those who began to visit him in the jungle were friendly treated by the saint. Ultimately Dayaram Shah became known to the local people as their well-wisher, as well as path-finder in the problematic situation. Dayaram Shah did not discriminate between the Hindus and the Muslims, between rich and the poor class and between high and low castes. He considered all the people equal. Dayaram was a very able singer of Fakiri songs and people flocked to him to hear his songs. Dayaram used to prescribe folk medicines to the people with different diseases. In due course he could attract a large number of disciples and devotees. When it was well-known to the public the solitary spot in this jungle became the sacred place for all the people. The people belonging to both the religious communities used to come here for getting relief in mental anxieties, in familial troubles, as well as in curing different diseases. The Sufi Saint in question gradually became popular throughout the length and breadth of the country and he was well-known as the prophet with high spiritual power and miraculous deeds. Various activities relating to these spheres are still to be gathered from the rich folkloristic materials in this locality. He had profound love for the people as well as he loved the beasts of the jungle. He did many things for trouble-free life of the beasts living by his side in the jungle. Once a tiger became furious and used to approach the sacred stop even during day-time. At this the devotees and disciples who used to come to pay homage to the Saint became very much frightened. They intimated the matter to the Saint who later met the tiger in the jungle and asked him to spot his ferocious activities because love for all was the basic quality of leading trouble-free life in this world. But the tiger did not agree to it. He said that if he gave up predatory activities, he would die to starvation. The tiger asked the Saint if he could offer his son for his (tiger's) satisfaction of hunger, he would give up his ferocious nature once for all. The Saint did not react to this strange as well as panic-stricken proposal, rather his face was characterized by a serene smile. The Saint readily agreed to the proposal and he immediately offered his son for the satisfaction of the hunger of the tiger. From that moment the tiger became devoid of all sorts of ferocious nature. The places, where the Saint offered his son to the tiger, is still revered by the people and in the local folklore there is a complete picture of mental reflections of the Saint and the tiger in the perspective of offering and receiving the son of the former.

After the death of the Saint his body was buried under the banyan tree where he used to meditate and had serious discussions with his disciples. It is believed by the people of the locality that the soul of the great Saint has been sleeping in peace and a constant watch over the land and the people is being kept by the Saint. From time immemorial this particular religious centre has been arousing deep respect in the mind of the general public because of the multifarious activities of the Fakir various super-human procedures and above all, the greatness of site. It is strongly believed by all sections of people that the banyan tree under the shadow of which lies the mortal remains of the Muslim Saint, can, in no circumstances be cut by anybody excepting the members of the family of the Fakir. It has been seen from spot enquiry that a number of branches of the said tree have been dangerously extended over the Railway track. The Railway authorities have tried to check the extension of the tree over the track by erecting an iron fencing on that side. But the small branches with leaves of the tree have been gradually extending neglecting the barriers and the continuous rubbing with the boggies of the passenger and the goods trains has given it a well-shaped structure. The workers under this section of the Railways are very much conscious about the super-natural affairs connected with this religious centre and they are reluctant to cut down its branches even if they are ordered to do so. Formerly,

Railway authorities used to sanction annual grants to the Fakir family to cut out the branches learned over the Railway track. The present Fakir-in-Charge has reported that owing to the sudden stoppage of the annual grant they have completely stopped cutting down the extended branches. It is regularly observed that when the passenger trains cross this *majar* a section of passengers regularly throw small coins on this sacred spot in memory of the great Saint. Nobody other than the Fakir family, looking after the *majar* can dare picking up these thrown away coins as it is believed that unauthorised persons making a attempt to it would face dire consequences. At present three brothers namely Jalal Shah, Piya Shah and Badal Shah, have been looking into the affairs of the religious unit. They claim that they are the great grandsons of the renowned Saint and they have been residing here for three generations. All of them follow Fakiri way of life and their main occupations are centred round this particular religious unit and affairs connected with it. They have got a large number of disciples, who are inhabitants of the different villages. These disciples regularly pay visit to the sacred *majar* and especially during ceremonial occasions they come here in large number. The Fakirs also visit the families of the disciples for the performance of ritualistic activities, as well as to treat the diseases in occult way. They roam about here and there riding on the horses which they keep in the *majar*. The Fakirs living here are very good singers of Fakiri songs. Their songs indicate the triumph of humanity and selfless love above every thing. Some of the songs are highly influenced by the Radha-Krishna philosophy and the Vaishnava line of thinking. The life and activities of these Fakirs is the symbol of unification of Islam and Hindu religious beliefs and ideas, and they themselves consider that the artificial difference in religious sentiments obstruct the smooth progress of the devotees towards attaining divine favour a number of Fakiri songs have been collected in this perspective which depicts the exact line of thinking of the Muslim Fakirs. When other similar songs composed and sung by the Vaishnava Bauls are kept in parallel position and compared analytically, it is crystal clear that both the procedures, though processed in two different religious faiths, are based on the same line of thinking. The *majar* is occasionally visited by the Bauls and they pay their respect to the great Saint through the singing of songs. They sing here the essence of love and the love philosophy of Radha and Krishna. At times they sing with the fakirs, who also emphasise the importance of love and respect to humanity for getting the grace of God. The attempt of comparison of the minor details of the songs sung by both the groups of singers in very much helpful in drawing the analogy between the two.

Every year on the last Friday of the Bengali month of *Ashar* (June-July) the *majar* of Alam Saheb is swarmed with a huge number of disciples and devotees belonging to the two major religious path communities. This place is far from the main road and there is no distinct path leading to the *majar*. But on the festive day all types of conveyance assemble in the vicinity of the *majar*. Devotees belonging to the Muslim communities offer *chadar* with procession on the *majar* of the Saint. The non-Muslim devotees offer flowers and sweets asking benediction of the Saint. A medium-sized fair is held for the day on which a number of shops with diverse merchandise visit the place. A *mancha* or platform is erected at an open place away from the Banyan tree where the night long performance of Fakiri, as well as Baul songs are arranged. By the side of this there is a *kunda* for lighting up the sacred fire where the Fakir preceptor take their seats and offer homage in the fire in sacred memory of the Saint Alam Shah. It is done throughout the day and night. The song performances are attended by the listeners belonging to both the Hindu and the Muslim communities. On the platform the Fakirs dance and sing when the Bauls do not hesitate to present their own songs based on the theme of Vaishnava philosophy of love. The Fakirs also present songs of love for humanity centred round the Vaishnava way of thinking. Their songs on *dehatawa* run parallel to those popularly sung by the Bauls. Thus on the very festive day the *majar* of Alam Saheb becomes the meeting place of Hindu and Muslim line of thinking. The participating ordinary people can understand through various practical instances that distinct and rigid boundary line between the two communities - Hindu and Muslim - has got no practical value when the whole thing is evaluated in the background of love philosophy whether it be in the Islamic line or the Hindu line of thinking. When the Vaishnava Bauls and the Muslim Fakirs join their voices here to sing songs in honour of the Man of the Heart, it seems that the problems of religious differences and communal misunderstanding is overcome. There is no reason to think themselves in two separate branches all are the same in the heart and soul.

The Fakirs visit the *Pous-mela* at Santiniketan through the direct invitation from the organizers of the *mela* committee. Some eminent Fakirs like Tahid Shah of Santa (Birbhum), Musan Shah Kalindar of

Fakirs like Tahid Shah of Santa (Birbhum), Musan Shah Kalindar of Makdamnagar (Birbhum), Behetar Shah of Hatia (Birbhum), Sheikh Billan Chisti of Belenda (Burdwan), Sheikh Taher and Abu Hasan of Pandaveswar (Burdwan) reached here on the day following the inauguration of *Pous-mela.* A Few Fakirs attached to them in either Preceptor-Disciple or Preceptor-Devotee relationship also came to the fair but they did not receive any formal invitation. The *mela* committee arranged for accommodation and meals for the Fakirs but that was restricted to the invitees only. The non-invitee Fakirs were to arrange for their own meals and other allied matters. In the *mela* campus the accommodation for the Fakirs was arranged along with the Bauls under the same *pandal.* The Fakirs were seen to stay side by side with the Bauls. But they performed their own ritualistic activities separately. They were also seen to engage in group-singing to the accompaniment of their characteristic musical instruments like *Pakhoaj, Khanjani, Dotara,* Harmonium, *Dugi* and large and small tongs. During this organised singing performance the Fakirs were all along singing the songs related to *dehatatwa.* With these, a few Islamic songs were also presented. The Fakirs were all along engaged in dancing and showing various feats. Mubar Shah Fakir was an expert in playing with fire. He was showing the feat of swallowing burnt charcoal from the fire kindled in a large *dhuni* or sacred fire spot. This fire swallowing feat was enjoyed by all the attending people including the Bauls.

The *Guru* or preceptor of the Fakirs came here and he was engaged in organising certain basic formalities relating to the Fakir way of life. Many people belonging to all the communities approached him to seek his advice to tide over different crises in life. He was seen to give patient hearing to all the description of problems put forward by the ordinary people. After thorough discussions he was offering various types of amulets and stones to the persons facing problems. Sometime he was found reciting spells before the person concerned and fequently applying the large tongs over his head. Most of the time he was uttering the name of Data Saheb of Patharchapuri. The side-walls of the camp were decorated with the *chadars* that were offered to them during the fair at Patharchapuri. They were very much addicted to the smoking of hemp. Some were seen used to chain smoking. Sometimes Bauls were also accompanying them in the smoking of hemp. Through close interaction with the Fakirs, it was seen that they were totally free from any rigidity of religion. When they were offering any stone to the Hindu clients, they asked them to wear these on any Thursday, i.e. *gurubar* (a day of the *guru)* after ceremonially purifying these by a Brahmin priest. Moreover, the clients were instructed to observe the Thursday by prohibiting the non-vegetarian meals. When enquired, it was explained by the Fakir concerned that Data Saheb himself was a Brahmin and so Brahmin tradition should necessarily be preserved. They were the staunch followers of Datababa and, therefore, no trace of narrowness regarding the religious beliefs was to be maintained in any of their behaviour-pattern.

Thus the Fakirs and the Bauls think in the parallel horizon. They are not the followers of antithetical ideas, rather they come very close to each other in their ways of *sadhana* through love for humanity. The principles of the worship of the Man of the Heart are based on similar view-points and in following these the Fakirs and the Bauls stand on parallel grounds. They sing each other's song composed on the subject matters of both Vaishnavite and Islamic religious thcughts. The Fakirs very often sing the songs that are composed on the themes relating to the love philosophy of Chaitannyadeva. Sometimes they show profound respect to the divine couple Radha-Krishna centering round divine love which is the essence of everything. The Bauls feel satisfied in singing the songs of *Murshid.* They feel it a sacred duty to visit the Sufi centres and to show due respect to the Sufi Saints through their usual way of singing and dancing. In this regard the Bauls are very progressive and readily they can not cast aside all the artificial barriers of religion and communal thinking. In the different Sufi dominated fairs it has been seen that the Bauls come to the limelight. They come to these places not only in large number but also they get opportunity to exert immense influence on the festivals as a whole. On the other hand, the Fakirs are seen to visit the Vaishnavite centres but their activities are not seen to be widespread. They are found in great number in *the Jayadeva-Kenduli mela*, but they fail to acqauire any prominent position there to attarct the general public though they sing the love philosophy of Vaishnava way of thinking. The rigidity of the Vaishnavite thinking, it may be the fact, does not allow the Fakirs or Islam dominated mendicants to come to the sphere of this religious field in spite of their total dependence on love for man in the way of *sadhana.* Though these two groups - the Bauls and the Fakirs -

run parallel, yet the people following or sponsoring the Vashnavism cannot accept the Fakirs as the true followers of Vaishnavite love philosophy rather they think them as the part and parcel of the rigorous Islamic spheres of thinking based on conflicts with the general tenets of Hinduism. It is because of this fact a difference has automatically been created in the minds of the people and naturally a local usage has been developed which tries to see the Fakirs as different from the Bauls in the internal phases of philosophy. Where the rigidity of Vaishnavism or similar religious trend is weak or more or less absent as in *Pous-mela* at Santiniketan the free mixing of the Bauls and the Fakirs is highly illustrative.

6

Bauls in Integrational Contrivance

The songs form an indispensable part of Baul life as these play the essential roles of his *sadhana,* these help them in their eternal quest for the Man of the Heart, and also these are the only ways to communicate his ideas to the ordinary men of the world. In short, the Baul does everything through his songs, he lives in his songs, he meditates in his songs, he sleeps in his songs and he dies in his songs. The songs act as the reflectors of many events of history - these are the store-houses of diverse thoughts and ideas. These are also the medium of recreation for the common people. They get tremendous joy and merriment in the peculiar modes of presentations of these; also they derive solace and mental peace in times of their depression and agony. The songs of the Bauls are really the wonder of wonders. In these one can find the systematic illustration of the Baul mind and to understand the Baul their songs must be comprehended through proper analysis. Attempts have been made here to explore the different horizons of Baul thinking through the categorical understanding of their songs collected from the different places and in different situations. These songs have been collected in original Bengali and which have been translated into English for sake of convenience. Some representative songs have been picked up from the original collection to put the focus on the different corners of the vast and complex Baul way of life and thinking.

The Bauls explore the spiritual perspectives in all walks of their life through the application of their songs, the wordings of which always contain some hidden meaning. These are like the sweet fruits covered by a thick skin. When this thick skin is peeled off, the sweet taste of the fleshy and juicy part of the fruit can be obtained. When a listener of these songs can reach the hidden meaning of these songs penetrating the superficial or outer layers, his mind is filled up with heavenly pleasure. The uniqueness of these songs lies in the fact that the profoundest philosophy of the world is found to be embedded in the simple and rural languages composed by the unsophisticated people belonging to the backward section of the society. The composer-singers of these songs emerge from the common village folk and it is very natural that their creative ability and observational perspective would be limited to that particular social and cultural environment where they have been born and brought up. It is quite natural that their freedom of expression is not extensive and in the study and evaluation of these songs these factors are to be borne in mind. The songs of the Bauls are meant to unveil the world of the invisible and the unattainable, but these are not characterized by the organised expressions of feelings with relevant poetic expressions. These express true creative intuition of the people of rural setting. There are no traces of any sophisticated poetic consciousness in the songs sung by the Bauls. But the contents and the magic of music places them in a significant position in the music as well as spiritual world.

The Bauls have special reverence for their songs and dances. These are regarded by them as blossoms of the forests. The flowers are plucked and gathered by the general devotees to pay homage through the offerings of handful of flowers to the deities. Baul songs are like these flowers which are dedicated to the feet of the Ultimate Being through sincerity and devotion. The main aim of singing and dancing is to submit oneself in the propitiation of the Ultimate Being though they outwardly engage these in asking alms from the general public. Baul songs are so delicately composed that these focus dual meaning. The internal theme of these songs is deep-rooted where a high psycho-philosophical horizon is categorically opened, but this becomes out of reach of the common people. They enjoy only the outward general meaning of the songs that are sung so elegantly to the accompaniment of rhythmic *anandlahari* and sometimes *ektara* which beggars description. The flow of sound that emits from the especially-designed *anandlahari* really oscillates the mind of the general people and when it is accompanied by the highly specialized tone of the Bauls, characterized by sudden ups and downs, the audience are held spell-bound. The wordings of the songs are simple and restricted to the worldly activities and thinking pattern of the common people. What the common people observe in their day-to-day life is reflected in the very wordings of the songs. Naturally these people do appreciate from the core of their hearts and which very naturally have become the part and parcel of the folk mind. But the Bauls do not stop here--they are not satisfied with what the common people have drawn from these. They move forward and surpassing the general way of living they reach the realm of the basic philosophy of life.

The Bauls belonging to all the categories try to master themselves in song and dance which they regard as the medium of propitiation of the Ultimate Being. Baul engages himself in three kinds of activities *viz.* singing, dancing and playing the music. Generally he does not want the help of any expert to enable him in focussing the three angles of the recital. The Baul songs have got their own specialities.It is the song which has made the Bauls famous throughout the world. The Baul song has two different aspect (i) the special tuning and peculiar mode of presentation, (ii) the literary value and lyricism. During the field study various representative types of songs have been recorded at the time of their presentation by the singers. A few songs were collected on request. Sometimes group singing was initiated and through the organization of group singing some discussions were made on the nature and extent of different types of songs. The central theme of the Baul songs is the particular outlook towards life and their philosophical and realistic orientation. These two approaches have been fused in the subject-matter of the songs. The Baul songs have got a common central theme and these are devotional in character. If one analyses the general trend of the theme, he will see that it is of three types - (i) the particular goal to be reached is expressed in these, (ii) it describes the different difficulties that are to be faced by the followers of this spiritual path, and (iii) it suggests measures to overcome these difficulties. Above all there is a clear covering of ritualistic and humanistic understandings. The Baul songs are composed on the same thematic principle - similar spiritual aspect, similar method of ascetic practices and identical principles on the phenomenon of *Guru*. It is due to this reason various composers of Baul songs focus the same horizon. Through an analytical study of the Baul song composed by many composers, it is seen that though the wordings vary and the compositions differ, there is a close unity and basic likeness amongst these songs. All the Bauls in the former period, were totally illiterate. They represented the lower section of the society before entering this sect. After thorough enquiry so far made it has been seen that no appreciable change is to be recorded in the sphere of literacy of the Bauls. Still they represent the illiterate mass of our country. But they effectively bear the age-old tradition characterized by deep-rooted philosophy of life connected activities. In spite of utter illiteracy the Bauls themselves are the spontaneous composers of songs. Backed by a rich tradition and initiated by selfless love for humanity the Bauls are all along the possessors of the eyes in which the concrete reflections of all happenings of the nature and society are detected. This experience has, in reality, found place in the composition of songs which are given shapes orally and are handed down through generations. Owing to the closed-set central theme of Baul life and thought, the nature of songs presented by diverse composers remains the same. Here lies the root of basic unity amongst the Bauls composed by diverse composers through the ages. The Table No. 6.1 illustrates the multiple perspectives of the singers of these traditional songs of Bengal. A close-set person-to-person enquiry into the different behaviour-patterns of the Bauls adopted in respect of the songs which are regarded as the life-force of their particular spheres of *sadhana* or simply the way of life. Amongst the total number of Bauls so far interrogated, 69.47% belonging to the Ascetic, 89.11% belonging to the Domestic and 90.01% of the other categories are active singers. 50.49% of the singers belonging to the Domestic group sing songs in the public vehicles like trains and buses regularly. 39.39% of the Other sections practise this, whereas a few of the Ascetic group (15.78%) present their songs in the public vehicles. 84.22% of the Ascetic Bauls have expressed their opinion against this practice as it injures the very sanctity of the Baul *sadhana*. Regarding composing of songs, this table reveals that 25.26% amongst the Ascetic and 25.74% amongst the Domestic Bauls are able to compose songs themselves. Amongst the Others category the percentage of the composers stands the same as is seen among the Ascetic and Domestic Bauls. 82.12% of the Domestic Bauls think that dance is the essential part of Baul songs and therefore, all types of songs should be accompanied by relevant dances. Their opinion is highly supported by the Bauls belonging to Others category. Most of the respondents (60.60%) are in favour of the situation that dance is the indispensable part of Baul songs, though 21.21% of them remain indifferent. But amongst Ascetic Bauls only 41.06% pass their opinion in the indispensability of dance during the presentation of Baul songs. They believe that the songs should be

TABLE NO. 6.1

Baul Songs and the Bauls--Multiple Behaviour-Patterns

Type	Actively sing Baul songs			Sing songs in trains & buses			Sing songs in professional singing troupes			Can compose songs			Dance is indispensable part of Baul songs.				Baul song should be sung in meditative mood			
	Yes	*No*	*Total*	*Yes*	*No*	*Total*	*Yes*	*No*	*Total*	*Yes*	*No*	*Total*	*Yes*	*No*	*Indif-ferent*	*Total*	*Yes*	*No*	*Indif-ferent*	*Total*
Ascetic ..	66	29	95	15	80	95	17	78	95	24	71	95	39	40	16	95	66	16	13	95
Percentage..	69.47	30.53	100.00	15.78	84.22	100.00	17.99	82.01	100.00	25.26	74.74	100.00	41.06	42.10	16.84	100.00	69.47	16.85	13.68	100.00
Domestic..	90	11	101	51	50	101	47	54	101	26	75	101	83	9	9	101	60	26	15	101
Percentage ..	89.11	10.89	100.00	50.49	49.51	100.00	46.54	53.46	100.00	25.74	74.26	100.00	82.18	8.91	8.91	100.00	59.40	25.75	14.85	100.00
Others ..	30	3	33	13	20	33	14	19	33	8	25	33	20	6	7	33	20	7	6	33
Percentage..	90.91	9.09	100.00	39.39	60.61	100.00	42.43	57.57	100.00	24.25	75.75	100.00	60.60	18.19	21.21	100.00	60.60	21.21	18.19	100.00

presented in meditative mood and during which a calm and quiet atmosphere must prevail. 69.47% of the Ascetic Bauls are in favour of this trend. 59.40 and 60.60% of the Domestic and Other sections, respectively, of the Bauls think that the Baul songs should be presented in meditative mood. The Table concerned pin-points the different other types of responses in all the minor details of the songs and dances.

The Baul songs have got necessary literary implication and sometimes it is so imbued with intellectuality that it surpasses the literary appeal of various well-integrated compositions authored by educated and sophisticated persons of the present period. These songs are free from any artificiality - all the examples, metaphors and very wordings are taken from the natural surroundings, as well as life and thought of the rural folk. These speak for and on behalf of these rural people and naturally folk sentiment is highly conspicuous in the Baul songs. On this ground the Baul songs have been classed by many scholars as typical folk songs of Bengal. There is a section of scholars who are reluctant to call Baul songs as folk songs simply because of the fact that these songs are highly philosophical. But it is not reasonable. The common folk is not out of philosophical thinking. Rather, the philosophical aspects present in Baul songs are so simply presented and so finely illustrated through the common events in the life and activities of the family men that one readily identifies these as direct reflections of folk mind. But at the same time it should be noted that the Baul songs are basically different from the other types of folk songs in content and character. These are conspicuous in some of their features.--

(1) The high literary value of the Baul songs is specially characterized by multiple meanings;

(2) these are heavily centralized on the general events of the day-to-day realistic life of common people;

(3) these reflect the patterns of interactions of the diverse faiths of the different factions of the Hindu religion and also of the Hinduism and Islamic beliefs and practices, and

(4) the changing situations of the society conditioned by the socio-economic changes are categorically reflected in the Baul songs.

In course of this study a good number of Baul songs have been collected as well as tape-recorded. Attempts have been made elsewhere in this treatise to analyse these songs in the perspective of the different stages of the society as a whole. The songs have been collected from--

(a) the solitary Bauls who move from door to door for soliciting alms,

(b) the organized Baul groups who categorically maintain *ashramite* character,

(c) the platform singers during spontaneous Baul gatherings, and

(d) the internationally famous individual Bauls who have been conspicuous by their newly-oriented outlook.

While studying, a number of representative songs have been recorded in black and white to focus discernible light on the exact nature and extent of these tradition-bound songs. The above mentioned Bauls of different categories were approached to make a good record of these songs. Uninterrupted presentation of Baul songs needs a befitting environment and for this reason the Bauls are to be provided with the necessary atmosphere. In order to serve the purpose, we had made some special arrangements for the assemblage of the Bauls coming from different places, and in those gatherings an atmosphere of *mahotsab* had been created centring round different Baul *ashrams*. Bauls of different categories had been invited ceremonially to attend the *mahotsab* and thereby present different varieties of songs. Sometimes group-songs were arranged in which a good number of Bauls took active part. The collected Baul songs were being studied and analysed primarily in the three different ways:-

(i) The trend of integration of diverse religious thoughts and ideas;

(ii) The attempt of averting social disintegration caused by caste and class feelings; and

(iii) The clarion call given by the Bauls through their songs to prepare a platform for universal brotherhood.

TABLE NO. 6.2

Situational Perspectives and the Presentation of Baul Songs

Sl. No.	*Particulars*	*Ascetic*	*Percentage*	*Domestic*	*Percentage*	*Others*	*Percentage*	*Grand Total*	*Percentage*
1.	Very Solitary Place..	44	46.31	17	16.83	5	15.16	66	28.82
2.	Solitary River Banks ..	4	4.21	6	5.94	2	6.06	12	5.24
3.	Populated Market Place ..	4	4.21	6	5.94	3	9.09	13	5.67
4.	Road-side Tea Stalls ..	4	4.21	6	5.94	1	3.03	11	4.80
5.	Temple and like Religious Centres ..	30	31.59	35	34.65	11	33.33	76	33.20
6.	Organized Musical Conference ..	5	5.26	22	21.78	9	27.27	36	15.72
7.	Other Places..	4	4.21	9	8.92	2	6.06	15	6.55
	Total..	95	100.00	101	100.00	33	100.00	229	100.00

The Baul songs have a very strongly applied aspect and these are provided with special characteristics of their own. The songs are so neatly composed and so beautifully presented that these leave a prominent impression in the inner recess of the hearts of the people. The long-drawn struggle amongst the three sects of the Hindus family--the Sakta, the Vaishnava and the Shaiva,-- has been washed away by the Baul philosophy. There are many songs in which the Bauls communicate their earnest desire to ward off the artificial barriers that have been raised for meaningless grounds. In some of their songs the Bauls go against the heavily conflicting attitudes that are present amongst the different religious faith like Hinduism, Islamism and Christianity. Social stratifications as exemplified by castes and classes are against Baul line of thinking. The Bauls learn to adore the man of the Heart and which is present in each and every human being, irrespective of castes, classes and religions. This Man of the Heart is unique in Himself. He is far away from differentiation,--He does not come under any sort of artificial barrier created by man at different times to serve many purposes. The Bauls inspire the people to establish brotherly feeling in their minds at the time of dealing with any human being. Universal brotherhood is the motto of the Bauls and some of their songs are composed and song with the particular philosophy in view.

Thus the Baul sings, -

Man exists in man
Man exists in sense
Man gets birth and dies out
Look at him through the eyes.

Simple and complex he may be
King and subject he may be
Man is fostered by man
Do enjoy it with pleasure and pain.

Man is the father
Man is the mother
Man is the child
friend and brother.

Man cries and man laughs
But he is all the above
Man is friendly, man is cruel
He is both preceptor and disciple
Come to him and have a look.

Man comes to this earth and goes
Only to establish his works
Man is the killer of man,
Again he is the catcher of man
And it is this man who worships man
From the core of his heart.

The Bauls understand man in this way. Man is his subject of veneration - his essence of *sadhana*. It is very difficult to reach the man. There are many steps to arrive at the threshold of the so-called 'temple' of man. In this journey to the path of man the Baul accepts female consort though male and female concepts run in a parallel line. Still the Bauls enter in conjugal life. The male and the female Bauls do enter in material relations. They have got their own marital regulations which are conditioned by their own line of thinking. It is far from the customs performed by the common people around them. Before the short ceremony information of the matrimonial union is circulated to the different Baul-*akhras*. It is customary for them to attend the ceremony and convey good wishes. The *Guru* plays the role of priest. Leaves of plants, flowers, sandle-paste and garlands of *tulsi* beads are the essential articles for the marriage. The male and female Bauls stand side by side in courtyard of the *akhra* in presence of the attending Bauls when the *Guru* places the *tulsi*- bead garlands round their necks. After that they exchange each other's garland. This function, in common term, is known as *Kanthibadal*. It is followed by a ceremonial feast in which the invited Bauls, Vaishnavas and other mendicants are served with profound respect. This sort of marital ceremony is also held in the different Baul gatherings, Baul *mahotsab* and fairs. When any domestic Baul wants to marry the female Baul belonging to ascetic sect, the former is to go through a formal initiation form the *Guru* concerned.

In a particular marriage ceremony held during the course of this investigation it was found that from the very morning the Bauls from different *akhras* began to assemble at the *Tamaltala Akhra* of Sudhir Das

Baul in Jaydeva-Kenduli. The Baul *Guru* Phulchand Das presided over the performance. In the evening the ceremony was held at the *Gosaintala* when all the invitees attended. The Baul Guru, first of all, offered two pieces of white cloth and they were asked to wear those. Then through the utterance of the sacred name of 'Nitai-Gour' the *tulsi-bead* necklace, after smearing it with sanddle-paste was handed over to the female Baul. Then she was asked to offer the bead necklace to the male Baul. She placed it round his neck and the male Baul was instructed to place the same round the neck of the female Baul. In this way the exchange of the bead-necklace or *Kanthibadal* was affected. Then the male Baul reached the feet of the female Baul. The female Baul readily held his arms and picked him up. It was followed by the joint ceremonial begging before the attending Bauls, Vaishnavas and *Sadhus*. All the invitees were then served with ceremonial meals.

Marital life of the Bauls is highly restricted. The male and the female Bauls are to go through a process of *sadhana* based on bodily perspective. They are to know the physiology and philosophy of the body and to understand deeply the technique of enjoying the bodily passions with such a particular type of bodily union that keep them away from worldly phenomenon. It is for this reason the scene of Divine - Pair of Radha-Krishna is so meaningful and symbolic to them. They are very much sensitive to the celebrated Platonic love of Villwamangal-Chintamoni, Jaydeva-Padmavati and Chandidas - Rami. The peculiar thing is that the education of Platonic love, the bodily *sadhna* or the acts and procedures for special bodily union of opposite sexes is not received from any formal training centre. They are to receive everything in the philosophy of life which is seen to be embedded in the traditional songs of the Bauls. Thus the Baul sings on the love union of Villwamangal and Chintamoni -

Oh, my mind, go to Vrindaban of Bengal
    If you like to have the experience of divine love
Where Chintamoni-Villwamangal are always
    Overwhelmed with the influence of love.

Celebrated Villwamangal and Chintamoni
Glorified by the love of Krishna
    Madden with Krishana consciousness all through
    the time.

In that band of eroded bank of Ajay
Double *tamal* in paired existence
Where Chintamoni purveys strength in her divine love
Underneath that immortal banyan tree
By dint of father's sacred last rite
Villwamangal was blessed with the kindness of Almighty.

Chinta was so thought-provoking
That the living snake forgot biting
It became a rope - the last means to climb up the high wall.

Chintamoni was so inevitable for Thakur
That he mistook floating corpse for plank
No obstacle could resist him, even the torrents of Ajay.

Thakurdas thinks, a holy bath in Radhakunda
Brings the immediate peace in mind
And the red feet of Krishna can be achieved
Through this devotional holy dip.

Through songs the Baul sings the mechanism of body of the women especially linked up with sexual patterns. It is not only for letting the people know the facts about this mystery but for his own understanding of the situation. From the very childhood days he has been singing as well as hearing these from others.

The female consort of the Baul is not considered only a woman, but a co-worker in the field of meditation. This particular field is full of hurdles and to overcome these the united strength of the male and the female is needed. The Bauls are characteristically free in the maintenance of family life. The attachment between the married couple is not so rigid and the theoretical concept is always applicable in the Baul life. They keep themselves out of social norms and customs and naturally are free from familial bondage. Thus disunion between the married couple is a common phenomenon. There are many a Baul who have got more than two wives. Generally the ascetic Bauls have no children in spite of their conjugal life and bodily union. They consider it their sacred duty to control the birth of children. The methods for the checking of this natural process lie in their deep-rooted *sadhana* which every Baul undergoes as well as in the following of certain techniques in day-to-day life and activities which come down through tradition. Thus they sing :

The flow tide results in every month in the women's body
Like the confluence of three rivers
The women represent the rivers Ganga, Jamuna and Saraswati.

Their celebrated sports continue for three days
One day in black, one day in white
Whereas the next day is full of loving activities.

When the follow tide reaches the tree,
Try to cut it down with dexterity
Be careful about your falling underneath it
Effected by the tear of the rope-support.

The method of birth control is one of the main essential items of behaviour-patterns of the Bauls. The Baul tries to free their body from passion through the control of the mind as well as by the application of a few indigenous herbal medicines. They firmly believe that if a man regularly takes some quantity of juice extracted from *bel* leaves in the empty stomach every morning, he will gradually lose the power for producing children. Similarly if a woman takes a pentapetalous China rose together with sugar every morning regularly for fifteen days after starting of menstruation, she will develop sterility, of course, temporarily. In this way they possess mutiplicity of ideas and carefully follow these to fulfil their purpose. But they maintain excessive secrecy of these features of activities as it is believed that any leak out of these secluded ideas would affect the very line of their *sadhana*. These can be collected through the application of various methodological principles but it would involve a very long-term and depth-oriented field work by some efficient field workers well-versed in the different lines of Baul *sadhana*.

The Bauls are very much devoted to know the body of man. They think the humnan body as the replica of the earth. Thus they say -

" Ja achhe Biswa Brahmande
Ta achhe Dehabhande."

"The elements that are present in the Universe
are to be exactly seen in the human body."

In *Dehatatwa* or spiritual knowledge of the body the Baul goes deep into the matter and tries to find out the different complexities which are characterized by their naturalistic procedure of simplification. In this way a Baul observes the human body as follows:-

How many persons can recognise him? Alas !
Who sprinkles the water of Jardan and Ganga
In the sandy Arabian territory.

In the stable of Bethlehem whose elegance
Has been sparkling like a ruby.
That very child was seen in the celebrated prison of Kangsa
It enlightened the lap of mother Devaki
How many persons can recognise him?

For whose expectation Maya, Chandramoni
wanted in anxious state of mind

And whose address as 'Mother' made
Mary, Sachi and Amina overwhelmed.
How many persons can recognise him?

In Palestine, Sarnath
In Tabani and Nadia
Who came to offer love was the person who
wandered in Mecca.
How many persons can recongnise him?

Granth Saheb, Gita, Koran, Tripitaka
Bible and *Purana*
All these are created by one God
Who is recongised by multiforms
How many persons can recognise him?

Not recognising, Oh my mind, this man
They became engaged forgetting the essence of religion
And crucified the revered personality

Who adored the Father of universe
How many persons can recognise him

From whom Ashanandan asks
Blessings for all

He is suspicious, lest he loses him
Whose eyes are full with tears of compassion.

Everybody in this world is the possessor of this type of body. In each body resides the Man of the Heart. The human body is his sacred seat. Thus there should not be any sort of discrimination amongst the people. Therefore, the Baul puts his life-long resistance to the organisation of caste, class and religion. Man is known by the term 'man' and he is to be understood through love. Then why this discrimination? Why one community quarrels with another? What are the bases of religious riots? The Bauls by virtue of their real understanding have been able to reach the root of the situation and have acquired perfect knowledge. It is for this reason they call the people not to be misled by ignorance. All men of the world are tied together by the common thinking pattern which is universal. This is to be properly evaluated. Thus the Bauls sing.

I hear, in the midst of this house exist
The fourteen worlds*
The bird which stays inside this
Is not seen by anybody.

Oh mind, on the expiry of the term of living
The bird flies in the sky-blue.
And his residence is then engulfed by
The blazing fire of the funeral pyre.

I hear, in the midst of this house exist
The fourteen worlds.

What exist in that Universe
(I hear) these can be found out
In this house.

* Mythological Seven Heavens and Seven Under Worlds.

Ashanandan says, Oh my Guru
When shall I meet the owner of the term?
I hear, in the midst of this house exist
the fourteen worlds.

The Bauls do not support the caste discriminations prevalent in India from the time immemorial. Whatever may be its uniqueness or applicability, the Bauls all through the time vehemently put their objections. The human body with all its precious elements is unique in itself and no society has got any authority to make any sort of differentiation amongst these bodies on the plea of their higher or lower statuses. Man has come to this earth to perform his sacred acts and as these acts are done for the service to man, these cannot be categorized as high or low. The Bauls become vocal in this perspective—

Oh my mind, do not think for any discrimination based on caste,
Open the *puranas* and see there is only one caste which is man
Just see that *Purusha* and *Prakriti* are the two human divisions
Then why is so excessive eagerness in *Veda, Bible* and *Koran*
to establish human differentiation?

Caste in man is never affected by the taking of food
Brahminism can never be established by mere sacred thread.
Chacha (uncle) can be recognised by identifying his beard
But what should be the identification mark of Chachi (aunt)?
Monastery, temple, mosque, church are resided by
God, Kali, Ram and Allah

Rites, rituals, *Jumma, rojah* all mean the same
Jerusalem, Mecca, Puri, *Pani,* water all indicate the water proper
Thakurdas says-In the name of caste discrimination
why we are quarreling with each other?

In this sphere of discussion the famous song of Lalan Fakir deserves mention. Lalan Fakir was a devoted Baul who wrote thousands of songs and thereby preached his ideas based on love for the people. His philosophy is highly notable for the total resistance to religious and caste clearages amongst the people of the world. He was a legendary figure in the Baul culture throughout Bengal. He sang on a conspicuous point of caste differentiation -

All people enquire about the caste of Lalan
In this worldly state
Lalan replies--I have not seen through my vision
the manner of caste
The *namaj* signifies the Muslim males
But what about the significance of the females?
The Brahmin is proved by his sacred thread
What is the criterion of female Brahmin?

Of late, we have been able to understand the futility of grading the people, high and low, touchable and untouchable according to the caste groups which are determined by birth and not by any action. Through continuous painstaking work done by the different national leaders under the direct inspiration of Mahatma Gandhi, a public opinion has been created against untouchability. It has been regarded as a sin. With the gradual changing of mentality of the people associated with many other changing situations of the world we have now been able to abolish the untouchability and give it a constitutional safeguard. The caste system in this country though practically present, has lost its rigidity and gradually it is becoming weaker.

The Bauls from the remote past have been putting resistance against this peculiar phenomenon. They called it peculiar because they did not find any justifiable ground behind that system. But this particular line of approach did never attract our attention. How and why this tradition-bound community put their joint objection against another tradition of India was not practically within our knowledge. Had it been so, we could have gathered active supportimpregnatedwith precious practical reasons to avert the human differences created by unreasonable ground. Thus it can be said without any hesitation that the Baul community has been nourishing a philanthropic idea since long and after passing through a long path we have joined our hands with them at least in thinking parallel with them in respect of the driving away of the human discrimination.

The Bauls have emerged from the basic rural society. This point has been established by so many former scholars and also during this field study it has been confirmed totally. It has been observed that the Bauls have come principally from four types of different levels of communities-

1) From Caste Hindu families,
2) From Vaishnava families,
3) From Muslim families, and
4) From Scheduled Caste families.

There are so many concrete examples of coming of the Bauls from various stratified social groups. It is said that the famous Baul of the ancient period, named Lalan Fakir, came from the Hindu community. He was a Kayastha by caste. During the present period this particular tradition is being maintained. Biswanath Das, an eminent Baul of Bolpur in Birbhum, came from Brahmin caste group. Sambhu Das Baul of Illumbazar was Hadi by caste (a very low caste-group) before he took initiation in the Baul community. A large number of Bauls have so far been interrogated and it is seen from the long list, appended to the Appendix, that persons from different castes ranging from the highest Brahmin to the lowest caste groups like Hadi, Muchi, *etc.*, have taken initiation into the Baul community, and from the very moment of their celebrated entry they have freed themselves from all sorts of caste distinction. The Bauls are, as a rule, very far from all types of social regulations, prohibitions as well as superstitions. The Bauls coming from different caste groups do not mind for their former caste affiliations. They designate themselves as Bauls and identify themselves as the persons belonging to the same level. They distribute and share food amongst themselves. Not only they eat and drink from a common vessel but also they do not hesitate to use the same bed for taking rest. They are totally free from all sorts of social prejudices which is reflected very much in their day-to-day behaviour-pattern and the themes of the songs sung by them. The Bauls, despite their original caste affiliations of various types, think themselves as belonging to equal status. Naturally they discourage all sorts of social inequality. The Bauls regularly attend many social, socio-religious ceremonies and folk festivals in which they try to communicate their life-philosophy not only by means of their songs but also through their mode of behaviour. The Bauls always talk with the common people in a round about way. They insert their philosophical view points in a simple way at the time of conversation with the people. It is very much attractive, as well as a matter of great importance in a study of interactions of the Bauls with the common people. As the Bauls have emerged from the different castes and communities of rural Bengal, so there is no communication gap in spite of the former's close alliance with high philosophical setting.

The Bauls visit all holy places without any discrimination. They go to temples, mosques and churches with same reverence as they do not find any basic difference in the various religious sentiments. They neglect all sorts of prejudices and mix with the men of all categories. Thus they sing.-

I am impatiently searching
the simple address
of that particular shop-
Where Allaha, Hari, Ram Kali, God
take meals from the common plate.
Where the fire has been lit in the form of
divine devotion,
Gora and Ramkrishna place the great iron tumbler
on the fire place,
And Mohammad, Gin, Jesus fry *mihidana**
In the love juice of sugar
I am impatiently searching the
simple address
of that particular shop.

Where knowledge-posset and duty-sugar
are being dabbed by Buddha and Nanak
Where by dint of kindness and forgiveness
the religion-based sweets develop

These can't be purchased through payment of money
Whereas these can be eaten without making any payment
The proper way of knowing the whereabouts of the real owner
Can be known through meditation and prayer.

Ashanandan informs more,
Search out the Universe
the particular place is situated there
where there is no abode of six rats.

I am patiently searching out the
simple address
of that particular shop.

---

*A kind of Sweet meat Consisting of very small globules.

The Bauls raise their voice against the existing trend of discrimination among different religious faiths. There is no inequality in religious spheres and naturally no boundary line can be drawn up amongst the activities of the different religious prophets, *Gurus* or preachers. All are one and the same and what is needed to reach the goal is to clarify and body and mind of the devotee. It is reflected in the following song:--

"Whether he is Ram or Rahim, Radha or Jesus
Where shall you get him through search?
As much as you involve in tracing their discrimination
So much you go far from your destination.
He is playing secretly
inside your mind daily.

Through groping in the dark chamber
Your effort will be futile for ever.

This is why Naga calls out
After smearing the conscious-turmeric on body
and having the knowledge-guru in your favour
O brother, unlock the door of the concerned chamber.

Generally, it is seen that a Brahmin is reluctant to show hospitality towards persons belonging to low-graded castes like Dom, Bauri, Hadi, *etc*.. But when they become Bauls, they are readily accepted by the Brahmins or other higher castes or groups with due honour.

The Bauls are not in favour of idol worship. They never pay homage with flowers to the deities. The Bauls adore man who is their centre of meditation. They are the real admirer of love. But at the same time it should be noted that the Bauls sometimes keep or install the images of deities. During the field study it has been observed that many *akhras* or the Bauls are provided with the pictures of divine pairs - Radha-Krishna or Jaydeva-Padmavati. Some keep the pictures of Chaitannya Deva or Nityananda Prabhu. But these are not kept there for routine worship. The idols or images are not the main points of focus - these are the media to adore the love, the substance of Baul philosophy. The divine love that exists between Radha and Krishna or Padmavati and Jaydeva is desirable to the Bauls.

The special characteristic feature of the Baul songs and Baul way of life is that it is enjoyed by various grades and statuses of people sitting on the same platform. A veteran scholar, a renowned litterateur enjoys the Baul songs with due seriousness. Sitting by the side of whom an illiterate villager may be similarly interested in hearing the songs and getting himself acquainted with the various modes of presentations of songs and dances. What is the actual cause behind it? Certainly this sort of question may crop up in mind. It is true that the meditations of the Bauls are principally centred on the deep-rooted philosophy of love for humanity. It is limited to the emotional perspectives of various nature, but its very nature of presentation is so simple that it attracts the common people. There are numerous scopes for the common men to enter into the very recess of Baul songs. The Bauls are their livelihood through *madhukari* or begging and for this they move about village to village spread over the large tract of land. They present their songs even in the crowded buses and trains, in the road-side stalls and fairs. During this the Bauls come in close contact with the common people who are very fond of their songs. The double entity of the Bauls--taking shelter in the emotional and celestial world for their *sadhana*, and wandering in the realistic field for the earning of livelihood--has made them conscious and experienced about man and his activities. It has been observed in various songs and dance recitals that through the unique pattern of presentation of songs and dances the Bauls can easily establish a tremendous influence on the mind of the audience who, for the time being, are held spell-bound. The Baul propitiates man, who is his *Guru,* the path-finder the soul's companion on the one hand, as well as his appreciator and supporter on the other. In the latter phase come all the common people ranging from rich to poor, and from erudite scholars to illiterates. Through his novel method of approach the Baul can easily roam about from one mind to another as a nomadic community moves through different places. The Bauls, in course of their *sadhana* to understand man, delve deep into the psychic features which orient human thought and mentality. It is because of this fact the Baul is regarded as the successful artist in drawing human nature and related perspectives which are reflected in his eternal search for the 'Man of the Heart.' To establish close relationship with man who is regarded as the central point in Baul philosophy and the *sadhana* of the Baul is nothing but life-long untiring zeal for unveiling the mystery of man. It is a difficult affair and the *sadhak* or meditator is to invest his intentness all through the time. It is reflected in the particular song-

It is troublesome to recognize the
Man of the Heart
It is with him I conduct my family life
Yet I cannot get his contact.
He builds his house in me
Where he stays daily
I hear daily the very sound of his
bell-oriented anklet
Yet, why he is formless?
It is troublesome to recognize the
Man of the Heart-
Ashanandan, the twice-born, says-
The heart becomes flooded with his lustre
Who wins over the mind through the 'dying' of it
O Guru! please give me his address.

It is troublesome to recognize the
Man of the Heart.

All through the attempt of investigation in the different Baul *akhras* or some other like centres it has been observed that the Baul life is largely dominated by the multiple influence of the *Guru* or preceptor. The Guru-based line of thinking of the Bauls has been investigated in detail, during various phases of study, through person-to-person enquiry as well as close observations during different assemblages of the Bauls and every-day life and activities of the individual Baul. Indian philosophy is very much influenced by the Guru-oriented procedures. In such religious beliefs and practices where practical functions are more prominent than theoretical knowledge and spiritual understandings, the necessity of the *Guru* is the essential. To understand all aspects of his *sadhana* the Baul approaches the *Guru* for clarification. Thus he sings--

O Guru ! I have failed to come
into the view of a man
"Man exists within this man"
O Guru! you always inform this to me
I hear, man is the prophet, man is the disciple,
Man is the rich and man is the destitute.

Again this man rules the Universe
Yet he is always invisible.
O Guru! I have failed to come
into the view of man.
Man is the king, man is the subject,
Man is satan, sadhu, ojha -
Yet it is not easy to recognize the man.
To search him, the whole life is spent.
O Guru, I have failed to come
into the view of a man

Man is the police,
Again, man is the thief.
Also, that man in the upstairs
constructs his own house.

Ashanandan says, O Guru! tell me
When I shall get his celebrated feet?
O Guru! I have failed to come
into the view of a man.

Baul philosophy is practical thought-oriented and, therefore, they need the help of *Guru* in passing through every stage of activity. They view the *Guru* in the two different forms--*Guru* as a man and *Guru* as an Absolute Being (God). These two aspects of viewing the *Guru* are clearly reflected in their songs. In order to reach the Absolute Being it is essential to show profound respect to the Man-*Guru* and to follow all his instructions. Man - *Guru* is regarded as the representative of the divine *Guru*. From the different enquiries and observations it has been clear to us that dependency of the Bauls on *Guru* is deep-rooted and it surpasses any other *Guru*-oriented religion and philosophy. The *Guru* has various functions to perform. He, first of all selects the disciple for *sadhana* after being satisfied that the disciple concerned has made himself fit for the same. The *Guru* helps the disciples in all affairs. He even attends sexo-yogic practices of the disciples and gives him advice if the disciple fails to perform the right activities. The *sadhak* and *sadhika* do not feel any hesitation in the sexo-yogic performances in the presence of the *Guru*. The *Guru* guides them in the peculiar *sadhana* based on the bodily union between the *Prakriti* and *Purusha*. In this way the perfect realization of the self is attained by the disciples. It leads to the domain of truth or the

Absolute Reality. It is compared with the moon in the clouded sky of mind. The clouds of ignorance, the wrong path of religious formalities, the mistaken procedures of the *sadhana* give a cover to the moon. It is the proper guidance and mercy of the True perceptor by which the clouds in the sky of mind disappear and the moon begins to shine in her full form. A few eminent *Gurus* have been interviewed during investigation and through a structured questionnaire some internal basic activities could have been brought to light. Bauls are of the opinion that the Baul *sadhana* is based on *Guru*-based knowledge to unveil the truth of the Universe. The particular knowledge is centred round the attempt of exposition of the Absolute Reality. It has got three features - one is reflected as the *Purusha* or Male, the other one is known as *Sakti* or *Prakriti* of Female, and the third one is the tremendous enjoyment and satisfaction arising out of the union of the former two forms. The principal *sadhana* of the Bauls lies in the attainment of this third state of affair through the celebrated union of these two separate entities. Krishna is known as the *Purusha*, Radha is *Prakriti* and the deep love-based union is recognized as the Guru-oriented knowledge. This deep and all-rounded love gives rise to the indescribable feeling of pleasure, an ecstatic state. This is regarded as the ultimate and prime condition of love. The unique and joyous entity is the normal state of the real *Guru*.

For the purpose his sadhana the Baul is always conscious of receiving direct help and co-operation from the *Guru*. Without *Guru* a'' Baul is distracted from his celebrated path to the "Man of the Heart. Thus he sings,-

Oh my Guru! please tune up
 my favourite *ektara*
My mind has become worried
That's why! now I can do nothing
And on turning into this side I see
The time is slowly rolling down.

Oh my Guru! please tune up
 my favourite *ektara*.
If the instrument goes out of tune
Does emotion reign over the core of the heart ?
And without that emotion how can I
 address you through singing of songs ?

Oh my Guru, please tune up
my favourite *ektara*

Ashanandan tells you, tie this mind with the
single string
so that life becomes overwhelmed by your adoration
through the use of that tuning in repeated succession.

Oh my Guru! please tune up
my favourite *ektara*.

The life and thinking of the Bauls are full of hopes and desires, love and affection, and with these there are instances of the will of acquiring many things of material as well as spiritual nature. The Bauls are keen in the realistic view of life and through all their allured ideas given to the people they remind them the last day of their life when all will be equal in status and power. The world is characterized by impermanence. Nothing will last long. But in human beings there are profound longing, there are excessive arrogance. These are short-lived and everything ends with the death of a man. The cremation ground levels up all the ups and downs in man, it sets men belonging to the different categories in a line. Thus the Baul sings-

All are equal in that premises of crematorium,
When the life-sun covers its glittering face
through setting down in the west horizon.
When that body burns to ashes,
nobody likes to note
who have come here on bamboo-made bier,
or on a golden carriage.

All are equal in that premises of crematorium,
Kings, ministers, middle-class people
and poor beggars
All are to receive the sticks by bamboo poles
lying down on the pyre.

At last by mixing in the soil
they are to sacrifice the self-conceit in all.

Ashanandan says, we enhance our personal value
on coming to this world
All are equal in that premises of crematorium.

Besides various theological subject-matters and other allied features of importance the Baul songs centre round the simple folk mind. They depict the different reverse happenings in the world very close to the rural folk and try to pinpoint the activities of supernaturalism in these respects. Most of the narrations are bizarre and do nothing but create joyous mood in the mentality of the folk. Still these are impregnated with philosophic trend as per very nature of Baul songs. A few songs in this respect may clarify the points-

O mind ascetic, do Gosainji know
the inner recess of mind ?
The bamboo plants bear tamarind
And *Jhingey* is seen to hang in tamarind tree.

There is no water in the sea
but the waves strike the market place
When the father is yet to be married
the daughter - in - law is in the lap of the son.

Thus the Baul songs focus the diverse horizon of human understanding. After going through a large number of songs and analysing their modes of approach and inner significance the songs of the Bauls may be grouped under the following broad heads for the convenience of study:

(i) *Prayers made of the Guru:*

In these songs the Baul appeals to the *Guru* for his help, co-operation and guidance in the understanding of the various phenomena of life and death including natural happenings. Everything of his life is sacrificed to him - he is the pivot of his making round through the world.

(ii) *Metaphysical Analysis of Human Body:*

The Baul makes a sincere attempt to study and analyse the body of man through metaphysical way. The body is described as the microcosm

of the Universe and the songs are composed and sung in this line of approach.

(iii) *Categorical Focussing of Divine Love:*

The Baul expresses his ideas and principles of *sadhana* through the examples of love which is always divine. He imparts the idea that love inundates all smallness of human life. The love which binds the divine couple through the ages is the central theme of these songs.

(iv) *An Emotional Search for Man:*

The Baul sets out on a journey in search for man and during which he tries to understand the different roles played by man in different situations. He goes through the different spheres of human activities and then evaluates these in the background of man.

(v) *Putting Hints on the Hidden Mysteries:*

The ways of Baul *sadhana* are characterized by multiple mysteries which are always kept secret. The secrecy of understanding is sometimes expressed through some hints and these are found to be reflected in the songs sung by them. These are expressed through symbolic representation.

(vi) *Impermanence of Life and Desires:*

In course of his life man desires for many things of worldly nature. He earns money, loves the beloved, extends affections to sons and daughters, quarrels with each other. But the Baul sings that the life and desires are extremely temporary. He alerts the people as regards the last day of life - everything is impermanent.

(vii) *Resistance against Social Inequality:*

The Baul believes in the philosophy of universal brotherhood. Therefore, in his songs he revolts against the existing artificial barriers, created by man, through the imposition of caste, class and religion. It is futile to think in terms of inequality in human society.

TABLE NO. 6.3

Time-based Perspectives in the Presentation of Baul Songs

Type	*Presentation of Different Types of Baul Songs should follow strict time-based perspectives*					*Time-based perspectives of Presentation is strictly followed*				
	Yes	*No*	*Partial*	*Not Definite*	*Total*	*Yes*	*No*	*Partial.*	*Not Definite*	*Total*
Ascetic..	68	13	8	6	95	36	17	22	20	95
Percentage..	71.57	13.68	8.44	6.31	100.00	37.89	17.89	23.15	21.07	100.00
Domestic ..	36	41	11	13	101	16	47	18	20	101
Percentage ..	35.64	40.59	10.99	12.87	100.00	15.84	46.53	17.83	19.80	100.00
Others ..	15	12	2	4	33	9	13	7	4	33
Percentage ..	45.45	36.36	6.06	12.13	100.00	27.27	39.39	21.22	12.12	100.00

(viii) *Efforts for gaining Practical Experience about Unknown:*

Throughout his life-long *sadhana* the Baul makes serious attempts to have the experience of many events which remain unknown in the worldly perspective. He wants to have the experience of death while the body is in the living state. A large number of songs depict the experience.

The Bauls are keen observers and they explain various phenomena of the society according to the various principles of Baul philosophy. It is seen that they not only explain these but are always in the mood in ventilating their observations and explanations in the minds of the people. A very interesting feature has been noticed during the collection and analysis of the different views of the Bauls. The songs of the Bauls are nothing but the media of heartfelt homage to the Absolute Reality. It is also used for the performance of *madhukari* to maintain the livelihood. It is never to be utilized for worldly fame of the Baul concerned and to earn money through public performance. The Baul songs, largely conditioned by the philosophical understandings, are regarded as the wealth of the Baul community and everybody within the community is promised to maintain the sanctity of the songs through their proper utilization. They are in favour of presenting the songs in befitting environment, failing which a gross injustice will be made on these songs which are regarded as the integral part of Baul *sadhana*. In an investigation into the various liking patterns of the Baul singers as regards the situational perspective in the presentation of songs it has been revealed, in Table No. 6.3, that 46.31% and 31.59% of the Ascetic singers like "very solitary place" the "temple and like religious centres" for the presentation of their songs. Amongst the Domestic category 34.65% of the respondents like the religious centres very much and 21.78% are in favour of presenting songs in musical conferences. 16.83% of the respondents have opined that they prefer singing in very solitary place. Amongst the Others category of Bauls, 33.20% went to sing in the temple and other religious centres, 28.82% of the respondents give their opinion in favour of 'very solitary place'. 27.27% of the respondents prefer organized musical sittings in presenting their songs.

The singers always feel that the different types of songs should be sung after maintaining the time-schedule meant for the purpose. The songs possess particular appeals which are conditioned by the specific time of presentation. The singers are under the obligation to follow this principle to maintain the ideal of song-based Baul philosophy. But during the present period most of the singers do not maintain this principle due to obvious reasons and naturally opinions regarding this have differed. In the Table No. 6.4, it is seen that though 71.57% of the respondents belonging to the Ascetic group feel that they should follow the strict time-based perspective in the presentation of songs yet 37.89% of them are able to maintain it strictly. 23.15% of the respondents try to follow these but fail to fulfil the condition completely. Amongst the Domestic category 40.59% do not feel the necessity for maintaining the time-based perspective of the presentation of songs, but some of them (15.84%) have reported that they follow it strictly. 17.83% of the respondents belonging to this category try to follow the principle as mentioned. The respondents belonging to the other category also show some inclination towards the traditional belief. 45.45% of the respondents have expressed their opinion in favour of time-based perspective of the singing of Baul songs, and 27.27% maintain it at their level best. The table also points out that a conspicuous number of the respondents have no definite idea about the situation in question.

The effort for maintaining the sanctity of the songs as per traditional background has now-a-days faced a challenge. In consequence of this, the outlook has been changed to a considerable extent. The impact of modernism characterized by various urban contacts have caused a great deal in changing the outlook of the Bauls. The popularity of folk songs and related folkloric materials is being increased throughout the world and these have received due importance in focussing the culture and historical perspective of a particular community or country. The different mass media like Radio and Television programmes have played a very important role in giving it wide publicity amongst all classes of audience.

The Baul singers belonging to the different categories have definite attitudinal behaviour--towards the programmes broadcast or telecast through the Radio and Television. A thorough investigation was conducted amongst the Bauls covering this attitudinal perspective. The results have been summarised in Table No. 6.4 It reveals that 65.50% of the respondents belonging to the three categories of the Bauls believe that the Radio/ T.V. programmes ennance the popularity of the singers amongst the general public, whereas a few of them (15.73%) think that

TABLE NO. 6.4

Attitude towards Radio/T. V Programme Popularity

Particulars	*Ascetic*	*Percentage*	*Domestic*	*Percentage*	*Others*	*Percentage*	*Grand Total*	*Percentage*
Popularity of the Singer enhanced directly by Radio/T.V. Programmes ..	50	52.63	73	72.27	27	81.81	150	65.50
Does not exert any influence on popularity by Radio/T.V. Programmes..	21	22.11	13	12.87	2	6.06	36	15.73
Baul songs become vitiated through these media ..	8	8.42	6	5.95	1	3.03	15	6.55
Not definite.. ..	8	8.42	5	4.95	1	3.03	14	6.11
Quite indifferent idea ..	8	8.42	4	3.96	2	6.06	14	6.11
Total ..	95	100	101	100	33	100	229	100

it does not exert any significant influence on the popularity of the singers. It is noted that amongst the Domestic category as many as 72.27% of the respondents feel that the popularity of the singers enhances through the Radio/T.V. programmes. It is for this reason they are very much eager to have the opportunity for broadcasting and telecasting their songs all through the time. 6.55 of the total respondents think that these programmes can do nothing but to vitiate the life of the Baul songs developed through traditions. Almost the same number of persons (6.11%) have got no definite idea and also quite indifferent ideas on the influence of these programmes.

In the Table No. 6.5, it is seen that 72.05% of the respondents belonging to all the categories consider it as a matter of profound prestige to broadcast and telecast songs through the media of Radio and Television. 81.18% of the Domestic Bauls support this view wholeheartedly. Out of the total respondents 18.78% do not possess any definite idea about these and only a few respondents (9.17%) consider the practice of broadcasting and telecasting of songs as an embarrassing matter. The Ascetic Bauls are to some extent (12.64%) show embarrassment in this affair, though 27.36% of the respondents exhibit indifferent attitude.

The present study reveals that in course of time one or two eminent Bauls have managed to go over the western countries to present their songs. They have been highly accepted by the people of those countries owing to the same reason--the deep appealing features in the songs and connected music performed through specialized musical instruments. Gradually more Bauls have procured the chance to present their songs in various western countries. Ultimately, it has been seen that amongst the public these foreign-returned Bauls, as well as the Radio and Television artistes have become the most dominating figures. This particular situation has attracted many Bauls who have been trying to get the chance to make themselves famous through the presentation of songs in foreign countries as well as in broadcasting through Radio and Telecasting through the Television sets. This changed world-view has brought conspicuous influence in the mode of behaviour of Bauls. Sometimes it has led to cause injurious effect on the life of the Bauls. During present time many young Bauls are looking for a chance to go over to foreign countries. It has become the centre of attraction of a large number of Bauls. It is very often seen that a good number of innocent and top-level Baul singers has fallen in the traps of some clever agents of Calcutta and have become frustrated after their return from the foreign countries. These agents are appreciators of Baul songs and have got good influence in making contact with the different countries. They generally move about from village to village, from *akhra* to *akhra* to search out the promising Bauls and on getting so they make contact with the different foreign countries for presenting Baul songs belonging to rural Bengal. It is, no doubt, an alluring affair for the rural singers and they readily accept the offer through any kind of personal contact with the agents. These agents, by means of their well-organized procedures, can manage to arrange different internationally famous stages for the presentation of Baul songs and thereby collect a very good amount of money through selling of tickets to the audiences. The Baul singers, the pivots of the whole arrangements, generally receive a nominal amount even after their completion of long-drawn programmes. Gour Kshepa, a famous Baul of Birbhum, is totally against this sort of arrangement. He himself went out to visit the different western countries and there he presented numerous songs at the well-known centres of the world. During the time, according to him, he was totally utilised by the organizers of India, who picked him up to the several countries of the world. He was even directed to present his songs at the busy road crossing. According to Gour, it is demeaning for the Bauls to present their songs in this fashion as these are not mere songs but are regarded as medium of propitiation to the God. These should be presented with due regard and seriousness. No doubt, there are many connoisseurs in these countries and he has received due respect from many persons; but the main intention of the organizers concerned was centred round the earning of money. After being misutilised, as he described it, in these foreign countries, Gour came back with nothing worth-mentioning in the perspective of his time-long *sadhana* in Baul way of life. Gour was of opinion that the allurement for going abroad and earning of profuse money had given a severe blow to the very interest of the Baul songs and singers. He expressed that he could get nothing in course of his long stay in European countries, rather he had been feeling himself empty-minded. He thought that he had gone against the regulations of Baul way of life and it naturally deviated him from the main line of Baul philosophy. He, in course of discussion, informed that a good number of young and promising Bauls were being attracted to this type of allurement and it caused a great deal in deviating the Bauls from their rich tradition. It must be resisted, said Gour, otherwise Baul community would be able to retain its hard-earned fame and cultural traditions.

In this connection another bitter experience faced by the *Pather* Baul Dinabandhu Das of Lakshmanpur *ashram* in the district of Howrah deserves mention. A few years ago a team from Japan visited India to study folk songs of this country. In course of their wandering through the rural areas they made contact with Dinabandhu Das and he was requested to present a few of his songs for recording them. Dinabandhu Das was taken over to Japan Embassy in Calcutta where the team arranged for an interview with him to be telecast in the Television programme of Japan and recorded a bunch of Baul songs. After this he left for his *ashram* at Lakshmanpur. A few months later, Mr. Bakshi, an employee of the Japan Embassy in Calcutta, gave him Rs. 500/- as his remuneration. Next year the said cultural team from Japan again visited India and they did not forget to make contact with Dinabandhu Das. Dinabandhu could collect from them that he had been awarded ten thousand rupees as his remuneration for recording the bunch of songs in a long playing disc record as well as for his interview with comments and discussions telecast through the television network of the country. Dinabandhu Das communicated his position to them and they were very much shocked to know the nature of evil activities of the middlemen in this respect. Their surprise reached the climax when they knew that the artist had not been given the particular disc record as a symbol of courtesy. It was lost in the midway. The interpreter, Mr. Unishi, gave the artist a hope on behalf of the Japanese team that on their return to their homeland they would immediately make an arrangement to send the record in question. Ultimately, Dinabandhu Das received the record as a token of regard but he did not receive the full payment due to evil activities of some middlemen.

It is high time to look into these affairs. From our extensive field survey we have come across a number of such phenomena. One close associate of the Bauls is of opinion that this sort of Baul-hunting by some sophisticated urban agents should be totally stopped forthwith so the innocent Bauls may not be distracted. As citizens of India, it is our national duty to go against this type of planned activities. It is quite natural that the Bauls, though not all, are eager to present their songs in the different countries and thereby earn good reputation. If some arrangements are made through the authentic and philanthropic organizations to help the Bauls in this connection, the Baul tradition, in the strict sense of the term, can be retained as well as the promising Bauls can be saved from frustration.

The Baul song is now at the cross roads. From our earlier discussions it has been cleared that the nature and extent of Baul songs is totally dependent on the time, society and environment of the Baul land concerned. Besides this the influence of personal life of the Baul concerned is seen to be reflected in the song. Generally it is felt that the two Bauls belonging to two different categories sing the same song in completely different ways even in the perspective of similar time and environment. In Baul songs the singers and the audience know each other which may be social, psychological or spiritual. It is for this reason the mental attitude of one is readily understood by the other. This is the uniqueness of Baul songs, and which is absent in other spheres of Indian musical traditions. It is seen that in classical music there must be a harmonious relation amongst the time of presentation, particular tuning, rhythm and the *raga*. In *kirtan* songs there must be the atmosphere of spiritualism associated with total absorbedness in emotion. But in Baul song there is no such bindings. These songs can be sung at any time and at any place. It can be attained to any situation and not only so, the untoward situation can be brought in favour of the song. Sometimes Baul songs are sung through the musical mood of *raga* of classical songs. It is also sung in the tuning of *kirtan*. The eminent female Baul Chintamani Das of Birbhum is expert in this line. Her nature of Baul song presentation deserves mention. She tries to exert spiritual emotion in her voice and with systematic clapping she creates passionate atmosphere. Gour Kshepa deserves credit in presenting Baul songs through the tuning and pattern of Santali music and dance. The Baul songs are extensively dynamic in nature and due to this these have experienced substantial alteration through the ages. Rabindranath extensively used this forceful nature of Baul songs in his numerous poetic works. Various rhythms and gestures of dancing patterns of the Bauls have influenced Rabindra-dance. Rabindranath did these deliberately, being highly attracted by the magnanimity of the Baul song and dance. The Baul songs spontaneously open the total perspective of life-situation because these are dedicated in honour of life. In consequence of this fact the Bauls are always able to bring under the sweet and melodious tuning the love, affection, desire, sorrow, despair and disappointment and give the song a full motion as if it is pulsated with life.

From an extensive field work throughout the region it is seen that at present the character of the Baul songs is rapidly changing. Though the central appeal remains the same; the wordings and tunings have witnessed tremendous change. The nature of the audience is also changing and the devoted Bauls hardly get any chance to present their songs from the core of their heart. Biswanath Das of Bolpur raised his voice strongly in this regard. He told that the present-day rural audience were being overruled by the *baboos* (urban audience) who came with tape-recorders at the different gatherings and started recording the songs one after another. They are not the genuine lovers of these songs and had no mind to show proper respect to these songs. It was for that reason Biswanath was reluctant to offer any song of spiritual importance in public gathering. He vehemently objected to the activities of these *baboos*, who were in the habit of enjoying the recorded songs during leisure time giving no respect to these.

A large section of the present-day Bauls have changed their line of action by accepting the professional musical programmes in the urban sittings. Most of the times the fake representatives of the Bauls are being introduced as the successful carriers of their artistic tradition. The fake Bauls sometimes find out various means to adopt different techniques to attract the minds of the present-day audience who are especially interested in superficial approaches. Ultimately, these songs with the impositions of various light tuning imitated from other spheres gain popularity. Many of the serious Bauls are of opinion that this 'popularity' of the Baul songs is exerting severe blow to the Baul songs as well as on the Baul community. The renowned and devoted Baul Pankaj Bandopadhyay has opined that this is not popularity but degradation of the Baul songs. The imposition of cheap tuning especially from the hit film songs to these is not only unfair but a criminal offense. The general listeners do appreciate this attempt and who have got no background of evaluating the essence of these songs take these as the rural trend of Baul songs. This must be stopped, otherwise the tradition will die out. The senior Baul Sanatan Das of Bankura showed his overall strong protest against that kind of distortion of Baul song, what was going on in the name of popularity. He was of opinion that the Baul songs were to be presented in a meditative mood which might necessarily be accompanied by rhythmic movement of the body through the following of categorical dancing gestures, *i.e., mudra.* In no circumstances these would be presented with 'jumping and twisting the body'' as this practice ultimately hurt the very interest of the songs. He depicted the practice like the taking of *Rajbhoga* after smearing it with dust and dirt. As one of the seniormost leading Bauls, he felt that had he got the power of stopping these cheap practices, he would have done it with immediate effect. But it was far from practicability. At present the Bauls have started their own publicity and are extensively hankering after overall popularity throughout the country. They have made themselves *Baul Samrat, Baul Raj* or *Baul Churamani* and the like. But the singing of Baul songs in a melodious voice does not mean that a person concerned is devoted and top-ranking Baul. The Bauls and the Baul singers do not mean the same thing. A devoted Baul may be good singer, but a reputed Baul singer may not necessarily be a devoted Baul in the strict sense of the term. A sincere Baul thus sings in the following way :-

Now, all say, I am Baul. Oh, brother, I am Baul
Search out your room and feel that there is no Baul
Oh brother, all are counterfeited, they move through the way
    So they have become precautious
    Their *sadhana* is totally baseless.

All are overwhelmed in staging comic songs
They do not want to get their own taste
    To satisfy the hunger exclusively they have dressed up
    And that is why they are devoid of *sadhana*.

So, to-day the imitation and drollery have become wisdespread
    Their emotional state is to be noted
    And having known it I have nothing to wonder.

All say I am the Emperor, the lightly-found realiser of Truth
    World-ruler is the subject of mine
    Aul, Baul and Sain.
What is the fun of *Kalikal*, Baul becomes the subject of all
    The bogus personality becomes King of Baul
    There is no Baul in the land of Baul.
Therefore, following the easiest path Jhingey Kshepa cries,
    Oh mind, Oh Gossain, look into
    the different affairs and evaluate varieties.

Now there is a tendency to come under the sphere of Baul life, though in reality they are far from it. They have got no *sadhana* and have taken the easiest way to get the support of the people. For this they do not hesitate to imitate the activities of the Bauls and show these outwardly for conquering people's mind. It is gratifying to note that in the land of Bauls there is no Baul. The Bauls have been subjects to some particular Baul Emperor which is beyond the motto of Baul life.

In connection with the discussions on the nature and extent of Baul songs another class of people come to the limelight. They are the composers of Baul songs. There are many Bauls who compose songs spontaneously. Despite their illiteracy, they are efficient enough to compose songs, put these in tuning and sing these in melodious voice. But all the Bauls do not belong to the category as will be clear from Table No. 6.1. A large section of them is to depend on the composers who are not necessarily Bauls. They are village bards and most of them are talented in this sphere of activities. They compose Baul songs of diverse nature which are sung by the Bauls. From our close study it has been gathered that the rural composers have a special quality of observing various facts of the social phenomena. Most of them are not sufficiently educated. But still they are distinguished from the general public of the locality by their special aptitude for composing poems. Special arrangements have been made to take long-term interviews with these village poets specially those who compose Baul songs. Though they do not follow the Baul way of life yet they are well-versed in this line of thinking. It is because of this reason these composers are able to present the exact nature of Baul thinking in their composed songs. Their clear understanding of the Baul philosophy places themselves in line with the Bauls and the latter do not feel and hesitation to use songs composed by these rural poets.

The composers, no doubt, exert great influence on the overall Baul culture as they are interlinked with the Bauls through the regular supply of songs. An investigation into the nature and extent of life and traditions of the Baul song composers who are the inevitable factors in the sphere of Baul way of life and activities has been conducted in this phase of study. The composers of Baul songs belong to two different categories (1) first group of composers follow the ascetic way of life and they try to understand the Baul philosophy through *sadhana*. With this personal experience they compose Baul songs of different types. These composers have got practical knowledge in tuning and other allied features. They are not only composers, but also they are the experts in setting these songs of music; (2) Second group of composers are the common men who have got natural ability of composing lyrics. They do not enter into the *sadhana* of the Bauls. They simply compose songs and according to the merit of these the Bauls of different categories put tune to these and thereby present these in various situations.

The Baul composers of both the categories have got specific role in the sphere in question. There are a few characteristic features in the line of composition of songs-

(1) The composers must have got clear-cut idea and self-consciousness on Baul philosophy;

(2) Power of direct observations on the different happenings of the world at large is essential;

(3) Various roles played by the society, surrounding sceneries and patterns of person-to-person interactions are to be assessed properly;

(4) Special ability to apply these understandings based on knowledge and observation in the composition of songs;

(5) The skill to create poetical beauty; and

(6) The technique of actual putting up of the simple example to clarify the complicated philosophy centring round Baul life.

These songs are not only the medium of recreation, but also these acts as the explorations of social and religious perspectives in the background of time and place. The songs bear the name of the composers. Sometimes the composers like to put name of their *Guru* in the songs. There are some songs where the name of both the composer and the *Guru* are found. It has been collected during field study that the present composers of Baul songs belong to varieties of people who range from school teachers to mere tea-stall vendors. In the midst of their multifarious activities they compose Baul songs through practical observations that are made in their day-to-day life. It is to be noted that these composers always play the roles of impartial observers of the man and society. These observations are seen to be reflected in the Baul songs through melodious language, sweet tuning and befitting symbolic representations. The following are the eminent as well as popular composers of Baul songs in the present area of investigation.

TABLE NO. 6.5

Broadcasting/Telecasting of Baul Songs and its Impact on the Bauls:

Particulars	*Ascetic*	*Percentage*	*Domestic*	*Percentage*	*Others.*	*Percentage*	*Grand Total.*	*Percentage*
Broadcasting and Telecasting of Songs are regarded as an embarrassing matter ..	12	12.64	8	7.93	1	3.04	21	9.17
Broadcasting Telecasting of Songs are the matters of full pleasure and prestige ..	57	60.00	82	81.18	26	78.78	165	72.05
Totally indifferent idea ..	26	27.36	11	10.89	6	T8.18	43	18.78
No clear idea ..	..	-	-	-	-	-	-	-
Total ..	95	100.00	101	100.00	33	100.00	229	100.00

TABLE NO. 6.6

Name, Residence and Occupation of Different Composers of Baul Songs

Sl. No.	*Name of the Composer*		*Village/Town*	*District*	*Occupational Pattern*
1.	Ashanandan Chattaraj	..	Hetampur	Birbhum	School-Teacher
2.	Sudhir Das..	..	Jaydeva-Kenduli	"	Mendicant
3.	Ajit Kumar Das..	..	Tikarbeta	"	School-Teacher
4.	Arun Bauri ..	..	Hetampur	"	Cultivator
5.	Aswini Kumar Dutta	..	Gargara	"	Shop-keeper
6.	Jaydev Das	..	Tapsspur	"	Cultivator.
7.	Thakur Das ..	..	Dubrajpur	Birbhum	School-Teacher.
8.	Tarak Das	..	.Jaydeva-Kenduli	"	Mendicant
9.	Durgapada Das ..	..	Labpur	"	"
10.	Ratan Kahar ..	..	Suri	"	Professional Singer.
11.	Bhupen Chakravorty	..	"	"	Service-Holder
12.	Barun Kumar Ghose	..	Khandagram	"	Do
13.	Radhamoy Goswami	..	Jaydeva-Kenduli	"	Mendicant.
14.	Nagababa	..	Do	"	Prophet
15.	Subhas Kaviraj	..	Do	"	Grocer.
16.	Subodh Banerjee	..	Koga	"	Service-Holder
17.	Kshudiram Sen	..	Bolpur	"	School-Teacher
18.	Amulya Das ..	..	Durgapur	Burdwan	Service-Holder.
19.	Jaydev Saha..	..	Jamalpur	"	Do
20.	Dhiraj Chakravorty	..	Ara Shibtala	"	Priesthood
21.	Prasanta Roy	..	Chittaranjan	"	Service-Holder
22.	Manohar Kshepa	..	Purulia	Purulia	Prophet.
23.	Gourishankar Maharaj	..	Dubrajpur	Birbhum	"
24.	Dilip Banerjee	..	Sonamukhi	Bankura	School-Teacher.

7

Bauls : Continuity and Change

In the previous Chapters and life the activities of the Bauls have been evaluated both in their traditional perspectives as well as in the spheres of changes that have taken place in the background of the impact of modernism. The realistic nature of Baul life has been focussed here through the empirical data collected by continuous field investigations. This work claims to be the first of its kind where the spiritual life of the Bauls has been tried to focus in the perspective of the realistic life led by them. It is seen that Baul way of life has created a tremendous impact on the society and culture of the people of Bengal. From the different spheres of study on the Bauls and their patterns of living it can easily be said that this mendicant group of people is inextricably interwoven with the life and thought of the rural folk. By virtue of their keen observations and integrated outlook they have formed a particular culture ecology, which deserves uniqueness in India. The Bauls, as has emerged from the previous discussions, follow a line of philosophy which is of a very high order. In course of their meditation they go through some concrete paths much complicated as well as very hard to follow. From their mode of life it is seen that they live in a universe of their own and do various secret *sadhanas* and there by prepare the solid boundaries for that close universe. Though there are some points of differences between the ascetic and domestic Bauls, the line of approach is more or less the same. Both categories move about in their own spheres that have been established on a deep - rooted philosophical principle. The Bauls are very particular about their *sadhana*, and are much conscious about the subject-matters of the Baul philosophy which are jumbled up by the infliction of diverse religious thoughts and ideas of both Indian and foreign origin. The Jainism, the Buddhism, the Hinduism and the Islamic features have found their way in the Baul philosophy. These great traditional materials made conspicuous influence on the folk culture as exemplified by the Bauls. The rural folk-mendicant group had been accepting the various thoughts and ideas of the different religious sects during their respective supremacy through the ages. The Baul way of thinking was characteristically liberal in its approach to view the world from the very beginning and it was all along keen in assimilating the ideas of others. It was because of this fact that the Baul culture became the store-house of many events of history. All the characteristic features of diverse religious beliefs had become so intrinsically integrated in this particular way of life that it ultimately assumed very complicated shape. At the moment it is very difficult to trace the nature and extent of impact of different foreign beliefs on it separately. The lack of sufficient historical data is one of the main difficulties in tracing out the concrete features of the cultural integration. This excessively impedes the drawing up of social history of the region during the long span of items. In consequence of this state of affair the scholars in this line have given diverse opinions about the origin and development of the Baul cult. Some say that the Bauls are nothing but the offshoot of the Buddhism, which in course of time, have taken up different philosophies of life and have acquired distinctiveness. But they are silent about the exact nature of branching off from the main analogies between the two--the Buddhism and the Baul cult and sometimes it becomes so close that there arises a tendency to believe that the latter has developed directly from the former. Being the highly spread and tremendously influenced form of religious belief, the Buddhism has become conspicuous at the time of tracing analogy between the two. As a natural consequence, it is taken for granted that the Baul cult has borrowed ideas from the Buddhism. The Buddhism at one time became so influential and thus made itself conspicuous in the life of the people of the region under study that it overshadowed all spheres of life and activities of the people. As a religion sponsored by the rulers of the land, the Buddhism could spread all its influence in the inner recess of life of the people. The Baul cult received various thoughts and ideas of Buddhism in its sphere not to achieve any special end as was the case with the common, but because of its all-embracing attitude the Baul cult assimilated many features of Buddhist life and meditation. Amongst the scholars of the former period there was a special tendency to explain most of the happenings of history in the background of Buddhism and similar other religious beliefs and practices. The large scale impact of Buddhistic ideas and thoughts of behaviour on indigenous patterns of life made them biased in thinking the whole phenomenon in the perspective of Buddhism. The concrete example in this respect as has been cited in Chapter 3 of the present book in connection with the exploration of the nature and extent of Dharmaraj - a rousing folk deity of the region. The Dharmaraj was considered by the scholars of that period the conspicuous Buddhistic deity because of the Buddhist nature of thinking attached to his worship. But after a thorough study through the nature of impact of the Buddhistic ideas and their individual elements, it became gradually known that despite many Buddhistic thoughts in the general mode of worship of Dharmaraj, he is nothing but an indigenous deity of rural Bengal. In course of his journey through the ages, the Dhrarmaraj might have received many Buddhistic beliefs through imposition. The impositions of different ideas cannot be properly analysed from their roots until and unless these are evaluated on an unbiased critical view-point.

In the Vaishnavite literature the frequent reference of the term 'Baul' is to be met with. It has been meant to understand a particular state of mind which is helpful in the adoration of God. When the devotee becomes free from all worldly affairs, he can uplift himself from the level of realistic life, *i.e.*, he becomes crazy or mad, he will be suitable in getting the grace of God. It is for this reason that the great Vaishnavite Sri Chaitannya Deva has been depicted as *Maha Baul* or Baul the Great. There are some indications in the life and living of the then period, that is, when Vaishnavism began to spread its influence over Bengal, that a community known as Bauls started inflicting its influence on the way of life of the people. The enigmatic rhyme sent by Adwaityacharya to Lord Gouranga through Pundit Jagadananda, proves the broad-based influence of the Baul way of life in the then society of Bengal. It runs as follows :-

> "Baulke Kahio, lokey haila Bāul
> Bāulke kahio, hātey na bikāy chāul

Bāulkey kahio, kājey nahika āul
Bāulke kahio, ihā kahiachhe Bāul''.

Tell the Baul that the people have embraced Baul way of life
Tell the Baul that rice does not sell in the market
Tell the Baul that do not keep indifferent attitude
Tell the Baul that is has been informed by the Baul''.

The internal meaning of this puzzling rhyme is nothing but the presentation of a realistic picture of spread of the Baul way of life amongst the people. People in large numbers were coming forward to embrace the Baul line of thinking. All of them started *madhukari* or begging, and therefore, there was no need of selling rice in the market. It was thus referred in order to communicate the gravity of the situation. In that state of affair Lord Gauranga was requested to shake off his indifferent attitude. The informer became very much impatiently eager to communicate it to Baul the Great, *i.e.*, Lord Gouranga.

Thus the Baul line of thinking ran parallel to the Vaishnavite way of life. In later periods due to large-scale impact of Vaishnavite life and thought on the people of Bengal many contemporary religious patterns had been effectively influenced. The Baul community was not an exception to this. It so happened that the community in question allowed all possible infiltrations of Vaishnavite thoughts and ideas into its own central line of thinking. Owing to the tremendous strength of conquering human hearts by dint of its philosophy of love the Vaishnavism could cast a layer of Vaishnavite thinking on the overall behaviour-patterns of the Bauls, the life-philosophy of whom was focussed on the similar background. In this way a large scale imposition of Vaishnavite idea was effected and especially it became deep-rooted in the western part of West Bengal, where Vaishnavism flourished to its full content, the Baul life was highly moulded by the direct impact of Vaishnavism. The Bauls are not offshoots of Vaishnavism as is popularly believed by many. It is true that at times the Vaishnavite idea can be so close to the Bauls that it seemed as if the two had been fused to form one single whole. On the other hand, many orthodox Vaishnavites were allured to embrace Baul way of life and as the Baul philosophy was also based on the principle of love, there was no difficulty in following the main Vaishnavite principle even after their coming into the fold of Baul life-ways. The Baul way of life can never be termed as the later development of Vaishnavism because of the fact that in addition to Vaishnava philosophy the Bauls follow many other aspects which are not included in the Vaishnava line of thinking. A few concrete illustrations may be put forward here to support this view. Firstly, the Bauls do not support pollution through physical contact and people belonging to all social categories are placed by them in the same level - according to them, there is no in-equality amongst the caste groups. They are always vocal to some extent, in this context through the singing of many songs composed in this line of approach. The Vaishnavas, on the other hand, maintain this concept of purity-pollution in their daily mode of life. There is a conspicuous feeling of inequality unlike the Bauls, amongst the Vaishnava believers. They readily contribute to the idea of social inequàlity based on the stratification of castes. Secondly, the Vaishnavas are the orthodox believers in the line of their own religious thinking. The love-philosophy of Radha-Krishna is considered by them as the sanctified feature of their religion and they, in no circumstances, believe in the integration of different religious ideas. They are the staunch believers in the Vaishnava line of thinking. But the Bauls sing in favour of religious integration - they communicate the idea of equality in man. The Bauls, with concrete Vaishnava influence, go against purity-pollution concept based on caste stratification. Thirdly, the Bauls possess, in addition to many Vaishnavite beliefs and features of action, various folk-based traditions that are not present amongst the orthodox Vaishnavies.It is for this reason the Baul religion is sometimes called as the various folk-religion. The Baul line of thinking is far-reaching in its nature and extent. The Vaishnavas' stand against the other religious factions like *Sakta* and *Shaiva*, and the former does not like to make a compromise with others. But the Bauls, on the other hand, behave in a completely different way. They always move in the line of total integration based on free exchange of ideas. It becomes very much illustrative when we come across the case of the Fakirs or in other words the Sufistic Bauls. These Bauls are the followers of Sufism and to a large extent they maintain the basic philosophy of the Bauls. They think that their origin is rooted to the same stalk as the Bauls and by some incidence they have been channelised through a distinct path. Whatever may be the distinction that exists between the Sufis and the Bauls, it is clear from the close set discussions in Chapter 5 that the Sufis resemble the Bauls in many respects and in one essential basic fature, *i.e.*, the infliction of love for humanity they are very close to each other. Owing to the excellent adaptive nature of the Bauls many Sufi-oriented ideas have found place in the Baul line of thinking. The Bauls, as a rule, do not exert any differential attitude towards the Sufistic Fakirs because of their bearing of different religious traditon. Rather they receive, in course of their wanderings with the Fakirs, many Sufistic ideas to implant these into their own. The songs sung by the Fakirs are based on parallel thinking with those of the Bauls. At times, they sing the love-philosophy of Radha-Krishna and the preachings of Chaitannya Deva on the love for humanity. The Bauls are seen to join their voices with them during these song performances. The Bauls regularly visit the different *majars* of the Muslim saints and pay their homage through songs. Thus the Baul line of thinking is seen to be packed up with many diverse and sometimes contradictory thoughts and ideas which have been received by it through the ages. The Baul ideas might have developed in the long time past and it took a particular shape before the advent of other religious and cultural spheres. At the very early phase of its development the Baul thoughts and ideas were wholly based on the folk religion. These were centered round the indigenous beliefs and practices. These, in course of time, had been heavily influenced by other spheres and owing to large-scale imposition of diverse thoughts and ideas the Baul line of thinking became highly complicated. It is due to this compliciated nature many scholars who came to throw light on the Baul way of life became misguided. Many of them tried to analyse the imposed ideas of different spheres of thinking or religion on the Bauls, and, taking these as the original matters, started discussing the general trend of the Bauls. Their attention was characteristically centered round the various imposed beliefs and ideas, and naturally the total effort went away from the exact situation. The Bauls have never been studied from the root of their developement though it is very difficult to trace it out. It requires inter-disciplinary research with the close support of the analytical study of the historical and contemporary societies and their lines of actions through multiple spheres of life. As has been already discussed in Chapter 1 of this book the Bual line of thinking should be focussed right from the advent of Aryanization of Bengal the particular phenomenon which brought conspicuous changes in the philosophy of life in the then Bengal with tremendous effect on the economy and religion. The social history of Bengal is highly characterized by the atmosphere of conflict and compromise and in order to understand the actual nature of it one should start studying from the very origin of it. The Bauls effectively play the role of the living history of Bengal as amongst them the clear indication of conflict and compromise of different thoughts and ideas is reflected. The Bauls have never been studied in this particular line of approach. The Baul line of thinking can easily be utilized as a specific methodology in finding out the trends of interactions of different diverse beliefs and ideas of Indian and foreign origin on the soil of India. The Bauls, no doubt, bear a high-level philosophical thinking and all the former works on this particular community have been highly focussed on this issue - these philosophical thinkings were carefully compared with those of the Upanishad and other religious texts, and the Bauls were evaluated in the background of these levels of understandings. In some work, though very negligible, there are, no doubt, some reference of the indigenous nature of the Bauls. A few scholars have pointed out that the Bauls represent the peasant community of Bengal. But no attempt has been made by anybody to focus discernible light on this point through concrete facts collected from mode of living.

From the factual evidences as laid down in the different chapters it can be said with certainty that the Bauls are the living emobdiments of cultural conflict and compromise. They are not the offshoots of any religious faction or cultural tradition. They developed independently long time past in the soil of India and are characterized by distinct features of their own which have been either covered up by other thoughts and ideas or totally metamorphosed to fit the situation.

The idea that the Bauls are closely related to the folk-Bengal can easily be established by a few points noted from field observations. These are such as follows :-

(1) The Baul singers collect the subject-matter of their songs mostly from the rural surroundings of Bengal. Even in high philosophical songs or discussions they set various examples from the folk society. In setting these examples the Bauls are very keen in drawing the concrete facts from amongst the insignificant spheres of activities that are performed in the day-to-day family life.

(2) From a thorough investigation it has been gathered that in most of the time the lower caste groups come to embrace the Baul way of life in large number. Though there are evidences of coming of the persons from high caste groups yet the trend of coming into the Baul way of life from the lower castes and communities is highly

noticeable. The Bauls all through the time maintain close think with the life and thinking pattern of these lower caste communities.

(3) After passing through a long journey for a continuous span of time, and in spite of facing so many obstructions caused by various untoward incidents of religio-philosophical standpoints, the Bauls still exert tremendous influence on the life and activities of the rural folk of Bengal. This influence is so integrated that it seems that the Bauls are the part and parcel of the rural sentiments of Bengal.

(4) Because of the genuine indigenous nature and inartificial folk-based outlook the Baul way of life is still inseparable from the life of that of the rural folk of Bengal when all other contemporary beliefs and ideas have already totally disappeared from the scene or at times have left a few residues of the original matters.

Through painstaking investigations into the Baul gatherings over a broad area and the behaviour-patterns of the attending people the above four points have been illustrated critically. The different descriptive accounts that have been given in the earlier chapters speak for themselves. These categorically highlight the depth of Baul way of life and how it influences the rural folk of Bengal irrespective of castes, classes and religion. This study has effectively shown the power of the Baul line of thinking in controlling the movement of the large mass of the rural folk. The Baul gatherings surpass everything in rural society. The people belonging to the rural society forget their basic needs and problems for the time being. The annual assemblage of the Bauls in a particular village or region engenders an atmosphere of co-operation and compromise. On the eve of any Baul *mahotsab* the stratified village society becomes an integrated whole and during the actual performance the stratification is obliterated for some time. Man is recognised as 'man' and not as a representative of any social or religious faction. During *mahotsab* at Jaydeva-Kenduli people forget the formality of invitaition to them, whereas in other spheres these rural folk are very much sensitive in respect of invitation during any assemblage. People belonging to all castes and classes, sit side by side to take food spread over the *sal*-leaf plates. At this time the Brahmin does not make any enquiry about the caste affiliations of the cooks and the distributors of food. He does not bother about the caste affiliation of the person who sits besides him. But he is the man who is very much alert about these enquiries in other fields of activities. The organisers of these ceremonial feeding centres are eager to collect the used leaf-plates to throw away these in the rubbish-heaps. The dining ground is cleared by themselves. In general cases, it is seen that when a person belonging to the lower caste takes food in the courtyard of a higher caste person, the former must clean the place of his taking food with cowdung and water. But in these *mahotsabs* there are occasions when the same higher caste people are unhesitatingly engaged in cleaning the place where people of the lower caste take food. It is really surprising how it happens in the rigid caste society of the rural folk. But it regularly happens like this. In Dubrajpur Darbesh *Ashram* the attending people from all higher caste-groups deliberately take the residues of boiled rice from the leaf-plates of the Bauls as *prasad.* These have been possible for the tremendous force of Baul philosophy of love and respect which obliterates all the social inequalities and closes down the formalities of castes and religion, of course, for the time being. This force is tremendous as well as far-reaching. Many people contribute to their mite for the service of man. And this man is really 'Man' in the strict sense of the term as he is not designated by any other artificial nomenclature like caste, class or religion. There is no denying the fact that owing to the high potentiality of the Baul line of thinking the formal rural society with diverse obligations has become free from all sorts of obstacles and man begins to serve man. During the period of these three days, it becomes the routine affair which acts spontaneously on the people as a whole.

This functional aspect of Baul life has not been taken up in any of the former studies so far made on this community. As a pioneering approach to this field the present study not only tries to explore the origin of the Baul cult but it devotees itself in the sphere of direct influence exerted by this cult on the life of the people as a whole. The Bauls have not been separated from the society in which they wander about, rather their mode of behaviour has been analysed and evaluated in the direct background of the folk society of Bengal. In so doing the day-to-day behaviour-patterns of both the groups--the Bauls and the rural folk, have been observed from close quarters through field study.

Amongst the three categories of the Bauls, the Domestic Bauls come very close to the people. They live in village homes and become the partners of the graded society of the villages concerned. The Ashramite Bauls are not so close. Owing to their nature and way of life these Bauls keep a distance from the rural folk. Though the *ashrams* are very often visited by these folk and they get easy access to these, yet there exists a distance between these two groups which keeps one away from the other. But the Domestic Bauls have a close interaction with the common folk. They move with the common people, work with them and share their joys and sorrows. The Bauls belonging to the particular category designated as Others are not given any such importance as is attached to the Ascetic and Domestic groups. The Domestic Bauls are very commonly found amongst the people all through the time. By gathering in-depth information from house to house it has come up that despite Baul way of thinking these persons do all the jobs the common people do. Many of them possess agricultural lands of their own and they are directly attached to cultivation. There are a few craftsmen who practise their traditional craft-based occupation. There are a few *bidi*-makers, some businessmen and daily labourers. All the necessary findings in relation to these have been summarized in the Tables of different nature that have been appended to the Appendix of this treatise. They conduct all these activities to maintain the respective families. The family members are not necessarily Bauls and they are free to perform any sort of work they like. But the Bauls belonging to these families must perform some definite duties. They should conduct the *sadhana* and should go out for *madhukari*. Those who have got melodious voice, regularly go out to present their songs in the trains and buses, and beg for payments from the audience. In the district of Birbhum this practice is largely met with. The Domestic Bauls in a considerable number travel in the trains on Andal-Sainthia and Rampurhat-Burdwan routes and sing melodious songs to the accompaniment of *gabgubi* and *ektara*. At times they travel in the Howrah - bound trains like Viswabharati Fast Passenger and Mayurakshi Fast Passenger and go up to Howrah Railway station singing diverse songs composed on the themes of the important events of the region. These Bauls very often come closest to the people during various economic activities, marriages of their sons and daughters and also during any sort of village feuds. But during *sadhana* they create a particular distance with the commoners and in this spheres they maintain their distinct entity. This is the nature of the double-sided roles played by these Domestic Bauls as has been discussed earlier.

The Bauls belonging to the different categories are, as a rule, against all sorts of social regulations. They do not support the traditional pattern of the society based on caste hierarchy. The Bauls are the worshippers of man and this man is not to be put in the scale of differentiation based on artificial social stratifications conditioned by the concept of purity-pollution. But this state of affairs of the Bauls has never been tested through personal interrogation or through close observations of their behaviour-patterns. The earlier authors in this line have take it as an eternal truth and with the support of the Baul songs concerned they have tried to enunciate this aspect of the Bauls as a universal behaviour-pattern of them. But the present study reveals that despite their sectarian identity the Bauls cannot remain strictly aloof from the social atmosphere of the society in which they stay and work. After personal enquiries made with as many as 227 Bauls, it has been collected that a good number of them still contribute to the general customs of the society in terms of caste and ritualistic patterns. Sometimes it acts in their unconscious mind. A particular Baul may talk and sing depicting the oneness of human being, but in his general behaviour he may be seen to act in a different way. 38.42% of the respondents still believe that the Brahmins are the supreme caste-group of the graded society. 33.62% of them used to support the caste hierarchical system in their former life and they had requisite respect for the caste-based regulations before entering into the sphere of the Baul way of life. Being born and brought up in the caste-based society and having the general trend of mind in favour of the rites and regulations, which are thought to be sponsored by the divine world, the Bauls cannot shake off all the prejudices of their former life completely. Though they have theoretically thrown away all the customs and behaviours of the former life at the time of entering into the Bauls mode of life, yet the subdued remains of prior thought work in the unconscious mind. It is readily proved when they wholeheartedly support the supremacy of the Brahmins and unhesitatingly place them on the apex of the society. The Bauls go against the religious differentiation. There may be a good number of religious groups and each group may have got many factions, but ultimately all these are directed to the common aim. So, there should not be any sense of differentiation amongst the religions. The Bauls continuously sing in favour of the trend of religious integration and they speak against all sorts of tensions and conflicts in respect of religious beliefs and practices. The Bauls stand side by side with the Fakirs belonging mainly to the Islam. They sing in the common tune and discuss the different philosophical aspects under the same roof. Sometimes it seen that the Bauls and the Fakirs smoke hemp from the common bowl. But the Bauls are seen to be reluctant in taking food materials from the hands of the Muslims. During my visit to the *majar* of Alam Saheb at

Durbrajpur along with a number of Bauls I came across this particular event. The *majar* was attended by a large number of devotees belonging to both the Muslim and Hindu religious groups. A large fair was held on that day and all the shops there belonged to the Muslim community. Being requested by me, one of the attending Bauls went out to arrange for some sea and snacks for all of us. But after making a round through the fair the Bauls came back and expressed his utter disappointment. He told that there was no shop in the fair belonging to the Hindu community. He expressed his reluctance to take any food materials prepared by the Muslims. When I told him that they did not support the existence of any difference between religions, as the Bauls were promised, as per convention, to throw away all sorts of social inequalities and differences. The Bauls present there accepted the principle and they readily admitted their usual mode of behaviour would be in favour of my point. In no circumstance, they should reject the food materials from anybody on the plea of caste or community affiliation of the person concerned. But the things work here in a different way. The Bauls especially the Domestic Bauls live in the midst of caste-based society, which is highly characterized by various social norms and traditions. As members of this society the Bauls cannot totally flout the different social regulations and allied norms. They are to engage themselves in different agricultural works as day labour, contract workers, or *bargadars*. During this period of work of Domestic Bauls, most of the time, come very close to their land lords and participate in various socio-ritual performances that are connected with cultural activities. In this period the Bauls are compelled to abide by the customs and practices of the region despite their ceremonial commitment to waive away the rigid social regulations creating differentiation in the society of man. The Domestic Bauls are to make connection with the common people for sake of arranging matrimonial alliances for their sons and daughters, who are not necessarily Bauls. Overandabove these, as members of the village, they are to pay respect to the village organization even if it is characteristically processed by multiple social regulations based on the differentiation of castes, classes and religions. Coming to the Ascetic Bauls, it is seen that they are to some extent in a better position compared with their Domestic counterparts. As *ashramites* they maintain more or less secluded life. But due to the impact of Vaishnavism the purity-pollution concept has largely developed in them. From the behaviour-patterns of the *ashramite* Bauls it has been observed that they mostly try to avoid the close company of the *Fakirs* because of their Islamic beliefs and traditions. Also they show their reluctance in coming to direct contact with the lower caste groups. A few eminent Ascetic Bauls have gone to the extent of describing their way of *sadhana* as parallel to that categorized in the different Vedic literatures. Being influenced by the customs and practices of the region many of them silently support the phenomenon of untouchability. While discussing with a number of renowned Ascetic Bauls at Kotasur *Ashram* premises, we found that they were very much active in the work of imposition of different ideas from the *Vedas* and *Upanishads* on the folk-based Baul ideology. These Ascetic Bauls do not devote much time in singing which is the principal means of Baul *sadhana*, and they perform the spiritual activities through deep-rooted meditation as prescribed in the Vedic way of metaphysical performances. The two Bauls were interviewed extensively along with a few others of the same nature during Kotasur *Mahotsab* as has been discussed in Chapter 3 of this discourse. They claim that they have been raised to a particular height and through processed *sadhana* they have reached a level of an ideal spiritual sphere - very often they quote verses from the *Upanishads* and the *Gita* during explaining various events of Baul life. These Bauls feel that they have become upgraded through the shaking off the indigenous Baul characters, like singing of songs of diverse nature, a fully vagabond life with easy access given to everybody and utter negligence in the maintenance of customary principle of the religious sphere. On the other hand, they have been tempted to pick up a number of characteristic principles of *sadhana* as are followed in the other religious spheres especially the Vaishnavism. Thus a slow process of *sanskritization* into the web of indigenous folk-culture like the Baul way of life has become conspicuous. These Bauls perform the following activities in addition to their other modes of work in connection with their following of Baul way of life:-

(a) They sing devotional songs very often to the accompaniment of *khol* and *kartal* (Cymbal), and rarely with *gabgubi*.

(b) They paint sectarian marks on their forehead and on different parts of the body with the holy clay of the Ganges just like Vaishnavas.

(c) They adore Radha-Krishna and consider this divine pair as their spiritual guide

(d) They conspicuously relate the abstract idea of *Maner Manus* to Lord Krishna.

(e) They very often try to explain the Baul *tatwa* or philosophy in the direct perspective of Sanskritized religious texts and reciting different Sanskrit *slokas* or couplets.

If we analyse the above characteristic features thus adopted by some Ascetic Bauls, it will be clear that these Bauls are trying to Sanskritize themselves through the embrace of Vaishnavite features and giving up of their original indigenous characters. The Bauls decorate their bodies with different paints and dress up themselves before starting musical performance. But in no circumstances they put sectarian marks of the Vaishnava sect under purely ritualistic background. Amongst the Bauls the love-philosophy of Radha-Krishna, Padmavati-Jaydeva, Rami-Chandidas in the only point of showing due respect but they do never install the images of the divine pairs for practical worship after considering them as their spiritual preceptor. The Bauls never come forward to explain their philosophy with the direct or indirect support of *Sanskrit shlokas* or extracts from the Vedic literatures. The Bauls present everything as well as make efforts to solve the problems by quoting of common worldly events of the surroundings and expressing them through songs understandable to everybody.

The four-tier system of the Bauls, as discussed in Chapter 3, has been affected due to the conspicuous trends of *sanskritization, modernization and westernization* of Baul way of life. The Bauls in the Class A are the concrete examples of *sanskritization*. The Vaishnavite traditions have exerted tremendous influence on the Bauls and many of them have picked up a number of thoughts and ideas from the Vaishnava traditions and have tried to mould the indigenous patterns of Baul life. Thinking in terms of Sanskritic texts and exposition of different ideas in the background of *Vedic* literatures are regarded by these Bauls as highly desirable. The Domestic Bauls, on the other hand, are to adjust themselves with the various social obligations that generally arise in course of their living within the village society along with their family members. But in spite of all sorts of unfavourable situations to maintain the rigidity of Baul way of life, these Domestic Bauls very carefully keep themselves away from the obligatory perspectives of social life. The Bauls belonging to these classes have long been exposed to modernism due to the impact of which a number of Bauls has come out of the traditional spheres of activities. They have been attracted to the various type of modern media of publicity like the Radio and the Television. As a consequence of this publicity a few of them attained popularity and by virtue of the multitude of specialitiesin Baul songs as well as the quality and ability of the singers concerned, a few of the Bauls have got the opportunity to travel abroad for presenting Bauls songs. Owing to the direct contact of western thoughts, especially during their visits to the western countries, the Bauls have developed many ideas and ideologies that are completely new and sometimes are contradictory to their traditional thoughts and behaviour. There are a large number of instances that the Bauls after returning from the western countries have thoroughly changed their characteristic way of life and a few of them have started wearing westernized mod dresses. These Bauls belonging to Class C (please see Chapter 3), have established a new world of their own with changed values and ideas, and they have done a great deal in creating a new class of Bauls (described as Class D), who have rushed to their side from the non-Baul substratum. Thus it is seen that various circumstances have made the Bauls to find out themselves in the different Classes though traditionally they are far from any class or group discrimination.

At present the scholars as well as laymen complain that there are no Bauls in the strict sense of the term. They go to the extent of the saying that the Bauls have been vanished from this land and what we see in fact in recent times is nothing but the distorted type of the Bauls. But this complaint is to be analysed in the perspective of the factual data gathered during investigations. The Bauls are regarded as the living embodiments of the society. A systematic look into the past reveals the fact that the Bauls have always been highly adaptable in adjusting to the changes of the society. The Baul community presents itself as an unparallel unit in the process of assimilation of diverse cultural patterns with a proper synthesis. It is for this reason the changes in Baul life are so conspicuous and sometimes these are so rapid that the human mind fails to cope with it. When this happens, people complain for the non-existence of the Bauls with traditional cultural patterns. The Bauls were present in the former days and they are still in existence in full form. But during recent years the changes have occurred in many spheres emanating both from indigenous and foreign influence. Owing to the abrupt and continuous changes in the surroundings the Bauls have been successively moulding their forms and functions. From the mass of collected data it can be easily said that despite all sorts of changes the Baul way of life is continuous with its traditional patterns together with the new developments conditioned by the adjustments with changed sets of values of the society as a whole. The continuity of Baul way of life is conspicuous in different perspectives.

The Bauls irrespective of class or category, are dependents of *Guru*. The Guru-based philosophy of the Baul is still prevalent as before. The *Guru* is the path-finder of the Bauls and in all sorts of problems they approach the *Guru* for solution. The three different *Gurus* of three different types perform their joint activities on an individual Baul to make him fit for following the Baul way of life. The Bauls, every time sacrifice themselves at the feet of the respective *Guru* in their long-term *sadhana*. The *Guru* plays the role of a teacher and he teaches everything right from the procedure of *sadhana* up to the sexual behaviour. He teaches the Bauls to become always alert in adjusting everything with smiling face. They are specifically forbidden not to feel dissatisfied with any situation even if it goes against his personal interest. He must be alert in solving the whole situation by light talks but with due firmness. This sort of teaching of the *Guru* is still going on in the different *ashrams* or *akhras* of the Bauls.

The Bauls, in spite of many unfavourable circumstances, are equally active in the overall performance of their songs of different nature as before. They feel it as essential duty from the core of their hearts to attend different *mahotsabs* and fairs in connection with the Baul assemblages that are held all over the region. The Bauls of all the categories and from different localities flock, in large number, to various fairs and festivals. Recently the intensity of the Baul attendance is on the increase to their tradition-bound conferences. The Bauls still actively participate in singing the songs of religious integrations. They are even to-day the successful embodiments of circulation of the waves of compromise and tolerance in the minds of the general public. They communicate to the people the message of universal brotherhood. In their melodious songs Buddha, Jesus, Nanak, Mohammad became integrated to form a single whole. There is no different meaning and feeling for Ram, Allah, Hari, Kali and God. In these songs and also in the skilful presentations by the Bauls a beautiful compromising atmosphere prevails which reaches the inner recess of the hearts of the people. They advocate for the obliteration of untouchability because no man can be called inauspicious for the body of each man is the abode of God. The Baul is in communion with him at the extreme moment of his *sadhana* through song and dance, and he is known to the Baul as the Man of the Heart. When same type of Man of the Heart resides in every man, can one man be differentiated from the other by creating artificial barriers of caste, class or religion? The whole of the Baul philosophy centre round this pertinent question. Thus it is evident from the activities and thinking patterns of the Bauls that they have been contributing a deep-rooted feeling of national as well as international integration from time immemorial. They have been highly sensitive in propagating the feelings of universal brotherhood despite their lack of actual knowledge about the world due to illiteracy and other such limitations.

The Baul songs possess a rich cultural heritage and these are regarded as the invaluable wealth in the sphere of music and dance in this tradition-ridden country. From the presentation and overall analysis of a few representative and frequently sung Bauls song in the Chapter 7, it is manifested that the Baul singers have always tried to attract the attention of the folk listeners through the imposition of simpler life-situations in their everyday life. The Baul, in course of his singing of various songs, explores many events of the society. He sings for the praise of his *Guru*, he sings for the universal unity after spurning all the petty differences and boundaries. He sings against the caste discrimination and religious bigotry. Sometimes he points out the impermanence of life and thereby asks human beings to be wide awake. It is futile to desire anything more than your actual need. In this way the Baul works as the active factor for providing recreation to the people as well as he acts as their teacher. Thus they are the social teachers and they have been performing their specific duties spontaneously for the betterment of the general people.

Lately, there have been some changes affected in the total Baul culture. After the direct intervention of some unscrupulous agents from the urban settings into the Baul life a conspicuous alteration has set in. In Chapter 7, it has been pointed out that owing to the frequent visits of the Bauls to the different western countries, a "Fortunate" group has been evolved amongst them. They, by virtue of their tour and the opportunity for presenting the songs on the renowned stages of the world, have become famed and have begun to mould the songs and dances with the authoritarian motives. This particular act, on their part, has pained the orthodox Bauls much as they cannot withstand their act of twisting the originality of the songs and dances for gaining cheap popularity. In this way a wide gap has been created between the two sections of the Bauls. It is indeed a very bad indication and it must be nipped in the bud, if it is desired to maintain the rich cultural heritage of the country in its flourishing condition. The Bauls, who have gone abroad and earned due prestige and sufficient money, are not at all satisfied. From the various discussions in Chapter 7, it is evident that the foreign-returned Bauls feel embarrassed after coming back to this country. Their mental aptitude has been studied in full detail and by this it is understood that excepting a negligible number, all of them have been suffering from deep mental agony. Some say that they have been cheated by the agents. They admit that they have had to pay in terms of spiritual and mental wealth to get insignificant material benefit. This psychological conflict amongst the Bauls has made them practically imbalanced and infirm in the compact sphere of Baul life and activities.

The changes in Baul life are inevitable. The total canvas has been changed resulting from the alterations in the social perspectives. The Baul life had flourished in the background of the agriculture-based village society, where there was a dominant role of the village zamindars, the village headmen, and others in patronising them. In the lower sections of the community, the unlettered people were the principal connoisseurs. They used to extend their all sorts of co-operation including the regular contribution of crops for meeting the expenses incurred in the performances of songs and dances. But with the abolition of zamindary and the promulgation of Land Ceiling Act the age-old patrons became inactive. So to speak, owing to the sudden decrease of income from the agricultural fields. The agriculture-based patronization is being gradually transferred to the intellectual-oriented patronization. The intellectual patrons are very keen in the evaluation of Baul songs in the perspective of the national and international purchasers of manufactured merchandise. The advent of the educated and intellectuals as Baul-lovers has done a great deal in making the original and inherent art of the Baul as mere merchandise of the market under the total unawareness of the Bauls themselves. This particular untoward situation in Baul life, vis-a-vis, the rich cultural heritage of the country needs direct intervention of all the genuine well-wishers to save it from vitiation. It has been observed after thorough investigation of the situation that though the process of this sort of transformation of the philosophical indigenous songs and traditions of the Bauls into the profit based elements of art in the world market is slow, it is deep-rooted and we are afraid, this state of affairs would prove itself far-reaching in no time.

In fine, as a living embodiment of the rich cultural heritage of the country the Bauls need all-rounded protection from decay or distortion as well as effective nurturing of their highly valued philosophical principles based on the universal brotherhood of mankind. It is, no doubt, our sacred duty to give proper importance to these spontaneous and living heritage developed and communicated by the Bauls to the countrymen through the ages. In order to do this the following points are to be categorically noted with all due care and seriousness.

(a) The spontaneously providing of the message of cultural integration by the Bauls should be properly evaluated in their proper perspectives and these are to be effectively applied to the diverse Indian society.

(b) Proper publicity should be given to the basic philosophy of the Bauls based on the love for humanity, and due honour should be attached to these worshippers of man.

(c) The Baul community vis-a-vis their philosophical principles based on easiest understandings need be protected from distortion and destruction for the cause of national integration.

(d) The Baul community has never been given any befitting importance despite its silent work for the country and the people. It is high time to throw discernible light on the people belonging to this community still working against many adverse situations. All possible efforts should be made to help them in flourishing with full form, otherwise a rich tradition of the country will die out.

(e) The songs and dances of the Bauls are gradually vanishing with time. Though the new forms and patterns are emerging yet the old traditional techniques practised by the veteran singers are disappearing at a rapid pace. The different typical gestures of dancing by the Bauls are providing with special significance, and, it is to be noted, that this particular time-long art is vanishing. These deserve immediate recording and subsequent preservation.

Glossary

Achin Pakhi : The Unknown Bird. It indicates the Supreme Being which is considered incognito and without a particular form. The term 'Achin Pakhi' is frequently referred in the songs sung by the Bauls.

Adhar Manus : The Man Untouchable. It is represented by the Supreme Being and is out of direct reach of ordinary man. His existence is to be felt through deep meditation.

Adiguru : The Primary Preceptor.

Ajan Chakra : It is the highest Chakra situated in the human body just at the centre of the eye-brows.

Akhra : : This is seen in different villages and in the religious-Baul Centre. This is seen in different villages and in the religious spots throughout the region.

Alekh : It refers to the Supreme Being which cannot be described outwardly.

Alkhalla: A long loose type of garment used by the Bauls and Fakirs. It covers the body from the shoulders and hangs down the knees.

Ananda bhava : Blissful mood of joy.

Arhi : A measuring basket made of canes. It is extensively used in this region of study in measuring paddy.

Aryanization : The process of infliction of the thoughts and ideas carried by the Aryan -speaking groups on the indigenous communities in India. The direct and indirect impacts of this process have caused multifarious changes in the life and living of the indigenous caste groups.

Ascetic Baul : The Baul who strictly follows the mendicant life of *sannyasa* type. They stay in the *ashram* and perform ritualistic activities through rigid discipline.

Ashram : Celebrated hermitage. It is the essential feature of Baul life. They should perform all their activities of *sadhana* in *ashram* established by themselves or by others.

Atal Manus: Man Immovable.

Atma : Soul.

Aul : A particular category of the Bauls. The Muslim-originated Bauls are generally known by this term.

Aulia : The *Guru* of the Auls is known by this term.

Baka : One of the two principal aims of Sufism which is centred round the existence in the attributes of God.

Baul Sangit : The songs sung by the Bauls. They are of different types and impregnated with high philosophical thinking put forward in simple language though in twisted patterns. The subject-matter of these songs embraces multifarious fields of human life and activities. The songs are the real medium of Baul expression.

Bhaber Manus: Man of devotion.

Bible : The Christian Scripture.

Buddhism : The religion which has been established through the teachings of Lord Buddha. It is divided into many internal factions, each of which is characterized by some basic principles. The Buddhism exerted many-sided influence on the Baul cult during the former's flourishing phases in the soil of India, especially in the eastern part of the country.

Chadar : It means a sheet of cloth worn over the body. The sheet of fine cloth or *chadar* is ceremonially covered over the celebrated burial of the Muslim Saints by the devotees. It is a regular ritual followed by the Muslims. The offering of *chadar* is performed through colourful procession of the devotees associated with music.

Chaitannya Charitamrita : The celebrated poetical work in Bengali depicting the life and works of Chaitannya Deva written by Sri Krishnadas Kaviraj. It depicts in a broad perspective the life and thought of the people of Bengal during that period.

Chaitannya : One of the incarnations of the Vaishnava sect of Hindu religion. He was the founder of Gauriya Bhakti Yoga.

Chakra : The etymological meaning of this is wheel. It also indicates the network. The network of nerve centres in the body signifies the stages of spiritual development according to Tantra. These nerve-centres are the secret forces of the body.

Chandidas : A Vaishnava poet of legendary fame. He was famous for composing the book, entitled *"Vaishnava Padabali"*, depicting the love-based perspective of the Vaishnava religious ideas centering round Radha and Krishna--the Divine Pair.

Charichandrabhed : The etymological meaning of this is piercing of the four moons. It is an essential rite which is to be parformed in connection with the Baul *sadhana.* The four essential elements of the human body like semen, menstrual flow, stool and urine represent four moons. In a ceremonial performance the *Sadhika* and the *Sadhak* exchange these elements between each other, of course psychically. By doing this complete control over the body and mind can be established.

Dama : Action of breathing. It is a specialized form of *Pranayama* practised by the Bauls. Controlling capacity of *Dama* is regarded as the essential quality of the Baul without which he will not be able to exert his influence on the body.

Damer Manus : This represents the sincere and serious activities of the Baul arising through the action of breathing. Only the successful Baul can be able to feel His existence in the body.

Darbesh : A section of the Bauls. They are regarded as the *Gurus*, who, by vrirtue of their meditation, have reached the highest phase of *sadhana*.

Dehatatwa : The information and knowledge relating to different parts of the body and their integrated actions. The Baul songs that are composed on the subject-matter relating to the bodily aspects of man are known by the term 'Dehatatwa' songs. These are highly illustrative and pinpoint many secret events of human body.

Dharmaraj : A village deity seen extensively throughout the region under study. Both Brahmin and non-Brahmin priests perform his worship. In the patterns of worship of Dharmaraj the mixture of indigenous non-Aryan beliefs and Brahminical ideas is clearly seen to exist. This folk deity reflects the various stages of the slow process of Aryanization in the region of study.

Dhenki : The husking lever, extensively used in this region for husking paddy.

Dhuni : The sacred fire kindled with the help of heavy logs of wood by various types of saints during their stay and *sadhana* at a particular place.

Diksha : Initiation.

Diksha Guru : The Preceptor who gives intitiation to the Baul.

Domestic Baul :The Baul, who stays with his family even after his initiation and maintains family life all through.

Dotara : It is a four-stringed long-necked lute. A piece of goat skin covers the belly of this instrument. It is played with the help of a plectrum.

Dugi : The Kettle-drum. It is tied to the waist of the Baul singer while singing.

Ektara : It is so named because of having one string which is plucked by a wire plectrum fitted to the index finger. The belly of the instrument is constructed by an open-headed calabash. Sometimes it is also made of metal container. The neck is constructed by a metre-long bamboo which is split down the middle part. The two halves of the split bamboo neck are then attached symmetrically at the open end of the calabash or the metal container as the case may be. It is also known as *Gopijantra*.

Fakir : The Muslim Saint who follows Sufistic philosophy. These Fakirs are popularly known as the Muslim-variants of the Bauls. In their overall way of life these Fakirs come very close to the Bauls. In addition to performing various ritualistic activities the Fakirs prescribe and supply medicines of various diseases to the suffering public.

Fana : One of the two principal aims of Sufism. It is the total annihilation of the individual existence.

Folk deity : The deity propitiated through indigenous rites and rituals. Most of the time non-Brahmin priests worship this type of deity. The performance of worship is largely attended by the people belonging to the lower levels of Hindu society.

Freud : The famous psychologist who propounded the theory that all human activities are centred round sex-motivated and sex-oriented perspectives. The Bauls also believe in the sex-linked activities of human thoughts and ideas and their untiring effort is maintained in rechannelizing this sex-instinct to a high perfection.

Gabgubi : It is a kind of musical instrument, very commonly used by the Bauls. It is a plucking drum which is provided with a pair of gut strings attached to the foot-long drum with one head. This drum is held at the left side of the body under the left arm. The gut string is kept stretched. It is struck heavily by a plectrum and various vibrations are created by tightening and releasing the gut string. It is also known as *Anandalahari* or *Khamak*.

Ganja : Hemp. It is extensively used by the Bauls in smoking all through the time.

Gita : The celebrated song of life as expressed by Lord Sri Krishana Himself in the battle-field of Kurukshetra in front of Arjuna, the third Pandava of the Mahabharata fame. It has got profound impact of Vaishnavism, which, in turn, exerted tremendous influence on the Baul way of life.

Gosain-Ma : Gosain is the master in the Vaishnava sphere. The mistress is known by the term 'Gosain-Ma'.

Grihastha Ashram : The celebrated hermitage that is established in the family perspective. The Domestic Bauls perform their *sadhana* in the *Grihastha Ashram*.

Guru : The spiritual preceptor. *Guru* is held in the highest esteem in Baul way of life. He works as the mediator between man and the Absolute Being. The Bauls are to take initiation from different sections of *Gurus* and the former cannot move in the spiritual world without direct instruction of *Guru*. The *Guru* inserts the perfect form of realization in the minds of the Bauls.

Gurubar : Thursday. It is the day recognized through *Brihaspati* or Jupiter. The *Brihaspati* is known as the Preceptor or *Guru* of the gods. This is why the day is very often called *Gurubar*.

Guruvad : The doctrine of *Guru*. It is seriously followed by the Bauls in their day-to-day life and *sadhana*.

Hari : The name of Vishnu. The Bauls praise in the name of Hari by chanting the words "Hari Hari Bol" during the presentation of songs.

Hinduism : It is a kind of religious idea based on the Vedas and Puranas. It developed in India and at present, majority of the people of India follow Hinduism. The Bauls are directly influenced by the various trends of Hinduism.

Ida : It is a nerve current situated along the left side of the spine. The Bauls are very conscious about the workings of this nerve stream in the body.

Indriya : Sense organs. In Baul way of life the sense organs are given very much importance. According to them, these are to be perfectly known and subsequently controlled for trouble-free *sadhana*.

Islam : The religion that had been founded by Prophet Mohammad. A large number of people belonging to Islam have come under the Baul way of life through Sufism.

Jainism : A religious idea which took its formation through the teachings of Mahavira. In India it spread significant influence before Buddhism, broadly flourished in this country. In this religious belief more important is attached to man than to God. In this perspective the Bauls come very nearer to Jain thoughts and ideas.

Jayente mara : Death while alive. It is a particular phenomenon when the Baul reaches the level of deepest *sadhana* and ultimately loses his material existence. It indicates the mixing of the self with the Ultimate Being or in other word it is known as *'samadhi'*.

Jivatma : The finite soul in the human body.

Jyoti : It means the glow of light. In Bauls songs the word 'jyoti' is expressed in the full understanding of the world unknown.

Kaliyuga : According to the Hindu Shastras the stages of life on this earth are divided into four eras. *Kaliyuga* is one of those four eras which is continuing at present.

Kartabhaja : Karta means master of the family. *Kartabhaja* is a religious sect, the members of which perform their *sadhana* centering round the *Guru*, who is known by the term 'Karta' of the sect.

Katha : A measure of land. One katha indicates 320 sq. cubits of land.

Khirpa : A kind of dress with multicoloured patches used by the Sufi Saints.

Khanjani : The tambourine. It is sometimes used by the Bauls during singing performances.

Kirtan : The devotional songs sung in the praise of Radha-Krishna, Netai-Gour in the Vaishnava sphere.

Krishna : An incarnation of the Divine Sage, Narayana, who was one of the chief characters of the Mahabharata. The Baul philosophy is very much influenced by the love-oriented activities of Krishna with his consort Radha.

Kshepa : The literal meaning of this is mad. The Bauls identify themselves as *kshepa* or mad in the perspective of *sadhana*.

Kulachar : In Tantra the *kul* indicates the genital organ of woman. Thus the *achar* or rite relating to the *kul* or women is known as *kulachar*.

Kula Kundalini Sakti : It is a passive female force and is represented by a coiled serpent power. The Kundalini is sometimes called Jogamaya--a passive famale force characterized by the potential power of creation.

Kumbhaka : It is the suspension of exhalation and inhalation. It is extensively practised by the Bauls for controlling the courses of the vital wind.

Lalan : Lalan was a reputed Baul in East Bengal, who was popularly known as Lalan Fakir. According to some, Lalan came from a Hindu family though in later years he came under the fold of Islam. It is for this reason his life and philosophy are highly characterized by sober restraint on the controversial religious and caste problems. The name of Lalan in the Baul world has become a legend owing to multifarious ideas on the Baul way of life.

Lalan Gitika The lyrics composed by Lalan. He had the credit of composing more than a thousand songs on different subject-matters.

Lotus : The concept or Lotus or Padma in connection with human body highly characterizes the Baul philosophy. Different petalled lotuses starting from four to one thousand are seen at various important spots of the body. Each of these lotuses bears special meaning in the perspective of Yogic principles.

Madhukari : The celebrated act of begging from door to door like the bee gathering honey from flower to flower.

Mahamilan : The great union.

Mahotsab : The etymological meaning of it is the great festival. In colloquial language it is known by the term *'machhab'*. The *Mahotsab* is centred round the charitable supply of cooked rice and vegetables to the people along with the Bauls. These *mahotsabs* are the lively centres for enjoying Baul songs and feelings the Bauls way of life from close quarters.

Mahabharata : The Great Epic of India which focusses the multiple facets of Indian tradition. The values, attitudes and modes of behaviour of the people in general are clearly discussed here with critical and analytical outlook. The Baul way of life has drawn various thoughts and ideas from this Great Epic from time to time by means of which the particular pattern of life has been highly influenced by the variegated traditions as depicted in the Great Epic.

Majar : The celebrated burial place of the Muslim Saint. The *majar* is regularly visited by the people belonging to both the Muslim and the Hindu communities. The *majar* plays the role of establishing integrated outlook amongst the people with great inequalities.

Man of the Heart : The ideal of Baul life is centred round the Man of the Heart or *Maner Manus*. The human body is regarded by the Bauls as the sacred abode of the Absolute who cannot be understood through knowledge and intellect. It can be perceived only through subjective understanding. The Bauls are in the continuous search of this *Maner Manus* without whose perfect realization the Baul *sadhana* ends in futile attmpts.

Mancha : Platform. The raised platforms are constructed in the various Baul dominated fairs and Baul assemblages for presentation of Baul songs and dances.

Mela : Fair. The lively assemblage of diverse people on a particular spot centering round some special events or phenomena. In these assemblages sale and purchase of various commodities establish the economic perspective on a well-knit pattern. There are so many fairs which are attended by such a large number of Bauls that these readily turn into what is called Baul fair.

Mohanta : The head of a monastery.

Mudras : The gestures of dancing. The Bauls show various gestures while dancing and singing which are unique in their presentation.

Muladhar Chakra: The lowest chakra in the human body is known by this term. It is believed to exist in between the rectum and male organ in the abdominal region.

Murid: The disciple in the Sufistic perspective is called as *Murid.* The *Murshid-Murid* relationship in the Sufistic *sadhana* is based on a high esteem.

Murshid: The Preceptor in the Sufistic belief is known by the term 'Murshid'.

Nearar Fakir: The Fakirs who shave their heads. The shaven-headed Buddhists came under the influence of Sufistic beliefs caused by religious interactions of tremendous nature. Ultimately, the Buddhist personnel embraced the way of the life of a Fakir and continued the original practice of shaving the heads.

Nerha-Nerhi: Etymologically it means the male and female persons with shaven heads. But actually it indicates the community of devotees who came under the influence of Vaishnavism directly from Buddhist sphere through the direct initiation by eminent Vaishnava Saint.

Natmandir: The structure raised by means of wooden poles or brick-built pillars and thatched with straw or corrugated iron sheets in front of the temple of the deities. Generally, Kirtan and other devotional songs are organised here. It also plays the essential role of a public place where various discussions on intra-village and inter-village levels are seen to be made.

Parmatma: The Supreme Soul or God.

Pingala: The nerve current which flows inside the right side of the spine. The Bauls are alert all through the time in respect of the internal workings of this nerve current. All these are reflected in the Baul songs.

Pir: The Muslim Saint.

Pous-Mela : The fair which is held in the Bengali month of *Pous* (December-January). The fair held at Santiniketan on the 7th of *Pous*, which is the foundation day of this Institution, is popularly known as *Pous-Mela*.

Pous Sankranti : The last day of the month of *Pous* (December-January). It is a very auspicious day as it marks the end of *Lakshmi-Mas* or the month of Lakshmi. A large number of fairs, festivals and household ritual performances are held on this day.

Prakriti : Etymologically, it means Nature. Sometimes it is regarded as the phenomenal world conceived as a feminine entity. In the Baul thought Prakriti stands for female consort of the male saint.

Prana : The life force. It is highly influenced by the multifarious principles working internally to give rise to this integrated whole. The Bauls try to feel these interactions through their deep-rooted *sadhana*.

Prasad : The consecrated food offered to the deities during worship. The *Prasad* is believed to have some effective qualities in the ritualistic standpoint.

Puraka : It is one of the three vital winds of the human body.

Purusha : Stands for male. This *Purusha* in association with *Prakriti* has given the shape of this living world. Both are inevitable in the domain of life and to maintain it through the ages.

Radha-Krishna : The Divine Pair formed on the principle of deep-rooted love. In Vaishnava philosophy this means the mood of highest *Bhava*. Bauls have characteristically adopted this principle in their eternal philosophy.

Rashik Vaishnava : The Vaishnava-oriented devotee, who follows the divine principle of love in their day-to-day life. The Vaishnavite mendicants in and around Nabadwip form a definite community with specific characteristic features of love philosophy. This community is especially known as *Rashik Vaishnava*.

Rechaka : It is one of the three vital winds of the human body. The Bauls are very much attentive and serious in having a close knowledge on this wind to make an effective control over the body.

Ripu : Vices. There are six important ***ripus*** or vices in the human body. The Bauls always keep themselves alert about their existence and their evil influence on the activities of man. According to them, these *ripus* stand in the way of man's progress towards achieving Ultimate Reality.

Rudraksha : A kind of dried fruit which is used as a bead. The rosary is composed of these beads for using it is meditation.

Rupa and Svarupa : *Rupa* means form and the *Svarupa* indicates real nature. Every aspect of life has got these two features and until and unless these are evaluated properly, the realization will not be completed. The manifested and metaphysical existence are found to be reflected in the *Rupa* and *Svarupa*, respectively.

Sadhaka : The person who is engaged in meditation through the following of systematic principles.

Sadhika : The female meditator.

Sadhana : The course of spiritual practice. It is followed through rigid procedures.

Sadhu : The saintly person who dedicates his life for the adoration of God.

Sadhanbhumi : The place for performing austere ascetic practice.

Sahaj : Sahaj means easy. It also indicates the inborn, normal of natural as well as divine beloved.

Sahajiya : The Buddhists were the pioneers in giving the first shape to the Sahajiya concept of *sadhana*. At one time Buddhists started infusing *yoga* with sex so that this could be conducive to have higher realization. In course of time, the concept of Sahajiya passed on to the Vaishnavas.

Sahajyana : The Buddhist sect which came forward, first of all to imbibe *Tantra* into their doctrine of *sahaj*. Sahajyana is the last stage of *Tantric* Buddhism. In Sahajyana there is no place for worship of the deities, recitation of *mantras* and other connected rites.

Sahasrara : According to the meditational theology, the top of the head is looked upon as the ultimate goal of *sadhana*. It is here where the highest realization is effected. This is imagined to be the spot where the holy union of Siva and Sakti takes place. A lotus of thousand petals is believed to exist here.

Sahaj-Manus : Etymological meaning of this is Easy Man. Through the complicated path of sexo-yogic *sadhana* the Bauls feel an extreme pleasure of reaching the highest level of meditation. The *sahaj-manus* is regarded as the outcome of sincere and serious activities relating to the Baul cult. It is practically a state of mind which results from the overall satisfaction through the celebrated union of *Prakriti* and *Purusha*. *Sahaj-Manus* is also known by the term *'Bhaber-Manus'*.

Sain : One of the four categories of the Bauls. They are totally mendicant and wander about in search of the Man of the Heart without following any rigid path.

Samadhi : Self-absorbed meditation. In this state the meditator becomes completely lost in the sphere of *sadhana* in body and mind. During this time he is out of any external senses about the materialistic world around him. The

Ascetic Bauls very often observe this sort of *sadhana* and through it they enjoy a mood of divine pleasure.

Šangit-Guru : The Preceptor who teaches songs.

Sannyas- Guru : The Preceptor who gives initiation to *Sannyas* life.

Sannyasi : The man who has attained divine grace through austere religious practices.

Siksha-Guru : The Preceptor who imparts teaching of the Baul way of life.

Sinni : It is colloquial corruption of the term 'Sirni'. It means an oblation of sweets offered to deities or to the spirits of deceased holy persons.

Sevadasi : The female consort of the Ascetic Baul is known as *Sevadasi*. She acts as the helper of the Baul concerned in the smooth performance of the devotional practices. The relation between the Baul and his *Sevadasi* is not always well-knit though a good understanding works between them. Desertion and acceptance of *Sevadasi* by the Baul concerned is a very common phenomenon.

Sufism : It represents the spirituality or the mysticism of Islam. It is taken to be the central point constituting the Revelation of Islam. The idea of Sufism is based on the principle of sacredness. The complete freeness from the worldly self-centred activities and the purity in body and mind are regarded as the basic characteristics of the Sufi line of thinking. The love for humanity without any sort of discrimination as well as the total avoidance of outward rites and rituraals have become the bases to Sufi philosophy. In India, it brought tremendous influence on the life-philosophy of the people.

Susumna : It is the nerve current which flows in the centre of the spine starting from the bottom and going to the root of the Sahasrara.

Tagore : Tagore has brought the thinking and philosophy of the Bauls in the scholastic sphere. He came in direct touch with the Bauls and at that time he could enter into the actual nature of the cult and thereby brought out many interesting features of it. Tagore had continuously admired their unassuming form of expression through songs sung in simple language and in melodious tuning. He made use of many characteristic features of Baul songs and dances composed and planned by him.

Tantra : Hindu Tantra professes to originate from the conversation between Siva and Parbati, who is represented as the Sakti. Sakti is the root and Siva is her container. According to this principle, all the facets of life are regarded as natural but they need be transformed through the development of the *Chakras*. During the later phase of the Gupta period the Sakti worship through Tantra started gaining importance.Right from the 8th Century A.D. a new trend of Buddhism started flourishing which was known as Tantrayana or Tantric Buddhism. Bengal was heavily influenced by these Tantric beliefs and practices.

Triveni: The three essential nerve-flows of the whole body are known as *Ida, Pingala* and *Susumna*. These play the most important role of functioning the bodily system in systematic manner. These three streams of life-forces meet at a particular point of the body which is known as *Triveni*.

Ulta path : The reverse way. The Bauls always proceed forward through the reverse ways. They do not follow any social rules and regulations, rather they go against the convensional customs.

Upanishads : It is a religious scripture in which the Indian philosophy has been depicted in clear understanding. A number of ideas belonging to Upanishad is seen to be reflected in the life and activities of Bauls.

Urs : The death anniversary of the Muslim Saints or *Pirs*. The Urs of these saints becomes the meeting occasion for the people belonging to Muslim as well as Hindu communities. The Bauls also attend the Urs in large numbers and pay homage to the saint concerned through songs and dances.

Vaishnavism : A particular religious idea based on the principle of love. It believes that Vishnu incarnated as Krishna for setting an example for humanity. The celebrated activities of Krishna with Radha have established an ideal of divine love. Vaishnavism has spread over the large tract of Bengal centering round Nabadwip owing to the active sponsorship of Lord Gouranga and Srimat Nityananda. The Bauls are highly influenced by various thoughts and ideas of Vaishnavism.

Vajrayana : One of the various factions of Buddhism. In Buddhism there was no place for idol worship and it, all through the time, put severe resistance on the socio-religious formalities. During Pala dynasty a section of the Buddhists gradually got itself integrated with the Hindu beliefs and ideas, and thereby came out as Vajrayanists. They started establishing images of diverse deities through prolonged absorption in meditation. During Sena dynasty the Vajrayanists took shelter under the flourshing influence of the Hindu Tantra. The inter-mixture between these two concepts gave rise to a very powerful Tantra cult in that period.

Vrindaban : The holy place where the various celebrated activities between the Divine Pair, Radha and Krishna had taken place. The place is regarded as paradise for the Vaishnavites and it is believed that everything of Vrindaban, even the dust particles, are influenced by the concept of love the Vaishnavism draws its sustenance. The Bauls very commonly refer the name of this place in their songs to indicate the celebrated surroundings where the play between the finite and the infinite had taken place.

Yoga : A rigid method through which union with the Supreme Beloved can be effected. It is the only way to achieve desired materials in the spiritual world, and proper performance of it raises the *Sadhaka* to the highest level of spiritualism. There are different types of *Yoga*. The Bauls very often perform *Bhakti-Yoga*, in addition to other *Yogas*, which is unique procedure of uniting love with devotion.

Bibliography

Books and Articles in English

Bahtiar, L., *Suppressing of the Mystic Quest* ; Thames and Hudson, London, 1976.

Banerjee, Anil Chandra, *Buddhism in India and Abroad;* the World Press, Private Ltd., Calcutta, 1973.

Bandyopadhyay, Somen, "Baul Songs of Bengal and Their Modern Forms" in *Study of Changes in Traditional Culture,* Ed. by K. P. Chattopadhyay, University of Calcutta, 1957.

Basham, A.L., *The Wonder that was India;* Sidgwick and Jackson, London, 1954.

— *A Cultural History of India,* Clarendon Press, London, 1975.

Basu, Asoke, *Elementary Statistical Theory in Sociology,* R. J. Drill, London, 1976.

Behari, Bankey, *Sufis, Mystics and Yogis of India* ; Bharatiya Vidya Bhavan, Bombay, 1971.

Bhandarkar, R.G., *Vaishnavism, Saivism and Minor Religious Systems,* Indological Book House, Varanasi, 1965.

Bhattacharya. D., *The Mirror of the Sky* : Songs of the Bauls from Bengal, George Allen and Unwin, Limited, London, 1969.

Biswas, Hemanga - (ed.) *Folk Music and Folklore.*

Chakravorty, S.C., *The Bauls - The Spiritual Vikings,* Firma K.L. Mukhopadhyay, Calcutta, 1980.

Chaudhury, Roma, *Sufism and Vedanta;* J.B. Chaudhuri, Calcutta, 1945.

Collier J. (Jr.) *Visual Anthropology; Photography as a Research Method*; Holt, Rinehart and Winston Inc.: New York, 1967.

Dasgupta, S., *Obscure Religious Cult:* University of Calcutta, 1940.

Dasgupta A.R. and Dasgupta M.A.; *Roots in the Void* : Baul Songs of

Bengal. K.P. Bagchi & Co., Calcutta, 1977.

Desozin, N.K. *The Reasearch Act ; A Theoretical Introduction to Sociological Methods*, Mc Graw-Hill, New York, 1977.

Dorson, R.M. *Folklore and Folk-life : An Introduction*, The University of Chicago Press, Chicago, 1972.

Dumoulin, H. (ed.) *Buddhism in Modern World :* Collier-MacMillan Publishers, London, 1976.

Dutt, G.S., *The Folk Dances of Bengal ;* Bengal Bratachari Society, Calcutta, 1954.

Eckhardt, K.W. and Ermann, M.D. *Social Research Methods : Perspective, Theory and Analysis*; Random House, New York, 1977.

Forcese, D.P. and S. Richer *Social Research Methods :* Englewood Cliffs, New York, 1973.

Gangyopadhyay, Rabindranath "A Glimpse into the Baul Culture of Bengal" in "*The Contemporary*" Vol.16, No.9, 1972, New Delhi.

Hacmann, H.R. *Buddhism as a Religion :* Its Historical Development and Its Present Condition ; Neeraj Publishing House, Delhi, 1981.

Haq, M. Enamul *A History of Sufism in Bengal :* Asiatic Society of Bangladesh, Dacca, 1975.

Hackings, Paul (ed.) *Principles of Visual Anthropology :* Mouton Publishers, The Haque, Paris, 1975.

Leiter, K. *A Primer on Ethnomethodology :* Oxford University Press, New York, 1980.

Lings, Martin, *What is Sufism?* George Allen and Unwin, Ltd., London 1975.

Majumdar, R.C., *The Early History of Bengal;* Dacca University, Dacca, 1925.

Mahapatra, P.K. *The Folk Cults of Bengal* : Indian Publications, Calcutta, 1972.

Mitra, Sanat Kumar "Baul Songs of Bengal" in *Folk-Music and Folklore*, Ed. by Hemanga Biswas, Calcutta, 1978.

--do-- "The Bauls of Birbhum", in *West Bengal District Census Handbook*, Birbhum District, Census of India, 1961.

Nicholson, R.A. *The Idea of Personality in Sufism*, Idarah-I Adabiyat-I, Delhi, 1976.

Parshall, P., "An Overview of Sufism" in *Folk-lore* (Bangladesh), Vol.7, 1982.

Radfield, R. *The Folk Culture of Yucatan ;* The University of Chicago Press, 1941.

Redfield, R., Peasant Society and Culture : An Anthropological Approach to Civilization, The University of Chicago Press, Chicago, 1956.

--do-- *The Little Community* : The University of Chicago Press, Chicago, 1958.

Riley, M.W. and E.E. Nelson, *Sociological Observations : A New Strategy of New Social Knowledge*, Basic Books, New York, 1974.

Sarkar, R.M. "Conflict Compromise and Diversity-Unity Oriented life philosophy of a wandering Community" in *Indian Museum Bulletin*, Vol. XIX, 1964, Calcutta.

--do-- "The Bauls of Bengal - their diverse nature and patterns of thinking", in *Man In India*, Vol. 68, No.1, 1988, Ranchi.

Schimmel, A. *Mystical Dimensions of Islam* : The University of North Carolina press, Chapel Hill, 1975.

Shah, Idries, *The Way of the Sufis* : Jonathan Cape, London, 1968.

Siegel, Lee, *Sacred and Profane : Dimensions of Love in Indian Traditions as Exemplified in the Gita Govinda of Jaydeva*, Oxford University Press, Delhi, 1978.

Singer, Milton (ed.) *Traditional India* : The American Folk-lore Society, Philadelphia, 1909.

Singer, M. and B.S. Cohn (Ed.) *Structure and Change in Indian Society* : Aldine Publishing Company, Chicago, 1968.

Soloman, Carol, "A Contemporary Sahajiya Interpretation of the Bilvamangal - Chintamony Legend as sung by Sanatan Das Baul", in *Folklore* (Bangladesh), volume 7, 1982.

Stoddart William, *Sufism* : Thorsons Publishers Ltd., Wellingborough, Northamptonshire, 1976.

Tagore Rabindranath, *Creative Unity*, Macmillian & Co. Ltd., Calcutta, 1959 ; (First Published in 1922)

--do-- *The Religion of Man* : George Allen and Unwin Ltd., London, 1958. (First Published in 1931).

Trimingham, J.S., *The Sufi Orders in Islam* : Clarendon Press, Oxford, 1971.

Books and Articles in Bengali

Bandyopadhyay, Upendranath, *Banglar Baul O Baul Gan* (The Baul and the Baul Songs of Bengal) ; Orient Book Company, Calcutta, 1388 B.S.

Bandyopadhyay, Somendranath *Banglar Baul : Kavya O Darsan* (The Bauls of Bengal Lyric and Philosophy) ; Calcutta University Press, Calcutta, 1967

Bandyopadhyay, Debasis *Kshitimohan O Banglar Baul* (Kshitimohan and the Bauls of Bengal) - in *Sakuntala,* January, 1982, Calcutta.

Bardhan, Mani, *Banglar Loknritya O Gitibaichitra* (The Folk-Dances of Bengal and Diversities of songs) ; Government of West Bengal, Calcutta, 1963.

Bhattacharya, Asutosh, *Bangiya Loksangit Ratnakar* (Quarry of Gems of Bengali Folk Songs), Vol. 3. Paschim Banga Loksangit Gabesana Parishad, Calcutta, 1967.

Bhattacharya, Nilotpal, *Baul O Tattadarshi* (The Baul and the Investigator), *Birbhumi,* 1386 B.S., Suri/Birbhum.

Brahma, Tripti, *Sonamukhir Baul Mela* (The Baul Fair of Sonamukhi), *Samakalin,* Vol. 24, No.1, 1383 B.S., Calcutta.

- do - *Lokajibaney Banglar Laukik Dharmasangit O Dharmiya Mela* (Folk Religious Songs of Bengal in Folk-life and Religious Fairs), Calcutta, 1982.

Chakravorty, Tulsidas, *Baul Jiban : Darsaner Alokey* (The Baul Life : In the Light of Philosophy), *Brahmani,* Vol.3, No.1, 1384 B.S., Birbhum.

Chattaraj, Ashanandan, *Ashanandan Rachana Sangraha* (Collection of Eassays written by Ashanandan), An Anthology of Baul Songs, Birbhum Sahitya Parishad, Suri, 1384 B.S.

Das Matilal, and P.K. Mahapatra *Lalan Gitika* (The Ballads of Lalan), Calcutta University Press, Calcutta, 1958.

Deb, Chittaranjan *Palligiti O Purbabanga* (Village Songs and East Bengal) ; *Katakatha,* Calcutta, 1953.

Gangyopadhyay, Ramsambhu, *Birbhumer Aul-Baul* (The Aul-Baulof Birbhum) *Brahmani,* Vol.5, No.4, 1385 B.S., Birbhum.

Gupta, Amit, *Baul O Gabesak* (The Baul and the Researcher), *Samakalin,* January, 1982, Calcutta.

- do - *Bauler Dehatatwa*(The bodily knowledge of Baul), *Samakalin,* Calcutta, 1982.

- do - *Banglar Lokajibaney Baul,* (The Baul in the folk-life of Bengal), Sambad Publishers, Calcutta, 1983.

Jha, Sakti, *Aul* - in *Saptaha,* Vol. 16, No.27 Calcutta, 1983.

Kalkut, (Samaresh Bose) *Kothay Pabo Tarey* (Where shall I get him). Ananda Publishers, Calcutta, 1983.

Majumdar, Dipak, *Chhuti* - (The Holiday), Desh, Vol. 50, Nos. 41 and 42, Calcutta, 1983.

Mallick, Krisnanath, *Loksangiter Patabhumikay Baul Gan* (The Baul Songs in the Background of Folk-Song), *Agamani,* October, 1385, B.S., Dubrajpur/Birbhum.

Mitra, Sanat, *Kartabhaja : Dharmamat O Itihas* (Kartabhaja : Religious Faith and History), Pustak Bipani, Calcutta, 1975.

- do - *Lalan Fakir : Kavi O Kavya* (Lalan Fakir - the Poet and Poems), Pushtak Bipani, Calcutta, 1979.

Mukhopdhyay, Aditya, *Ei Samayar Alokey - Baul - Gan* (The Baul Songs in the light of present time), *Didibhai,* Vol.8, October, 1388 B.S., Kotasur/Birbhum.

Mukhopadhyay, Aditya *Baul Bhabna* (Baul Thinking) : *Brahmani,* vol.7, October 1388 B.S., Dharampur/Birbhum.

- do - *Baul Ki Tikbey?* (Whether Baul would retain?), *Ajkal* Daily, 31st August, 1982, Calcutta.

Mukhopadhyay Dilip, *Uttar Rarher Lok-Sangit* (Folk songs of North Rarh), Kalyani Prakasan, Calcutta, 1970.

Roy, Prasanta *Baul Sadhanar Kathamo* (The Framework of Baul Meditation), *Brahmani,* Vol.9, No. 2, 1389 B.S. Dharampur, Birbhum.

- do - *Kavi Jayadeva O Baul* (The Poet Jayadeva and Baul), *Sakuntala,* Vol. 8, January, 1982, Calcutta.

Sarkar Pabitra, *Baul O Samajik Sinri* (The Baul and the Social Ladder), *Sakuntala,* Vol. 10, January, 1982, Calcutta.

Sarkar, Rebati Mohan, *Birbhum Kahini* (The Story of Birbhum), Knowledge House, Calcutta, 1390 B.S.

- do - *Sarbadharma Sammannye Baul Darsaner Ruprekha* (Feature of Baul philosophy in the integration of all religions) in *Piramid,* Vol. 3, No. 4, 1393 B.S.

Sen Kshitimohan, *Banglar Baul* (The Bauls of Bengal), Calctutta University Press, Calcutta, 1954.

Siraj, Sayed Mustafa, *Aul-Baul*, *Sakuntala,* Vol. 10, January, 1984, Calcutta.

- do - *Sufi Darsan Prasange* (In connection with Sufi Philosophy), *Udbodhan,* Vol. 85, No. 9, Aswin, 1390 B.S., Calcutta.

Thakurdas, *Kheyali Baul* (The Whimsical Baul), Jophlai, Birbhum, 1380 B.S.

- do - *Kothay Pabo Tare* (Where shall I get him), Birbhum Sahitya Parishad, Suri, 1384 B.S.

Appendix I

List of Bauls and Fakirs who were brought under the sphere of direct investigation

The attached lists give the detailed information on the Bauls directly interviewed during field investigation. The ascetic Bauls were mostly contacted at their *akhras* or centres for meditation, and for the interview with the domestic Bauls their houses at different villages were visited frequently in addition to the effort made for meeting them all the different fair and festival sites. In order to look into the behaviour-patterns of the Bauls both in the noisy human congregations and in the calm and quite *ashram* environs as well as within the caste-oriented and formality-ridden village society this particular measure has been adopted with due seriousness. It is needless to say that this endeavour demands a painstaking fieldwork for a long period and, we do believe, until and unless this is done the realistic picture on this community would never be revealed in its proper perspective. These lists would provide a broad-based idea to the readers about the vastness of the field of study and the nature of inclusion of variegated Bauls living and wandering about this wide area under the endless sky. The name of the Bauls with respective village directories would no doubt, help the future scholars to trace them easily for further findings.

The Fakirs have also been similarly met with for interviews at their various sacred places during festive occasions as well as within the perspective of their individual meditational units and village homes.

Appendix I

TABLE NO. 1

List of Bauls who were brought under the Sphere of Direct Investigation

Sl. No.	Name of the Baul	Sex Male/Female	Belongs to the Village/Town	Police Station	District
1.	Chintamani Dasi	F	Radhaballavpur		Birbhum
2.	Gaur Das Baul (Khepa)	M	Nichubandhgora	Bolpur	--
3.	Bishwanath Das Baul	M	Bolpur	Bolpur	
4.	Madanananda Mahanta	M	Sahapur	Dubrajpur	--
5.	Rupdasi	F	Chandrahat	Sainthia	--
6.	Shyamsundar Mahanta	M	Aduri	--	--
7.	Nakshatra Das	M	Ahmadpur	Ahmadpur	--
8.	Lakshman Das Bairagya	M	Rabindrapalli	Suri	--
9.	Bahuballabh Das	M	Nandihat	--	--
10.	Bhakti Das	M	Iguni	Suri	--
11.	Rabi Das	M	Radhaballavpur	Bharatpur	Murshidabad.
12.	Satyacharan Das	M	Ruposphur	Khayrasole	Birbhum
13.	Suchitra Dasi	F	Bara	Sainthia	--
14.	Ashimananda Bairagy	M	Molian	Sainthia	--
15.	Dulaldas Baul	M	Gangulia-border (Bongaon)	Bongaon	24 Parganas

TABLE NO. 1 (Contd.)

Sl. No.	Name of the Baul	Sex Male/Female	Belongs to the Village/Town	Police Station	District
16.	Gouri Dasi	F	Bandhnabagram	Bolpur	Birbhum
17.	Sridam Das	M	Kurumsaha	Sainthia	--
18.	Gopal Das	M	Bautigol	Santiniketan	--
19.	Sanatan Das	M	Bandhnabagram	--	--
20.	Dinabandhu Das	M	Bautigol	--	--
21.	Chandicharan Das	M	Bandhnabagram	--	--
22.	Gandhi Das	M	--	--	--
23.	Sukumar Das	M	--	--	--
24.	Nimai Das	M	--	--	--
25.	Mayarani Dasi	F	--	--	--
26.	Gopal Das Bairagya	M	Babuija	Sainthia	--
27.	Adyaitadas Bairagya	M	Palpai	Khayrasole	--
28.	Gangadhar Das	M	Dubrajpur (Pahareswar)	Dubrajpur	--
29.	Ashalata Dasi	F	Palpai	Khayrasole	--
30.	Fakirdas Bairagy	M	--	--	--
31.	Nupurchandra Das Bairagya	M	Santiniketan	Santiniketan	--
32.	Radheshyam Das	M	Basuipara	Rampurhat	--
33.	Gadhadhar Das	M	Dubrajpur (Pahareswar)	Dubrajpur	--
34	Chandicharan Das (Bauri)	M	Amlakuri	Khayrasole	--
35.	Nirmal Chandra Majumdar	M	Midnapore	Midnapore	Midnapore

TABLE NO. 1 (Contd.)

Sl. No.	Name of the Baul	Sex Male/Female	Belongs to the Village/Town	Police Station	District.
36.	Lakshman Das	M	Hatikata	Khayrasole	Birbhum
37.	Ramchandra Das	M	--	--	--
38.	Santiram Das Baul	M	Marulidanga	Mayureswar	--
39.	Harekrishna Das	M	Kapistha	Raniswar	Santhal Pargana
40.	Narayan Chandra Das (Bairagya)	M	Dubrajpur	Dubrajpur	Birbhum
41.	Sudhir Das Baul	M	Sainthia	Sainthia	--
42.	Kumaresh Das	M	Barul	--	--
43.	Krishna Gopal Das	M	Parsundi	Khayrasole	--
44.	Ganesh Badyakar	M	Loba	Dubrajpur	--
45.	Harihar Goswami	M	Gangulia Border (Bongaon)	Bongaon	24 Parganas
46.	Dinabandhu Badyakar	M	Loba (Fakir-Bera)	Dubrajpur	Birbhum
47.	Nirnoy Das	M	Shankarpur (Raotara)	Suri	--
48.	Uttam Dom (Badyakar)	M	Loba	Dubrajpur	--
49.	Sukumar Das	M	Dholpur	Ilambazar	--
50.	Jamunadas Bairagya	M	Palpai	Khayrasole	--
51.	Ajit Das Baul	M	Gharua	Sainthia	--
52.	Gouridasi Vaishnavi	F	Bôlpur	Bolpur	--
53.	Sumibala Dasi	F	Lauberia	Khayrasole	--

TABLE NO. 1 (Contd.)

Sl. No.	*Name of the Baul*	*Sex Male/Female*	*Belongs to the Village/Town*	*Police Station*	*District*
54.	Narayan Chandra Das Vaishnav.	M	Lalberia	Khayrasole	Birbhum
55.	Purnachandra Sutradhar	M	Barsha	--	--
56.	Narayan Das Baul	M	Lauberia	--	--
57.	Manikdas Baul	M	Shankarpur	Dubrajpur	--
58.	Narayandas Vaishnav	M	Dharunia	Khayrasole	--
59.	Madhab Das	M	Lauberia	--	--
60.	Tinkari Das Baul	M	Paigara	--	--
61.	Parikshit Bala	F	Bara-Cobla	Purbasthali	Burdwan
62.	Narayan Baul	M	Prafulla Nagar Colony	Nabadwip	Nadia
63.	Ranjit Das Baul	M	Dignagar	Kotwali	Nadia
64.	Kanaidas Baul	M	--	--	--
65.	Rajanikanta Das (Ratan Saha)	M	Dhakanagar Colony	Nabadwip	--
66.	Satish Chandra Eatbar	M	Prafullanagar Colony	--	--
67.	Sanatan Das	M	South Serampore	Purbasthali	Burdwan.
68.	Lakshman Chandra Das Bairagy	M	Serampore	--	--
69.	Jagabandhu Das	M	Kharer Nath	Nabadwip	Nadia
70.	Madan Mohan Das	M	Serampore	Serampore	Burdwan
71.	Gobinda Mondal	M	Bara-Coble	Purbasthali	--

TABLE NO. 1 (Contd.)

Sl. No.	Name of the Baul	Sex Male/Female	Belongs to the Village/Town	Police Station	District
72.	Nitai Chandra Das	M	Nrisinghapur	Shantipur	Nadia
73.	Nityananda Das	M	Srifala	Rampurhat	Birbhum
74.	Rabi Das	M	--	--	--
75.	Deb Das	M	Sunripara (Bolpur)	Bolpur	--
76.	Sudhir Das	M	Railpara	Sainthia	--
77.	Nityananda Das (Roy)	M	Netajipalli	--	--
78.	Bishwanath Das	M	Sunripara	Bolpur	--
79.	Tarapada Mal	M	Kalipathar	Kundhahit	Santal Pargana
80.	Balu Chowdhury	M	Bagdohori	Bagdohori	--
81.	Surdas Baul	M	Mohammadbazar	Mohammadbazar	Birbhum
82.	Srinath Mukherjee	M	Lohapur	Muraroi	--
83.	Nakul Bauri	M	Gohaliara	Dubrajpur	--
84.	Sri Sri Amrita Giri (Borbhani Chotose Nagababaji)	M	Bharamaritala(Sujipur)	Kaliganya	Nadia
85.	Sadan Bauri	M	Bonhari		Birbhum
86.	Haridas Adhikari	M	Kanksa Colony	Kanksa	Burdwan
87.	Jiban Mahto	M	Nirchintapur	Barabazar	Purulia
88.	Sisir Chatterjee	M	Metala	Dubrajpur	Birbhum
89.	Krishna Chandra Mal	M	Metela	--	--
90.	Atul Mahto	M	Charakpathar	Patanga	Singhbhum (Bihar)

TABLE NO. 1 (Contd.)

Sl. No.	*Name of the Baul*	*Sex Male/Female*		*Belongs to the Village/Town*	*Police Station*	*District*
91.	Nikhil Goldar	M		Kanksa Colony	Kanksa	Burdwan
92.	Khepa Anilchandra Thakur (Lalbaba)	M		Baratola (Shaltora)	Nituria	Purulia
93.	Jadavendra Nath Das	M		Staff Quarters (Colliery)	Jharia	Dhanbad (Bihar)
94.	Shaktigiri Bhairabi (Nanibala Dasi)		F	Saraswatiganj	Kanksa	Burdwan
95.	Ananda Giri (Fakir Chandra Roy)	M		Akandara	::	::
96.	Gouribala Dasi		F	Kulkuri	Suri	Birbhum
97.	Bankashyam Das	M		Jaydev	Illumbazar	::
98.	Nagen Das	M		Kalipur	Suri	::
99.	Gurupada Das	M		Kanksa Camp	Kanksa	Burdwan.
100.	Atmaram Das	M		Khandagram	Dubrajpur	Birbhum
101.	Nilachai Giri	M		Gara	Illumbazar	::
	(Kartik Chandra Roy)	M		Khandagram	Dubrajpur	Birbhum.
102.	Sadhan Badyakar	M		Bagdohori	Bagdohri	Santal Pargana (Bihar.)
103.	Rupa Badyakar		F	Kalipathar	Kundahit	::
104.	Gopal Das Bairagya	M		Vilan	Sainthia	Birbhum.
105.	Nityananda Das	M		Kulkuri	Suri	::

TABLE NO. 1 (Contd.)

Sl. No.	Name of the Baul	Sex Male/Female	Belongs to the Village/Town	Police Station	District
106.	Arati Das	F	Jaydev	Illum bazar	Birbhum
107.	Bijay Das	M	Anandanagar	Khayrasole	--
108.	Subal Das	M	Kulkuri	Suri	--
109.	Sudeb Gorai	M	Saluka	Mohammadbazar	--
110.	Benimadhav Das	M	Pahareshwar (Dubrajpur)	Dubrajpur	--
111.	Adyaitadas Bairagya	M	Govindapur	Sainthia	--
112.	Tulsi Saha	M	Sahapara	Mohammadbazar	--
113.	Shibu Bagdi	M	Raipur	Rampurhat	--
114.	Haradhan Sarkar	M	Saluka	Mohammadbazar	--
115.	Harekrishnadas Bairagya	M	Barakuri (Panchra)	Dubrajpur	--
116	Kalidas Goswami	M	Rupasri Pally (Narmada plot)	Rainaghat	Nadia
117.	Ananta Das (Abhimannu Sarkar)	M	Jaydev	Illumbazar	Birbhum
118.	Bhajahari Das Baul	M	Maladanga	Suri	Birbhum
119.	Bimla Dasi	F	--	--	Birbhum
120.	Sitangshu Bhagat	M	Bunda	Suri	
121.	Shyamapada Mal	M	Kalipathar	Kundahit	Santal Pargana (Bihar)
122.	Gautam Garai	M	Bhaluka	Bagdohri	--

TABLE NO. 1 (Contd.)

Sl. No.	Name of the Baul	Sex Male/Female	Belongs to the Village/Town	Police Station	District
123.	Saradananda Goswami	M	Bakreshwar	Dubrajpur	Birbhum
124.	Jagabandhu Das	M	Muktatore		Purulia
125.	Kabi Haradhan Dhibar Baul	M	Ramkanali	Nirsha	Dhanbad (Bihar)
126.	Jiban Krishna Biswas	M	Asanunagar	Kotwali	Nadia
127.	Nityananda Das	M	Goal-lara	Dubrajpur	Birbhum
128.	Shankari Das	F	--	--	--
129.	Shashanka Das Baul	M	Sabuldaho	Baswa	Murshidabad
130.	Shashidas Bairagya	M	Ekemba	Baswa	--
131.	Narapati Das Baul	M	Bahadurpur	Jamuria	Burdwan
132.	Nimai Mondal	M	Metela	Dubrajpur	Birbhum
133.	Radharani Dasi	F	Gopalnagar	Bolpur	--
134.	Nimai Das	M	Panchthupi	Kandi	Murshidabad
135.	Khepa Chandrakantodas Baul	M	Sankarpur	Khayrasole	Birbhum
136.	Kalu Das	M	Dadpur	Mourisha	--
137.	Paramananda Brahmachari	M	Morjatpur	Sainthia	--
138.	Gourdas Mohanta	M	Nabadwip	Nabadwip	Nadia
139.	Narendra Das Baul	M	Dadpur	Mourisha	Birbhum
140.	Asimananda Bairagi	M	Sahapur	Khayrasole	--
141.	Niranjan Das Bairagi	M	Alema	Do	--
142.	Krishnadas Bairagi	M	Jayadeva-Kenduli	Illumbazar	--

TABLE NO. 1 (Contd.)

Sl. No.	*Name of the Baul*	*Sex Male/Female*	*Belongs to the Village/Town*	*Police Station*	*District*
143.	Prabhakar Das Bairagi	M	Sahapur	Khayrasole	Birbhum
144.	Narayani Bala Dasi	F	Kalipur	--	--
145.	Tarinidas Baul	M	Kinagalchandi	--	--
146.	Sanatan Mete-Baul	M F	Serampore	--	--
147.	Chandidas Bairagi	M	--	--	--
148.	Gopaldas Bairagi	M	--	--	--
149.	Dilipdas Bairagi	M	--	--	--
150.	Lakshmandas Bairagi	M	Dadpur	Mourisha	--
151.	Kalipada Das Bairagi	M	Jayadeva-Kenduli	Illumbazar	--
152.	Kalipada Baul	M	Dadpur	Mourisha	--
153.	Harish Chandra Das	M	--	--	--
154.	Adyaita Das Bairagi	M	Marugram	--	--
155.	Bhabananda Das	M	--	--	--
156.	Jagadananda Das	M	--	--	--
157.	Narottamdas Bairagi	M	Nirma	--	--
158.	Bankashyam Das Baul	M	Ballavpur	Santiniketan	--
159.	Anil Kumar Das Bairagi	M	Batur	Kendi	Murshidabad
160.	Gobardhan Das	M	Dhangara	Moureswar	Birbhum
161.	Sripati Ghosh	M	Shaboldah	Baswa	Murshidabad
162.	Gopi Khepa	M	Krishnanagar	Illumbazar	Birbhum
163.	Ramananda Das Bariagi	M	Jaydeva-Kenduli	--	--

TABLE NO. 1 (Contd.)

Sl. No.	Name of the Baul	Sex Male/Female	Belongs to the Village/Town	Police Station	District
164.	Haradhan Roy	M	Ahmedpur	Ahmedpur	Birbhum
165.	Sripada Das Baul	M	--	--	--
166.	Chandicharan Das Baul	M	--	--	--
167.	Ratandas Bahurupi	M	Rudranagar	Sainthia	--
168.	Sricharan Das	M	Nagirapara Colony	Krishnanagar	Nadia
169.	Harekrishna Sutradhar	M	Bankim Colony	Naihati	24 Parganas
170.	Kaluchand Mahanto	M	Debipur	Gouripur	Burdwan
171.	Sadananda Das	M	Serampore	Purbasthali	Burdwan
172.	Gopal Das	M	--	--	--
173.	Kashinath Das	M	--	--	--
174.	Mira Mahanto	F	Dainhat	--	--
175.	Gopalkrishna Das Mahanto	M	Ramkrishna Colony	Nabadwip	Nadia
176.	Haridas Khepa	M	No. 3 Rail Gate (Shantipur)	Shantipur	Nadia
177.	Prankrishna Khepa	M	Batanghachi	Ranaghat	Nadia
173.	Siddheswar Mandal	M	Simultala Doctor's House	Krishnanagar House	--
179.	Bhakta Goswami	M	Agradwip	Agradwip	Burdwan
180.	Parimal Baul	M	Nrisinghapur Colony	Shantipur	Nadia
181.	Atal Chandra Goswam.	M	Shyampur	Krishnanagar	Nadia

TABLE NO. 1 (Contd.)

Sl. No.	Name of the Baul	Sex Male/Female	Belongs to the Village/Town	Police Station	District
182.	Nityanandadas Bairagi	M	Kharrer Math	Nabadwip	Nadia.
183.	Chandramohan Mondal	M	Charbrahmyanagar Bazar.	--	--
184.	Subal Das Baul	M	Swarupganj	--	--
185.	Gostha-Gopal	M	Bagula	Ranaghat	--
186.	Madhab Das	M	Khidirpur	Sonamukhi	Bankura
187.	Naren Das Bairagi	M	Karasholi	--	--
188.	Basudeb Das	M	Moyuamuni	Bishnupur	--
189.	Brahmananda Das	M	Amral	Bishnupur	--
190.	Birbhadra Das	M	--	--	--
191.	Basan Das	M	--	--	--
192.	Narottam Das	M	Ghoshpara (Kalyani)	Kalyani	Nadia
193.	Sri Gopal Das Mahonta	M	Amarpur	Onda	Bankura
194.	Lakshman Das Baul	M	Bara-Cobla		Burdwan
195.	Narahari Das	M	Krishnapur Colony	Lalgola	Murshidabad
196.	Kanaklata Das	F	Memari	Memari	Burdwan
197.	Rabi Das	M	Palta		24 Parganas
198.	Arundas Baul	M	Kataganj Colony		Nadia
199.	Bishnudas Baul	M	Dhubulia		--

TABLE NO. 1 (Contd.)

Sl. No.	Name of the Baul	Sex Male/Female	Belongs to the Village/Town	Police Station	District
200.	Nimaidas Baul	M	Bhadurigram		Nadia
201.	Radhashyam Das	M	Basuipara	Nalhati	Burdwan
202.	Ananda Das	M	Shunripara	Bolpur	--
203.	Ramananda Das	M	Nechu-Bandhgora	--	--
204.	Lakshman Das	M	Mehednagar	Mallarpur	--
205.	Shantiram Das	M	Marudidangal	Mallarpur	--
206.	Chakradhar Das	M	Gopalnagar	Bolpur	--
207.	Keshav Das Baul	M	Kanksha	Kanksha	Burdwan
208.	Narottam Das	M	Char-Kashimpur		--
209.	Manohar Das	M	Paria		Santal Pargana (Bihar)
210.	Gouranga Das	M	Machibazar	Ultadanga	24 Parganas.
211.	Jagannath Koley	M	Metiaburuz	Gardenrich	--
212.	Lakshman Das	M	Aroa		Birbhum
213.	Suradhani Vaishnavi	F	Jayadeva-Kenduli	Illumbazar	--
214.	Sri Nirod Mal	M	Metela	Dubrajpur	--
215.	Sri Pradip Kunui	M	--	--	--
216.	Mohan Chandra Mal	M	--	--	--
217.	Sukumar Vaishnavi	M	Ulanga	Suri	--
218.	Sri Guiram Jamadar	M	Metela	Dubrajpur	Birbhum

TABLE NO. 1 (Contd.)

Sl. No.	Name of the Baul	Sex Male/Female		Belongs to the Village/Town	Police Station	District
219.	Sri Anilchandra Das	M		Kanksa	Kanksa	Burdwan
220.	Sri Sudhir Das Baul	M		Tikorbeta	Illumbazar	Birbhum
221.	Srimati Jogamaya Das		F	Jayadev	::	::
222.	Dilip Kumar Banerjee	M		Sonamukhi	Sonamukhi	Bankura
223.	Upen Das Baul	M		Agarpara	Agarpara	24 Parganas
224.	Prahlad Brahmachari	M		Kuntighat	Triveni	::
225.	Jagabandhu Das	M		Kalinarayanpur	Krishnanagar	Nadia
226.	Biswanath Das	M		Metidanga	Shantipur	::
227.	Rabilal Ankur	M		Gohaliara	Rajnagar	Birbhum
228.	Subol Baul	M		Aranghata	Badkolla	Nadia
229.	Satish Das Baul	M		Kalabagan	Nabadwip	::

TABLE NO. 2

List of Fakirs who were brought under the Sphere of Direct Investigation

Sl. No.	*Name of Fakir*	*Belongs to Village/Town*	*Police Station*	*District*
1.	Panchashaha Fakir-Umed Shaha.	Khanerdanga	Krishnanagar	Nadia
2.	Kanu Fakir	Sriniketan	Bolpur	Birbhum
3.	Makhsar Ansari	Katikhung	Amghachi	Dumka (Bihar)
4.	Ali Hussain	--	--	--
5.	Khoka Fakir	Nabagram	Mangalpur	Burdwan
6.	Moktar Ali Shah	Gunorha	Baghar	Burdwan
7.	Nawasar Shah	Darbarpur	Galshi	--
8.	Anawar Shah	Bhachcha	Irkuna	--
9.	Rezzak Shah	Darbarpur	Banharshi	--
10.	Abu Hassan	Marut	Ankhona	--
11.	Sheikh Ahammad Ali	Baze-Pratappur	Baze-Pratappur	--
12.	Shaha Sufi Mohammad Nagadh Ali Chistinigami	Pukurdihi	Pukurdihi	Birbhum
13.	Rahi	Shaktore	Shaktore	--
14.	Mok'ar Shaha	Hetia	Labhpur	--
15.	Moniar Hussain	Pilkundi	Salar	Murshidabad
16.	Sheikh Arshad	Madpur	Nasikgram	Burdwan
17.	Mollah Box	Barakalmi	Purshuri	--

TABLE NO. 2 (Contd.)

Sl. No.	Name of Fakir	Belongs to Village/Town	Police Station	District
18.	Mustaf Ahmad	Kalipur	Kalipur	Murshidabad
19.	Tahur Sheikh	Begumbari	Beladangi	Do
20.	Shiab Ali	Moureshwar	Moureshwar	Birbhum
21.	Abdul Mannan	Rowtara	Kaliganj	Nadia
22.	Nasiruddin Shah	Shanabandi	Shanabandi	Burdwan
23.	Khudu Khan	Karuikaitan	Karui	Burdwan
24.	Napha! Mondal	Kulgachia	Chotonaldar	Nadia
25.	Shaha Zohad Ali Chisti	Mondalpara	Katwa	Burdwan
26.	Abdul Bari Sheikh	Karuikaitan	Karui	--
27.	Fakir Babaji	Baracantua	Dubanpur	Nadia
28.	Sheikh Qutobuddin	Krishnarampur	Narudia	Burdwan
29.	Nocim	Krishnapur	--	--
30.	Dhanu Sheikh	Sahlar	Sahlar	Murshidabad
31.	Abul Khair Shaha	Patharchapuri	Dubrajpur	Birbhum
32.	Chist Afsar Rahim Mondal	Sangra	Bolpur	Birbhum
33.	Mohammad Billal Chistia	Bhatar	Belelda	Burdwan
34.	Mokambar Hussain	Lakshminarayanpur	Rajnagar	Birbhum
35.	Mohammad Nakir Ali Hussain	Nutangram	Kandi	Murshidabad
36.	Lalbaba Darbesh Shaha	Imamnagar	Rampurhat	Birbhum
37.	Abdul Alim	Moregram	Ketugram	Burdwan
38.	Abdul Momin Fakir	Dakeshinkhanda	Bharatpur	Murshidabad

TABLE NO. 2 (Contd.)

Sl. No.	*Name of Fakir*	*Belongs to Village/Town*	*police Station*	*District*
39.	Zohad Shah Darbesh	Municipality (Katwa)	Katwa	Burdwan
40.	Sirayul Islam Ali Chisti (Mondel)	Sonatola	Kotwali	Nadia
41.	Sabed Ali Mondal	Khairdrapota	Nakashi	Nadia
42.	Siraj Shaha Chisti	Baswa	Baswa	Murshidabad

Appendix II

A LIST OF FAIRS/MAHOTSABS CONNECTED WITH BAULS AND FAKIRS

The following are the principal fairs/*mahotsabs* (great festivals) at the different regions of West Bengal which occur, centering round various auspicious moments, throughout the year in specific times and sites. These fairs/*mahotsabs* are especially characterized by the celebrated presence of the Bauls, the Fakirs and other related religious mendicants. In most of these fairs/*mahotsabs* they assemble spontaneously, and they do not care any formal invitation from the organisers. These are traditional assemblages, and the Bauls and the Fakirs attend these, sing, dance, enjoy and then silently leave these praying for the well-being of mankind in general and the devotees and attending persons in these assemblages in particular.

	Name of the Fair/ Mahotsab	*Place of Occurrence*	*Date of Holding*	*Specific Purpose and Duration*
1.	Agradwiper *mela*	Agradwip, Nadia District	Ekadasi day-- following Dol-Purnima (Spring festival)	To observe the annual funeral rite of Ghose Thakur - a saint named Gopinath Ghose. The *mahotsab* is held for three days.
2.	Banamalipurer *mela*	Banamalipur, Burdwan district	Magh 5- (corresponding to January 19)	This place is believed to be blessed with the celebrated visit of Mahaprabhu the great Viashnava mendicant. The devotees and the Bauls come to show due regard to him. The fair is continued for four days.

APPENDIX II (Contd.)

	Name of the Fair/ Mahotsab	*Place of Occurrence*	*Date of Holding*	*Specific Purpose and Duration*
3.	Barunir *mela*	Krishnanagar, Nadia district	On the day of Baruni holy bath festival	The festival of holy bath in the Ganges at the auspicious movement of Baruni *tithi.* The fair is held for two days.
4.	Bipattarini Chandi *mela*	Sonarpur, 24 Parganas district	Ashar, Sukla Dwitiya (2nd day in the brighter half of the month of Ashar)	To worship the roaring deity - Bipattarini Chandi. It is accompanied by a large fair which continues for five days.
5.	Bhitarpara Pir *mela*	Bhitarpara, 24 Parganas district	Magh, 2 (corresponding to January 16)	To observe the death anniversary of the Muslim saint-Majdin Shah, popularly known as Pirbaba. The fair is held for one day.
6.	Darbesh Ashram *machchab*	Dubrajpur, Birbhum district	Magh, 3 (corresponding to January 17)	To commemorate the holy deeds of Darbeshji a prophet in the sphere of Baul *sadhana*. The festival is held for three days.
7.	Dadhibairagitalar *mela*	Bairagitala, Burdwan district	Maghi Saptami day (7th day in the brighter half of month of Magh)	To show specific regard to the spiritual *sadhana* done by Gopaldas vairagi - a great ascetic in the Vaishnava cult. The assemblage is continued for three days.
8.	Datapirer *mela*	Tollygunge, 24 Parganas district	Jaistha 8 (corresponding to June 22)	To celebrate the birth anniversary of Data Pir Saheb. It is attended by the

	Name of the Fair/ Mahotsab	Place of Occurrence	Date of Holding	Specific Purpose and Duration
				devotees belonging to the Muslim and the Hindu communities. The associated fair is held for a day.
9.	Datapirer *mela*	Dubrajpur, Birbhum district.	Chaitra, 9 (corresponding to March, 23)	To commemorate the sacred deeds of a famous Sufi Saint, Data Saheb, formerly known as Mehbub Shah. The fair is held for seven days and is attended by large number of Muslim and Hindu devotees.
10.	Devi Jogoddyar *mela*	Khirgram, Burdwan district	Vaisakh Sankranti (corresponding to May, 14)	It is based on the worship of Jogoddya Devi - a celebrated folk deity. The fair is held by the side of a large tank and is attended mainly by the people belonging to the lower caste groups. It is continued for three days.
11.	Fullara *mela*	Labhpur, Birbhum district	Maghi purnima (Full moon days in the month of Magh)	It is centred round the annual worship of the goddess Fullara on the Fullmoon day in the month of Magh (January-February). A fair is held for three days by the side of the celebrated tank in front of the temple of the goddess.
12.	Gajipirer *mela*	Ghutiari Sharif, 24-Parganas district	Falgoon, 24 (corresponding to March, 8)	To show specific regard to the celebrated memory of Gajipir - Mobarak Shah Gaji. It

APPENDIX II (Contd.)

	Name of the Fair/ Mahotsab	*Place of Occurrence*	*Date of Holding*	*Specific Purpose and Duration*
				is one of the largest fair in West Bengal and is continued for a week. It is extensively crowded by the Muslim and Hindu devotees.
13.	Godar Ashram *machchab*	Koridhya, Birbhum district	Aswin, 9 (corresponding to Sept. 26)	It is held to celebrate the memory of Godar Gossain - Vaishnava saint and founder of the *Ashram*. *Mahotsab* is held for a day.
14.	Gopalnagar *mela*	Gopalnagar, Birbhum district	Maghi purnima (Full-moon day in the month of Magh)	It is organised by the International Baul Conference established in recent years by Purna Chanda Das - the renowned Baul singer known throughout the world. It had a planning for reviving the traditional Baul culture and for organising research work on the Baul community. It is not functioning now.
15.	Jaydev-Kendulir *mela*	Jaydev-Kenduli Birbhum district	Pous Sankranti (corresponding to January 14)	To commemorate the celebrated event of coming of the Ganges at Kadamkhandi *ghat* in the course of the river Ajay as a divine grace to Jayadeva - the great Vaishnava saint. The fair is held for three days and is specifically characterized by taking of holy dip in the river by thousands of devotees.
16.	Jugalkishorer *mela*	Aranghata, 24 Parganas district	Jaistha Sankranti (corresponding to	It is centred round the annual worship of the deity Jugal Kishore placed in a temple by the

APPENDIX II (Contd.)

	Name of the Fair/ Mahotsab	Place of Occurrence	Date of Holding	Specific Purpose and Duration
			June, 15)	side of the river Churni. It is organised by the Vaishnava saints. The fair is held for two days.
17.	Kartabhaja *mela*	Ghosepara, Nadia district.	Dol purnima (Spring festival day)	To show special veneration to Satima - the consort of the saint Ram Saran Pal. Satima was believed to have got divine power. People belonging to all the communities pay their held for three days.
18.	Madhukari *machchab*	Kotasur, Birbhum district	Bhadra, 15 (Corresponding to September 1)	To commemorate the celebrated spiritual activities of Kshepama - a famous female Baul. The Ashrama is devoted to her and the *machchab* is held on the specific day of her departure from this mortal world. The Baul assemblage is continued for three days.
19.	Nabadwiper *mela*	Nabadwip, Nadia district	Ras purnima (A Vaishnavite festival day)	It is held on the occasion of Ras purnima centring round the celebration of a Vaishnavite festival connected with the divine play of Radha and Krishna. In Nabadwip the clash between Vaishnava and Sakta cults characterizes a conflicting situation of the traditional culture.
20.	Nabasan *machchab*	Nabasan, Bankura district	Full-moon day following Ram navami	The mahotsab is organised here to show respect to the Baul guru, Haripada Goswami.

APPENDIX II (Contd.)

	Name of the Fair/ Mahotsab	*Place of Occurrence*	*Date of Holding*	*Specific Purpose and Duration*
				It is observed for three days.
21.	Narayankuri Ashram *mahotsab*	Narayankuri, Burdwan	Radha Asthami day - the holy birth day of Radha.	The *mahotsab* is held to observe the foundation day of the Ashram. It is observed for three days and is attended by the people coming from inaccessible rural areas.
22.	Pakhannar *mela*	Pakhanna, Bankura	Maghi Panchami (5th day in the brighter half of month of Magh)	It is arranged for the celebration of the founder's day. Many devotees attend the three-day long ceremony and communicate their gratitude to the organiser of the Ashram.
23.	Pous *mela*	Santiniketan, Birbhum district	Pous, 7 (corresponding to December, 23)	It is held to commemorate the foundation day of Santiniketan. Pous mela has got international fame as it is the centre for nourishing many traditional cultural features and activities. The fair is held for three days.
24.	Ramkelir *mela*	Ramkeli, Maldah, district	Jaishtha Sanskrant (corresponding to June, 15)	*Ramkelirdham* is characterised by the celebrated visits of Chaitannya Deva and other Vaishnava ascetics. The festival is held here in the sweet memory of the Vaishnava saints. The ceremony is observed for three days.

APPENDIX II (Contd.)

	Name of the Fair/ Mahotsab	*Place of Occurrence*	*Date of Holding*	*Specific Purpose and Duration*
25.	Ram-navami *mela*	Sonamukhi, Bankura district.	Ramnavmi day - (the celebrated birth day of Rama of Ramayana fame)	To commemorate the celebrated birth anniversary of Sri Manohar Das- the worthy disciple of Mohan Chand - the great *guru*. The assemblage is continued for three days in twelve different *akhras*.
26.	Rasaraj Gossainer *mela*	Digrey, Nadia district	Chaitra, 26 (corresponding to April, 9)	It is celebrated in the memory of a famous Vaishnava saint Rasaraj Gossain. He had many worthy disciples. The mahotsab is held for a day.
27.	Rathajatrar *mela*	Mahesh, Hooghly district.	Rathajatra day - (the celebrated car festival)	It is held on the occasion of the celebrated Rathajatra (car festival) of Lord Jagannath at Mahesh. The fair is held for five days.
28.	Subol Gossainer *machchab*	Sanatanpur, Burdwan district	Chaitra, 19 (corresponding to April, 2)	It is observed to celebrate the birth anniversary of a Vaishnava ascetic Subol Gossain. The *mahotsab* is organised for this and is continued for a day.
29.	Tarapither *mela*	Tarapith, Birbhum district	Aswin Sukla Chaturthi - (4th day in the brighter half of the month for Aswin)	It is based on the worship of the goddess Kali at Tarapith - a famous centre of Sakta cult. During this annual festival a large fair is held for a week and the devotees from far and near visit it.

APPENDIX II (Contd.)

	Name of the Fair/ Mahotsab	*Place of Occurrence*	*Date of Holding*	*Specific Purpose and Duration*
30.	Ulaichandir *mela*	Birnagar, Nadia district.	Buddh purnima (the - Celebrated birth day of Lord Buddha)	This assemblage is centred the worship of a roaring folk deity Ulaichandi. The festival is observed for a day and is attended by many Hindu and Muslim devotees.
31.	Villamangal *machchab*	Villamangal, Birbhum district	Magh, 3 (Corresponding to January, 17)	To commemorate the divine activities of the celebrated poet Villamangal and his consort Chintamani. The place where the *mahotsab* is held is regarded as the birth place of Villamangal Thakur. The *mahotsab* is held for a day.

Index

Illustrations

1. The temple of Lord Radha Binode at Joydev Kenduli becomes the centre of all the visitors during Baul-*mela*.

2. The Baul and his consort offering worship to *Maner manus* through songs.

3. Biswanath Das Baul in a meditational posture.

4. Baul can sing, dance and play on music at a time.

5. (Above) Sanatan Das, a renowned Baul, with some female Bauls and Fakirs.

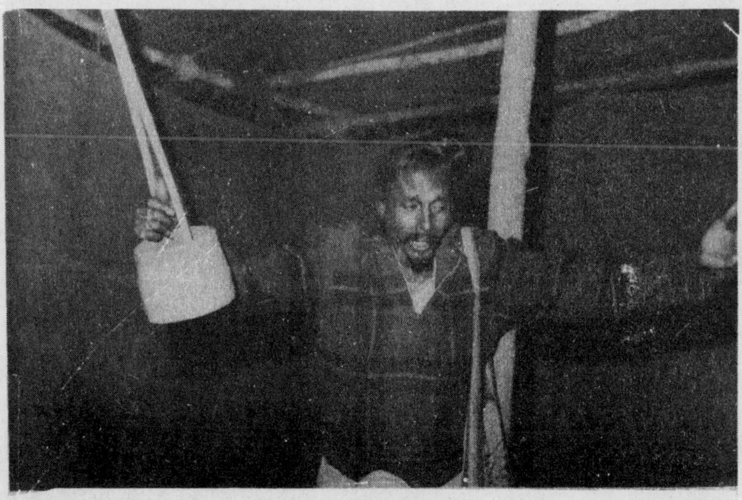

6. (Below) The singing Baul likes to embrace mankind in a brotherly feeling.

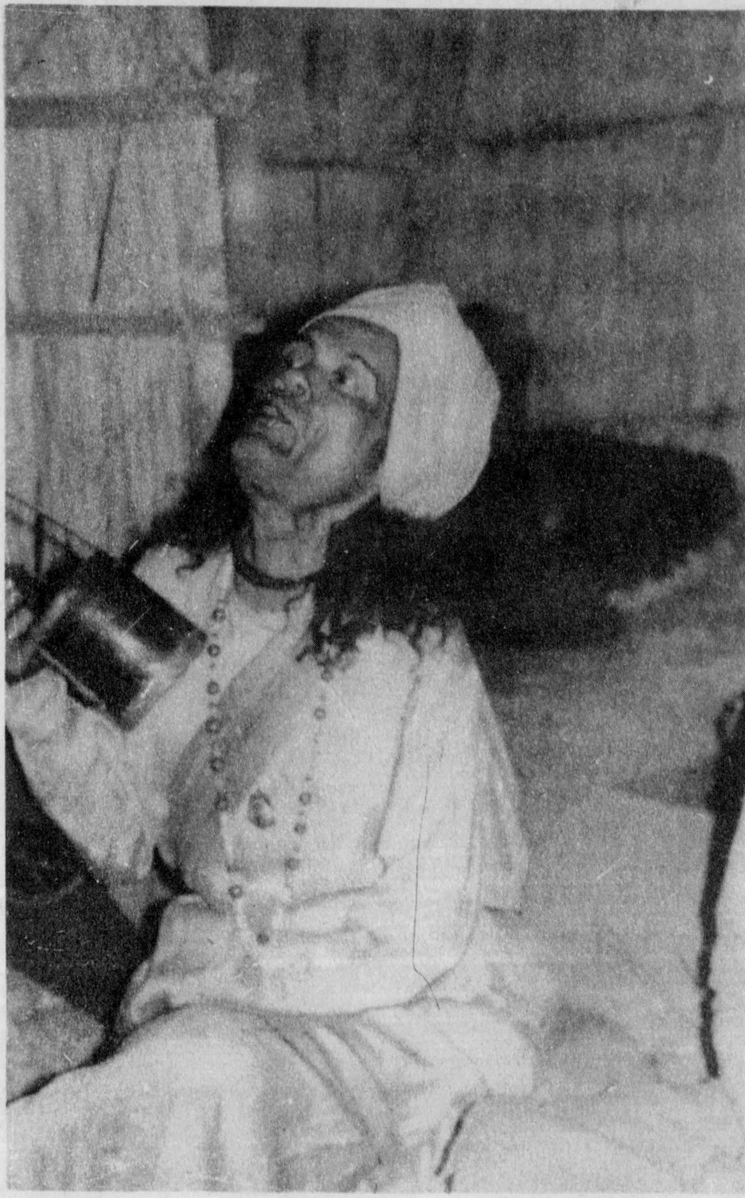

7. Sudhir Das Baul--a popular devotional singer of traditional songs.

8. Gour *Kshepa*, a melodious singer, in serious thinking mood.

9. Gour *Kshepa* in a jolly and laughing mood.

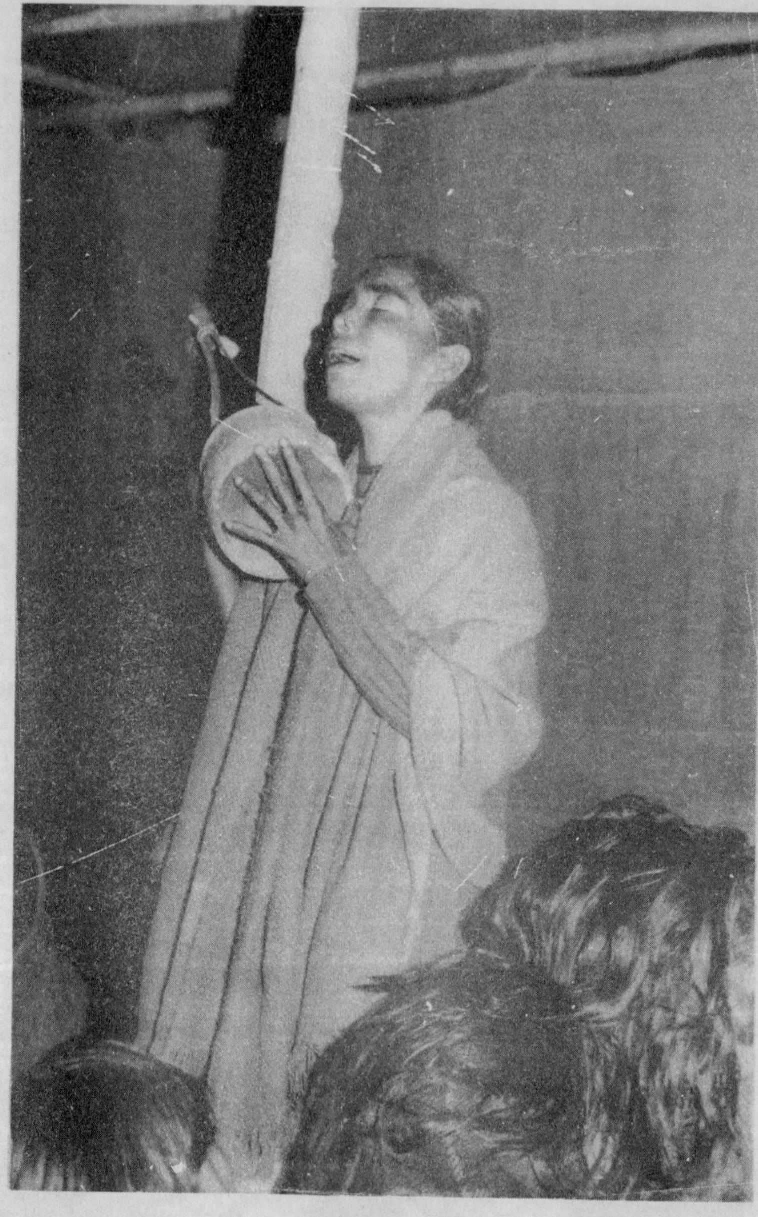

10. The female Baul lively participates in the recital.

11. During presentation of songs the singer very often becomes deeply concentrated.

12. Sometimes their open-hearted smiles create joyful situation amongst the audience.

13. The Baul duet in a public gathering.

14. The Baul singer in a specific gleeful posture.

15. The juvenile Baul receives training through continuous practice.

16. Kumaresh Das Baul and his companion presenting song at a professional dais.

17. Bauls, Fakirs and Song composer Ashanandan in a leisure-time discussion.

18. Hemp smoking helps the Bauls in self-controlling

19. The Baul in preparational mood before the start of recital.

20. 'Baul Samrat' Purna Das in a Baul *ashram* at Shantiniketan.

21. The author (just behind in juvenil.e Bauls) in association with some Bauls at Joydev-Kenduli.

22. A Fakir is showing his special feats of walking on fire.

Index to Sketches

1. The Baul in a singing mood with his *ektara* and *dugi.*

2. *Ektara,* one stringed instrument, is a symbol of Baul culture.

3. *Anandalahari* or *gabgubi* raises rhythmic sound during Baul song recital.

4. *Dubki* or kettle drum is an important musical instrument of the Bauls.

5. Playing bamboo flute is indispensable to Baul musical *performance.*

6. *Ghungur* or anklets set with ringing bells worn by the Baul singers.

7. *Sarinda* a specific musical instrument commonly used by Fakirs.

1

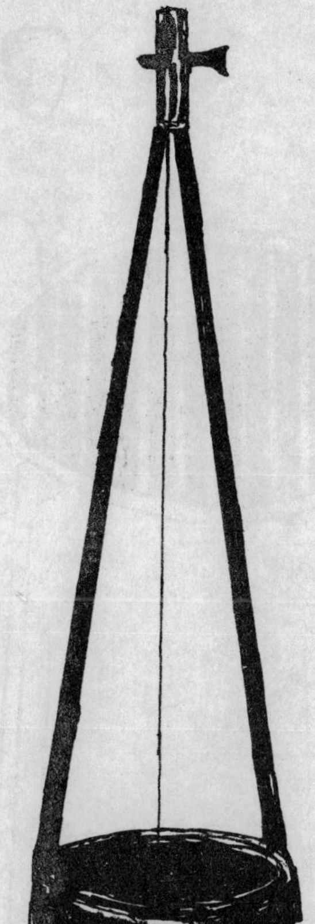

2

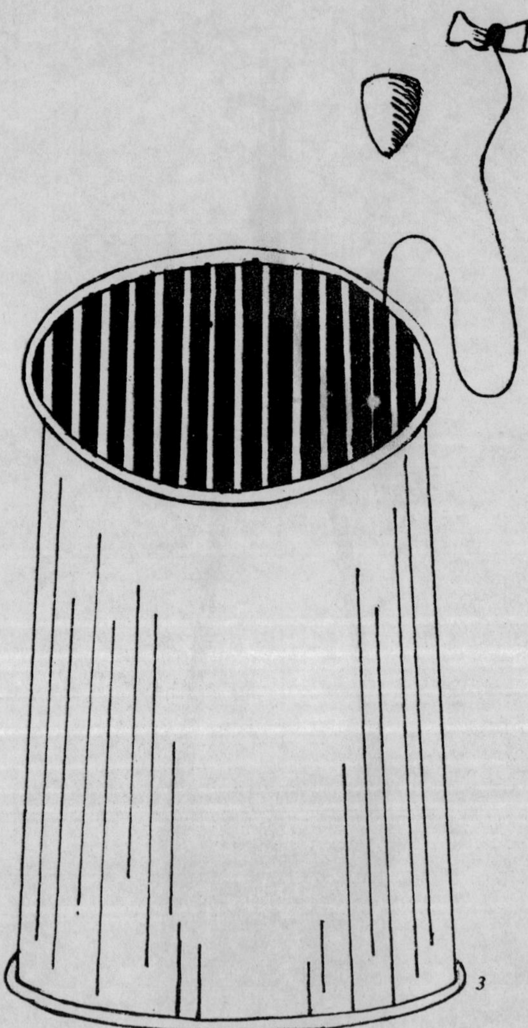

3

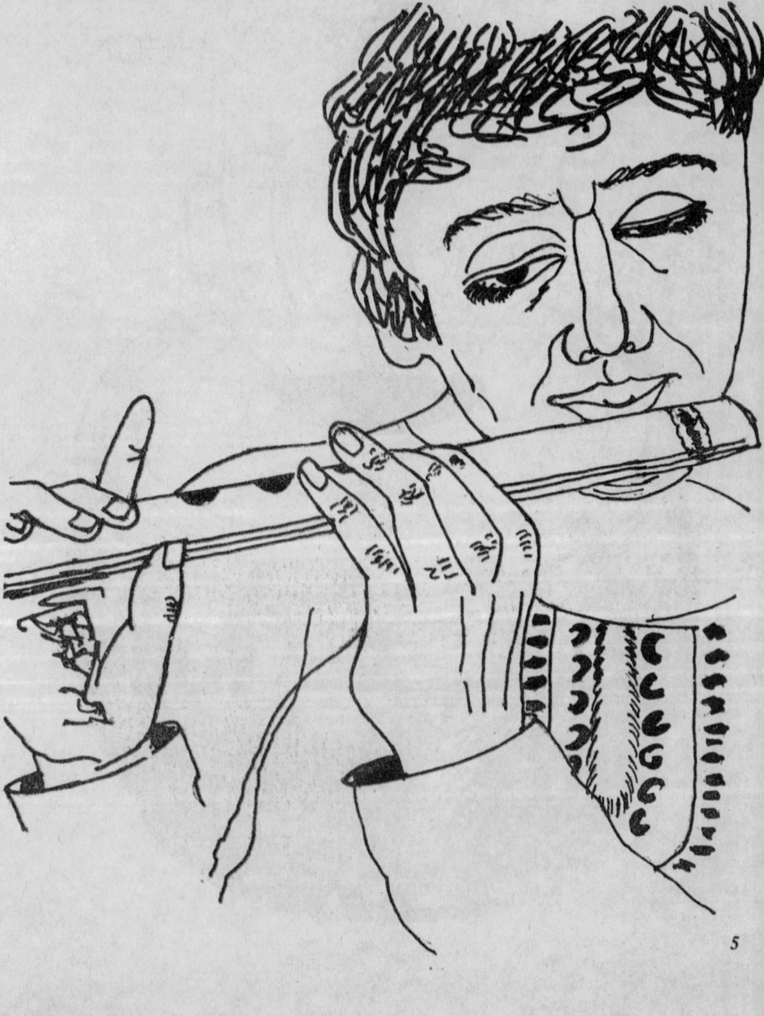

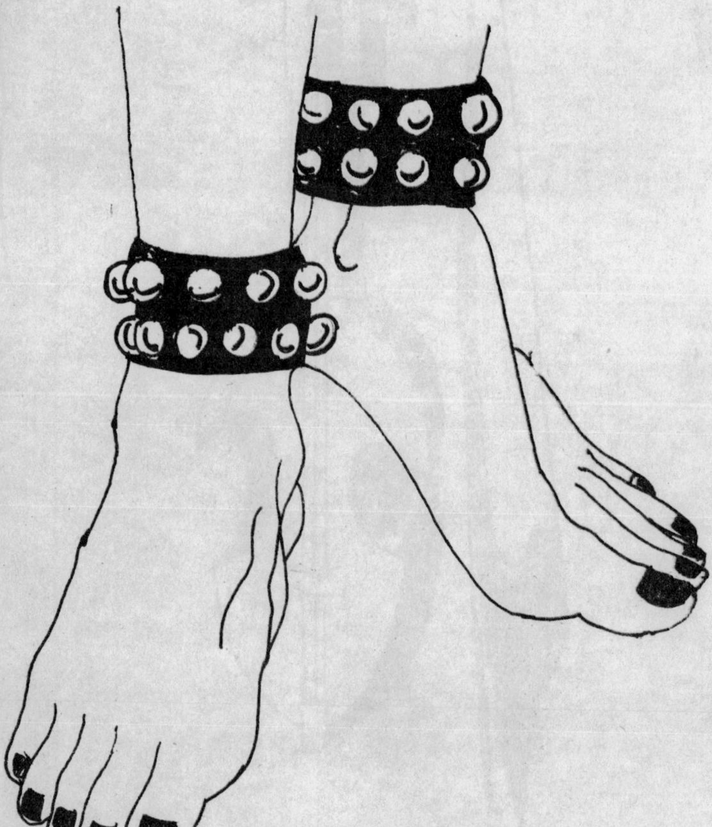

6

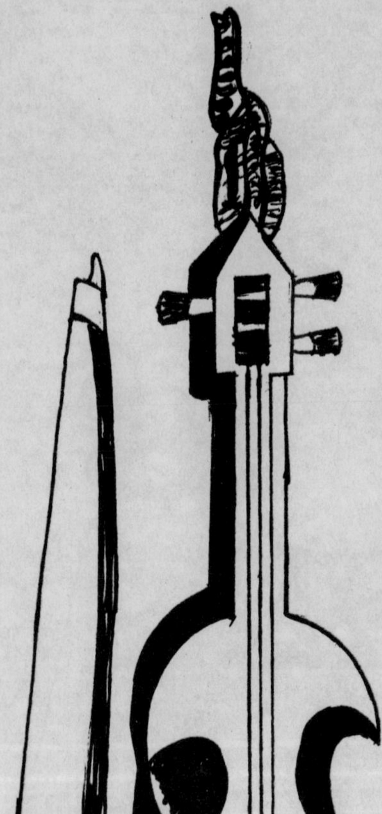

7